HISTORY, PHILOSOPHY AND SOCIOLOGY OF SCIENCE

Classics, Staples and Precursors

HISTORY, PHILOSOPHY AND SOCIOLOGY OF SCIENCE

Classics, Staples and Precursors

Selected By

YEHUDA ELKANA
ROBERT K. MERTON
ARNOLD THACKRAY
HARRIET ZUCKERMAN

THE WORLD-CONCEPTION
OF THE CHINESE

BY

ALFRED ⌐**FORKE**

ARNO PRESS

A New York Times Company

New York — 1975

Reprint Edition 1975 by Arno Press Inc.

HISTORY, PHILOSOPHY AND SOCIOLOGY OF SCIENCE:
Classics, Staples and Precursors
ISBN for complete set: 0-405-06575-2
See last pages of this volume for titles.

Manufactured in the United States of America

—————◆—————

Library of Congress Cataloging in Publication Data
Forke, Alfred, 1867-1944.
    The world-conception of the Chinese.

    (History, philosophy, and sociology of science)
    Reprint of the ed. published by A. Probsthain,
London, which was issued as v. 14 of Probsthain's
oriental series.
    1. Philosophy, Chinese. I. Title. II. Series.
B126.F6 1975   181'.11   74-26262
ISBN 0-405-06590-6

PROBSTHAIN'S ORIENTAL SERIES

VOL. XIV

THE WORLD-CONCEPTION
OF THE CHINESE

THE WORLD-CONCEPTION
OF THE CHINESE

THEIR ASTRONOMICAL, COSMOLOGICAL
AND PHYSICO-PHILOSOPHICAL
SPECULATIONS

BY

ALFRED FORKE

Professor of Chinese in the University of Hamburg.

ARTHUR PROBSTHAIN

(*Late* PROBSTHAIN & CO.),

41 GREAT RUSSELL STREET, LONDON, W.C.

1925

PRINTED IN GREAT BRITAIN BY
THE EASTERN PRESS, LTD., READING.

INTRODUCTION.

A GREAT deal has been written on the principal
philosophical systems of the Chinese, Confucianism and Taoism, much less on the independent
thinkers not falling under either of these two
heads and on the Neo-Confucianism of the Sung
time. From these writings we get a fairly good
idea of Chinese Ethics and Metaphysics, we learn
what the Chinese think of human life, man's
moral obligations, and the transcendental powers
supposed to rule the world, but obtain very little
information as to the Chinese conception of this
world and the phenomena of nature. We might
imagine that, as Chinese philosophy has produced
neither a logic nor a psychology, it did not concern
itself with speculations on the universe either.
Such a conclusion would be erroneous, for since
the dawn of their civilisation the Chinese have
philosophised on the world around them. In the
following we propose giving a systematical digest
of the ancient astronomical and cosmological con-
cepts of the Chinese and their attempts at natural
science. A history of civilisation and of the

gradual development of human thought cannot be written without taking into account the speculations of this important branch of the human family. The close resemblance which they bear to similar views of other nations, reasserts the fact now generally recognised that the Chinese are not a people apart and totally different from others, but intimately related to the other representatives of the human race.

There is a tendency to overrate the labours of the Sung philosophers, who are credited with having discovered the main parts of the philosophy of nature. With a view to determine how far these speculations are old and how far of modern origin, a distinction between ancient and modern times has been made, counting the latter from the Sung time in the 11th century A.D. This shows us that in most cases the efforts of these scholars have been limited to collecting and systematising ideas scattered in old literature, but that they have not produced anything quite new, being like their paragon Confucius rather transmitters of ancient thought than creators.

In ancient Chinese authors, science, religion, and philosophy are hopelessly mixed up. To bring more clearness into this medley, in treating of the various problems the scientific and religious-philosophical viewpoints have been separated.

Otherwise the division of the subject adopted by Chinese encyclopædias has been adhered to. A great many quotations are given, as it was deemed of interest to see how the various writers themselves plead their cause. A mere reference to them was in most cases not feasible, the texts not being accessible in translations. These quotations, moreover, enable us to fix the time when the Chinese mind first faced the diverse problems.

This book was originally written as a contribution to the Semicentennial Publications of the University of California (Berkeley), in commemoration of the Semicentenary Anniversary of this University, where the author was Agassiz Professor of Oriental Languages at the time (1918), and it was announced in the List of Semicentennial Publications (p. 40) as immediately forthcoming. Meanwhile the author was summarily dismissed from the University for imaginary inimical acts against the United States, on which he never could obtain any further information, and the manuscript was returned. It is most gratifying to him that after some delay his work is now incorporated into Probsthain's Oriental Series.

A. FORKE.

HAMBURG,
April, 1925.

CONTENTS.

BOOK I.

The Universe.

A. *ANCIENT TIMES.*

BOOK II.

Heaven.

A. *PHYSICAL VIEWPOINT*.

BOOK III.

Yin and Yang.

A. *ANCIENT TIMES.*

BOOK IV.

The Five Elements.

Book I.

THE UNIVERSE

BOOK I.

THE UNIVERSE.

A. ANCIENT TIMES.

I. BEGINNINGS OF CHINESE ASTRONOMY.

(a) *Earliest reference.*

THE oldest book mentioning Chinese astronomy is the
Shuking. In its oldest part, the Canon of *Yao*, we read,
" Thereupon *Yao* commanded *Hsi* and *Ho*, in reverent
accordance with their observation of the wide heavens, to
calculate and delineate the movements and appearances of
the sun, the moon, the stars, and the zodiacal spaces ; and
so to deliver respectfully the seasons to the people " (*a*).
The Hsi and Ho families seem to have been the court
astronomers of the emperor Yao. They had to make their
observations for the purpose of fixing the calendar from
which the people needed to know the seasons for their
agricultural labours. We further learn from the same
source that the younger brothers of the two families were
ordered to determine the vernal and autumnal equinoxes
and the summer and winter solstices from observations of
the sun and certain constellations (*b*). From a reference
to the constellation *Niao* (*c*) corresponding to *Cor Hydra*
of the West, which culminated at sunset on the day of
the vernal equinox in the time of Yao, it has been inferred

(*a*) *Legge*, Classics, Vol. III. Pt. I. p. 18 : 堯 典。乃 命 羲 和.
欽 若 昊 天. 曆 象 日 月 星 辰. 敬 授 人 時.

(*b*) *Loc. cit.* p. 18-21.

(*c*) 鳥

that this portion of the *Shuking* must have been written before 2254 B.C., the closing year of Yao's reign, and that it affords a strong confirmation of the reliability of Chinese chronology (*d*). After these remarks about equinoxes and solstices the text winds up this subject with the following words. The emperor said, " Ah ! you, Hsi and Hò, a round year consists of three hundred, sixty, and six days. By means of an intercalary month do you fix the four seasons, and complete the determination of the year. Thereafter, in exact accordance with this, regulàting the various officers, all the works of the year will be fully performed " (*e*). At such an early date did the Chinese make use of the method of intercalating months, in order to make their lunar year agree with the solar.

For the purpose of celestial observations the ancient Chinese astronomers are believed to have availed themselves of a kind of *armillary sphere* and a *triquetrum*. It is said of the Emperor Shun : " He examined the gem-adorned turning sphere, and the gem transverse tube, that he might regulate the seven Directors " (*f*), which means the sun, the moon, and the five planets.

(b) *Astronomers.*

Astronomers and astrologers were important officials in the early times of the Chou dynasty, viz., the eleventh century B.C. In the Chou-li we meet with the *T'ai-shih* (*g*).

(*d*) Cf. *eod.* p. 19, note.

(*e*) 帝曰。咨汝羲暨和, 朞三百有六旬有六日, 以閏月定四時成歲. 允釐百工. 庶績咸熙.

(*f*) *Legge*, Classics, Vol. III. Pt. I. p. 33 : 舜典。在璿璣玉衡. 以齊七政.

(*g*) 周禮春官 chap. 26 太史: 正歲年以序事頒之于官府及都鄙. 頒告朔于邦國. 閏月詔王居門終月. Cf. *E. Biot*, Le Tcheou Li, Vol. II. p. 106.

Among other functions he had to harmonise the solar and the lunar year by an intercalary month and inform the emperor, who during such a·month was obliged to sit within the gate of his private apartments (*h*), whereas during the regular months various palace halls were assigned to him for his residence. The T'ai-shih also announced the first month of the year. The emperor transmitted it to the feudal lords, who preserved it in their ancestor hall. Another official, the *P'ing-hsiang-shih* (*i*), was likewise entrusted with observations bearing on the calendar. He had to attend to the course of the planet Jupiter, making one revolution every twelve years, of the sun and the moon, to the twelve zodiacal spaces and the twenty-eight solar mansions. In winter and summer he measured the shadow of the sun and in spring and autumn that of the moon, and from their length determined the solstices and equinoxes. The functions of the *Pao-chang-shih* (*k*) were purely astrological. From the motions and changes of the planets and the stars, eclipses and parhelions, phases of the moon and the like they prognosticated lucky and unlucky auguries. The happiness of the empire depended on the gyrations of Jupiter, that of the various feudal states on their special stars. The five kinds of clouds around the sun at the time of the solstices and equinoxes were indicative of imminent blessings or disasters, and so were the

---

(*h*) 路 寢 門. The character 閨 shows the emperor sitting in his gate. The commentator of the Chou-li 鄭 司 農 says : 惟 閏 月 無 所 居 居 于 門 故 於 文 王 在 門 謂 之 閏 See also *S. Wells Williams*, Dictionary under 閏 and *Biot, loc. cit.*

(*i*) Chou-li, chap. 26 : 馮 相 氏 掌 十 有 二 歲 十 有 二 月 十 有 二 辰 十 日 二 十 有 八 星 之 位 辨 其 敍 事 以 會 天 位. 冬 夏 致 日 春 秋 致 月 以 辨 四 時 之 敍. *Biot*, Le Tcheou Li, Vol. II. p. 112.

(*k*) Chou-li, chap. 26 : 保 章 氏. *Biot, eod.* Vol. II. p. 113 seq.

twelve varieties of winds. Green clouds meant insects, white meant death, red meant devastation by war, black, inundations, and yellow, a rich harvest. The Tso-chuan, Duke Chao, seventeenth year = 525 B.C., has the following entry : The Viscount of T'an being asked at the court of Lu why it was that the Emperor Shao-hao, 2598-2514 B.C., named his officers after birds, replied that the old rulers gave to their officers the name of the thing which they regarded as the omen of their reign. " When my great ancestor *Shao-hao Chih* succeeded to the throne, there appeared just a phœnix at that time. Therefore, he took birds as the symbol of his reign, making bird officers and using the names of birds. The Phœnix Master had to arrange the calendar, the Dark-Bird Master to take charge of the equinoxes, the Shrike Master of the solstices, the Green Bird Master of the beginning, and the Carnation Bird Master of the close of the seasons " (*l*). If this passage were historical, all the afore-mentioned officials would have been engaged in fixing the various parts of the calendar. But in spite of T'an's pretending that *Shao-hao* was his ancestor and that he knew all about him, we can hardly award to this old mythical ruler and his court more than a legendary existence.

The oldest astronomers whose names have come down to us are : *K'un Wu* of the *Hsia* dynasty, *Wu Hsien* of the *Yin* dynasty, and *Shih I* of the *Chou* dynasty (*m*). Among

---

(*l*) 我 高 祖 少 皥 摰 之 立 也. 鳳 鳥 適 至. 故 紀 於 鳥. 爲 鳥 師 而 鳥 名. 鳳 鳥 氏. 歷 正 也. 玄 鳥 氏. 司 分 者 也. 伯 趙 氏. 司 至 者 也. 靑 鳥 氏. 司 啓 者 也. 丹 鳥 氏. 司 閉 者 也.

(*m*) Chin-shu XI. p. 1 r. 天文志: 昆吾, 巫咸, 史佚. *Wu Hsien* is believed to have been a Minister of the Emperor *T'ai Mou*, 1637, B.C., but another tradition makes him the astrologer of *Huang-ti*. Cf. *Mayers*, Reader No. 861.

the astronomers of the feudal states the best known are :
Tse Shên of *Lu*, *Yen* the Diviner of *Chin*, and *Tse Wei*
of *Sung* (*n*). The writings of *Wu Hsien*, *Kan Tê* and
Shih Shên were most appreciated by posterity. When
Shih-huang-ti burned the Classics he spared the astronomical works. In the *Han* time we have the two grand
astrologers, *Sse-ma T'an* and *Sse-ma Ch'ien* (*o*), father and
son, more celebrated as historians. Then there is the well-
known scholar *Liu Hsiang*, B.C. 77-6, the historian *Pan Ku*,
who died in A.D. 92, *T'sai Yung*, 133-192 A.D., and *Ch'iao
Chou* (*p*), 200-270 A.D., all of whom wrote on astronomy
as well as on history. *Sse-ma Piao* (*q*), 240-305 A.D., is the
last writer on astronomy mentioned in the *Chin-shu*. The
section on astronomy in the *Hou Han-shu* is his work.
None of the independent astronomical works of these times
has been preserved.

(c) *Astronomical observations.*

Quite a number of astronomical observations are
recorded in the *Shuking*, the *Ch'un-ch'iu*, and the *Tso-
chuan*, notably eclipses of the sun and the moon. In the
astronomical section (*r*) of all the later historical works all
extraordinary celestial phenomena such as the movements
of the planets, shooting stars, meteors and comets are

(*n*) The Chin-shu, *loc. cit.*, mentions : 梓愼 *Tse Shên* of *Lu*, 卜 偃
Yen of *Chin*, 裨竈 *P'i Tsao* of *Chêng*, 子 韋 *Tse Wei* of *Sung*, 甘 德
Kan Tê of *Ch'i*, 唐 昧 *T'ang Mei* of *Ch'u*, 尹 皋 *Yin Kao* of *Chao*,
and 石 申 *Shih Shên* of *Wei*. *Yen* of *Chin* is mentioned in the *Tso-
chuan*, Duke *Min* first year=B.C. 660. *Tse Wei* was grand astrologer
of Duke *Ching* of *Sung*, B.C. 515-451.

(*o*) 司 馬 談, died B.C. 110.　司 馬 遷, about B.C. 145-74.

(*p*) 劉 向, 班 固, 蔡 邕, 譙 周.

(*q*) 司 馬 彪.

(*r*) 天 文 志.

faithfully related.   From the eighth century B.C. solar and
lunar eclipses are regularly registered.   The Chinese could
pre-determine lunar eclipses, but their calculations were
often faulty.   They knew the *Metonic* and *Calippic* cycles
long before the Greeks (*s*).   As early as 1000 B.C. they had
discovered that nineteen revolutions of the sun of 365¼ days
each are equivalent to 235 revolutions of the moon (*t*).

Of comets observed in the earliest times there was one
in the year 613 B.C., near the Great Bear, another was
visible on November 5th, 526 B.C., one appeared in the
State of *Lu* in B.C. 482 (*u*).

Lu and other principalities had their special *observatories*.   At the solstices the princes would ascend these
observatories, survey the heavens and make a record.   As
we learn from the *Tso-chuan* this was done by Duke *Hsi* of
Lu in the fifth year of his reign, *i.e.*, B.C. 654 (*x*).

(d) *Astronomical works.*

The oldest astronomical treatise still extant is the *Chou-
pi suan-ching*, of which the oldest sections at least date
from the eleventh century B.C.   The latter part of the first
book seems to be later additions.   The works of all the other
astronomers of the ancient dynasties are lost.   The first
star-maps or *star-catalogues* are said to have been composed by *Wu Hsien, Kan Tê* and *Shih Shên*.   Under the
reign of the *Chin* emperor *Wu-ti*, 265-290 A.D., they were

(*s*) A. *Wylie*, Notes on the opinions of the Chinese with regard to
eclipses in Journ. R. Asiat. Soc. of Shanghai, Vol. III. 1866, p. 71; and
J. B. *Biot*, Etudes sur l'Astronomie indienne et sur l'astronomie chinoise,
1862, p. 351.

(*t*) 周髀算經卷下 p. 29 : 術曰置章月二百三十五
以章歲十九除之 Cf. E. *Biot*, Traduction du Tcheou-pei, in
Journal Asiatique, Juin, 1841, p. 632.

(*u*) *Gaubil*, Histoire de l'astronomie chinoise, in Lettres édifiantes,
vol. 26, 1783, pp. 193, 209, 222.

(*x*) 僖公五年。公既視朔.遂登觀臺.以望而書.禮也.

used by the grand astrologer *Ch'ên Cho* for his map containing 283 principal and 1,464 secondary stars (*y*). Already before this the great astronomer *Chang Hêng* seems to have known a greater number of stars, for, in addition to the sun and moon, the five planets and the twenty-eight solar mansions, he enumerates 124 ever-visible stars, 320 stars with names, 2,500 bigger and 11,520 smaller stars unnamed (*z*). *Chang Hêng*, A.D. 78-139, was perhaps the most eminent astronomer of ancient times. His work on astronomy was entitled *Ling-hsien* (*a*).

(e) *Astronomical instruments.*

About the construction of the *uranosphere* and the *triquetrum* of the time of *Yao* and *Shun* we have no information. For measuring the length of the shadow of the sun the ancient Chinese employed the *Gnomon* (*b*). This was a bamboo pole pierced by a hole one inch in diameter at the height of eight feet. Through this hole the sun was observed, which just covered it (*c*). This description is given in that portion of the *Chou-pi* which was added, but in the opinion of *Biot* cannot be later than the 2nd century B.C. (*d*), and may be much older. Presumably the Chinese

---

(*y*) Chin-shu, XI., 6 r., 武帝時太史令陳卓總甘石巫咸三家所著星圖大凡二百八十三官一千四百六十四星以爲定紀.

(*z*) Chin-shu, XI., 6 r., 張衡云 . . . . 官常明者百有二十四可名者三百二十爲星二千五百微星之數蓋萬有一千五百二十.

(*a*) 靈憲.

(*b*) 晷, 表 and 周髀.

(*c*) Chou-pi I., 26 r., 即取竹空徑一寸長八尺捕影而視之空正掩日而日應空之孔.

(*d*) *E. Biot*, Chou-pi, p. 595.

were acquainted with the gnomon at the beginning of the *Chou* epoch, when the *Chou-pi* was written, for in its old sections also, the gnomon is referred to, and the title of the book *Chou-pi* itself means gnomon. In the *Chou-li*, which is contemporary with the *Chou-pi*, an instrument *t'u-kuei* is mentioned (*e*). *Giles* calls it a sun-dial; *Couvreur* quotes *Chêng K'ang-Ch'êng* (*f*), A.D. 127-200, who says that it is a tablet fifteen inches long, which was placed horizontally from north to south to receive the shadow of the gnomon at noon. Consequently the use of the gnomon must have been known in the eleventh century B.C. Formerly, the Arabs were supposed to have introduced the gnomon into China in the thirteenth century A.D. (*g*). According to Herodotus, II., 109, the Babylonians had sun-dials, whence the Greeks received them. In the cuneiform inscriptions they are referred to likewise.

The *sphere* of antiquity remained known in later ages, passing from generation to generation, but the astrologers kept it concealed, so that their disciples did not see it. Its use thus gradually became lost, and the rival systems, *Kai-t'ien* and *Hsüan-yeh*, came into vogue. In the *T'ai-ch'u* period, 104-100 B.C., *Kêng Shou-ch'ang* (*h*) and others made again a sphere to measure degrees. From 89-101 *Chia K'uei* (*i*) corrected it and added the ecliptic. Finally, *Chang Hêng* perfected the instrument still further. He had

---

(*e*) Chou-li, chap. 9, 地官大司徒。以土圭之法測 土深正日景以求地中 " with the tablet he measured the depth of the earth, determined the shadow of the sun and thus tried to find the centre of the earth." Chou-li, chap. 20. 春官典瑞。土圭以 致四時日月 " the tablet is used to determine the height of the sun and the moon during the four seasons." Cf. *Biot*, Chou-li, Vol. I. pp. 200, 488.

(*f*) 鄭康成.

(*g*) *E. Biot*, Chou-pi, p. 594.

(*h*) 耿壽昌.

(*i*) 賈逵.

an inner and an outer sphere with a north pole and south pole, an ecliptic, the equator, twenty-four positions of the sun during the year, twenty-eight lunar stations, the sun, the moon, the five planets, the inner and outer stars. The whole was moved by water-power and placed in an upper room of the palace. Simultaneously it set in motion a wheel of fortune, whatever that was, and in front of the steps of the palace there was a monthly flower, which, conformably to the waxing and waning of the moon, every day had a new blossom or dropped one. This looks very much like a later embellishment. The instrument was made of copper. An assistant in a closed room had to take notice of all changes, and to call out to an observer on a high tower whether a star on the sphere was just appearing, culminating, or disappearing. The motions of the instrument were in exact accordance with the motions of the heavens (*k*). The time was measured by means of the *clepsydra* during the night and with the gnomon or sundial by daytime. The clepsydra was known as far back as the eleventh century B.C. A special official named in the *Chou-li* was in charge of it (*l*).

In a later description of the uranosphere dating from the *Wu* period (*m*), heaven has 365 145/589 degrees (*n*), and is half above, half below, the earth. The *north pole* protrudes 36 degrees from the earth, and so does the *south*

(*k*) Chin-shu, XI. 3 r. and 4 r.

(*l*) Chou-li, chap. 30, 夏官. 挈壺氏. The commentator *Chêng* of the *Han* time and the *Shuo-wên* say that the clepsydra 漏 was a copper vessel with one hundred marks 刻 or incisions, comprising night and day, and an arrow as a pointer. So one interval corresponded almost to a quarter of an hour, a meaning which 刻 still preserves to this day. *Vid. Biot*, Chou-li, II. 202.

(*m*) 吳時 A.D. 222-277.

(*n*) This division, differing from ours, corresponds to the number of days of a year. The Chou-pi reckoned the year at 365,'25 or more exactly at 365 235/940 days. *Biot, loc. cit.* p. 633.

pole. The distance between both is a little more than 182½ degrees. The upper hemisphere is always visible, the lower is covered. The *equator,* or the heavenly line, is about 90 degrees distant from each pole, the *ecliptic* (*o*), or the way of the sun, is half within, half without, the equator, which it intersects in the east about 5 degrees from the constellation " Horn," and in the west about 14 degrees from the constellation " Astride " (*p*).

II. THE SIX ASTRONOMICAL SYSTEMS.

With a view to explaining the universe as it appeared to them, the Chinese, from the earliest times, have propounded various theories. In the first centuries of our era six such attempts are recorded, denoted as follows :

(1) 蓋 天 *Kai-t'ien,* Heaven shaped like a cupola or a dome.

(2) 渾 天 *Hun-t'ien,* Heaven a complete sphere.

(3) 宣 夜 *Hsüan-yeh,* Heaven a void without any substance.

(4) 昕 天 *Hsin-t'ien,* Heaven of irregular form, in the north higher than in the south.

(5) 穹 天 *Ch'iung-t'ien,* Heaven ovoid, the apex above.

(6) 安 天 *An-t'ien,* Heaven motionless.

The first three systems date from pre-Christian times, the others from the first centuries of the Christian era.

(1) *Kai-t'ien System.*

This is the theory of the *Chou-pi,* the author of which, *Chou-kung,* however, is supposed to have derived it from the *Shang* dynasty, 1766-1122 B.C. It likens heaven to a covering umbrella and earth to an upturned bowl. Both

---

(*o*) 赤 道 and 黃 道.

(*p*) 角 and 奎.

are high in the centre and sloping at the periphery. The centres of heaven and earth are beneath the north pole. Owing to her declivity the rain flows down from the earth at her four sides. The distance between heaven and earth measures 80,000 Li. During the twelve months the sun describes six orbits of different sizes, which have been calculated with the help of the gnomon. Heaven is round, earth square, heaven has a dark blue colour, earth is yellowish brown (*a*). According to this description heaven and earth must be both half globes, one upon the other, but while heaven at its base is round, earth is rectangular. Heaven revolves along with the sun, the moon, and the stars, whereas earth is without motion.

The supporters of this view further hold that heaven is round like an opened umbrella and earth square like a chess-board. Heaven turns sideways to the left like a millstone, the sun and the moon move to the right—*i.e.*, eastward—but are carried along by heaven to the left—*i.e.*, westward. The real movements of the sun and the moon are towards the east, but heaven draws them to the west, where they go down. They resemble ants creeping to the left side on a millstone turning to the right. The millstone, being much faster than the ants, compels them to follow it to the right (*b*). This is quite a clever idea to illustrate the complex movements of the sun and the moon.

(*a*) Chin-shu, XI., 1 v., and Chou-pi, I., 17 : ¹方 屬 地 圓 屬 天 天 圓 地 方。²天 青 黑 地 黃 赤 天 數 之 爲 笠 也 青 黑 爲 表 丹 黃 爲 裏 以 象 天 之 位。II. ; 1 r.: ¹極 下 者 其 地 高 …… 滂 沱 四 隤 而 下 天 之 中 央 亦 高. ²天 象 蓋 笠 地 法 覆 槃. 天 離 地 八 萬 里。

For anybody not proficient in mathematics and astronomy the *Chou-pi* is very hard reading even in E. Biot's translation, especially the calculations are stumbling-blocks. Cf. *Biot*, pp. 602, 616, 619, 620.

(*b*) This comparison of the two luminaries with ants on a millstone was first used by *Wang Ch'ung* (see my translation Lun-hêng, Part I. p. 266). By a curious coincidence the planets are compared to ants

Heaven, however, is not a regular vault or hemisphere, but elevated in the south and depressed in the north. Consequently, the sun is visible when staying in the altitude of the south, and invisible when sojourning in the depth of the north. The sloping part of the earth, where the sun then stays, is not inhabited, and cannot be seen from above.

Heaven resembles a reclining umbrella; therefore the pole is north of the inhabited earth. Being at the same time the centre of heaven, the latter must be inclined. This is meant to account for the inclination of the axis of the world, which, as observed, passes through the polar star.

In the morning the sun issues from the *Yang*, and in the evening vanishes in the *Yin*, the dark fluid. In summer the *Yang* fluid is in the ascendant and the *Yin* weak; consequently the light of the *Yang* combines with the sunlight, and the sun is not obscured, hence the length of the days. Conversely, in winter the *Yin* fluid is excessive, therefore the sun is shaded and invisible though shining, whence the shortness of the days. Here light and darkness, Yin and Yang, are considered as two independent states not affected

---

creeping in opposite direction on a rotating potter's wheel by Vitruv. IX. 1 (15) : " Quemadmodum, si in rota, qua figuli utuntur, impositae fuerint septem formicae canalesque totidem in rota facti sint circum centrum imo adcrescentes ad extremum, in quibus hae cogantur circinationem facere, verseturque rota in alteram partem, necesse erit eas contra rotae versationem nihilominus adversus itinera perficere . . . similiter astra nitentia contra mundi cursum suis itineribus perficiunt circumitum, sed caeli versatione redundationibus referuntur cotidiana temporis circumlatione." Lun Hêng, XI. 8 r., reads : 其 喩 若 蟻 行 於 磑 上 日 月 行 遲 天 行 疾 持 日 月 轉 故 日 月 實 東 行 而 反 西 旋 也. The simile of the celestial sphere and a quickly rotating potter's wheel is also used by *Nigidius*, who from this incident received the sobriquet *Figulus* (*Augustini De Civitate Dei*, Lib. V. cap. 3). In Chinese the expression 大 鈞 " great potter's wheel," is in common use for " heaven, nature, creator." It occurs in the *Ch'ien Han-shu* (Couvreur) and *Wang Ch'ung*, Lun-hêng, XI. 8 v., compares the motion of the sky with 陶 鈞 之 運.

by the sun (*c*), an opinion combated a ready by *Wang Ch'ung.*

The *Kai-t'ien* theory was impugned in the *Han* time by the philosopher *Yang Hsiung*, 53 B.C.—A.D. 18, with eight arguments. Subsequently, *Huan Tan*, a contemporary of Yang Hsiung, *Chêng Hsüan*, A.D. 127—200, *T'sai Yung* and *Lu Chi* (*d*), third century, all votaries of the *Hun-t'ien* doctrine, raised objections.

Wang Ch'ung, A.D. 27-97, is looked upon as an energetic advocate of the *Kai-t'ien* system (*e*), but without sufficient reason, for he differs from it on almost every point. Wang Ch'ung disclaims (1) that light and darkness are produced by Yin and Yang, because darkness is never able to extinguish a light; (2) that heaven is like a reclining umbrella; for in that case it must strike against the earth with its lower edge; (3) that heaven is elevated in the south and depressed in the north; (4) heaven and earth are both flat, their vaulted shape and their junction are illusive. Wang Ch'ung has his own theory, *viz.*, that heaven and earth are two round disks, of which the uppermost turns westward like a millstone, on which the sun and the moon as ants creep eastward. Only by reason of this movement is he regarded as a supporter of the Kai-t'ien hypothesis. The disappearance of the sun and the moon in the evening is explained by their great distance. At a distance of ten Li already heaven and earth seem to meet together, and we do not see any more things still farther. When to us the sun appears to set in the west, then for people living in the west it culminates, and they have noon. In like manner a big torch at night becomes invisible at a Li's distance. The same is true of the sun. Neither the sun nor the moon

---

(*c*) Chin-shu, IX. 2 r.
(*d*) 揚 雄, 桓 譚, 鄭 玄, 陸 績.
(*e*) Chin-shu, IX. 2 v.; and Sui-shu, XIX. 3 v.

are round in *Wang Ch'ung's* opinion, they merely appear so.   Both are the essence of fire and water, which are not round on earth either (*f*).

To the horizontal movement of the sky *Huan Tan* already had taken exception.   At the spring and autumn equinoxes, he says, the sun rises exactly in the east and goes down in the west.   The celestial pole being north of us, we must be nearer to the south than to the north.   The north is farther away from us, and the course of the sun during the night from the west by north to the east, according to the Kai-t'ien theory, ought to be of longer duration than its course at day time.   Day and night, therefore, could not be equal.

Once of an afternoon *Huan Tan* was sitting in an open hall and had his back warmed by the sunshine, for it was very cold.   A short while afterwards the sunlight disappeared completely and did not warm him any more. Huan Tan then said to the adherents of the Kai-t'ien theory : " If your view concerning the millstone movement were correct, then at the westward progress of the sun its light could only be slightly shifted to the east, but not disappear completely.   Ergo the Hun-t'ien theory is right " (*g*).

Ko Hung (*h*), of the fourth century A.D., assails *Wang Ch'ung* directly, urging the following arguments : (1) If heaven moved sideways like a millstone, the sun, the moon and the stars ought to turn along with heaven from the

---

(*f*) Translation of Lun-hêng, Vol. I. pp. 258, 260-262, 271.

(*g*) 桓君山乃告信蓋天者曰天若如推磨右轉而日西行者其光景當照此廊下稍而東耳不當拔出去拔出去是應渾天法也渾爲天之眞形於是可知矣. Chin-shu XI., 3 r.

(*h*) 葛洪.

east to the south, west, and north, and back to the east. Instead of that they rise in the east, ascend heaven towards the south, and descend again towards the west, where they set. Even the stars of the west go down forthwith and do not proceed to the north first. They move in a slanting curve across the sky. (2) Against Wang Ch'ung's argument that the sun, during the night, becomes invisible owing to its great distance, Ko Hung points out that the size of the sun is as big as numerous stars combined, its diameter measuring 1,000 Li and its circumference 3,000 Li. Now the small polar star remains visible throughout; why then should the sun, which is so much greater, vanish in the north? If this was owing to distance, the sun ought gradually to decrease in size, whereas when setting it appeared even greater. (3) The comparison of the sun with a torch is out of place too, for a torch carried away grows smaller and smaller; the sun and the moon, however, do not alter their size during their whole course. (4) Just before going down the sun looks like a mirror broken horizontally. If, as Wang Ch'ung supposes, it disappeared towards the north, it might well resemble a mirror broken vertically, but there is no reason why there should be the shape of a disk divided horizontally. The assertion of Wang Ch'ung that the sun and the moon are not round and only appear so, he controverts with great ability (i).

We see from the above how zealously questions regarding the form of the cosmos were discussed by the Chinese, and how the partisans of the two principal theories carried on the controversy. Under the reign of *Liang Wu-ti*, 502-550 A.D., the problem was again scrutinised in the *Ch'ang-ch'un* palace, and a view officially adopted which was in

---

(i) Chin-shu, XI. 2 v.-4 r.

harmony with the *Kai-t'ien* system of the *Chou-pi* and rejected the *Hun-t'ien theory* (*k*).

(2) *Hun-t'ien System.*

This theory of the spheroid shape of heaven, in whose centre earth reposes, had already found expression in the uranospheres of ancient times.   During the disturbances of the *Ch'in* epoch most astronomers are said to have perished and their books were lost.   The uranosphere was still in existence, but the scholars did not understand it, and the theory had to be rediscovered.

The author of the *Huang-ti shu,* quoted by the *Chin-shu,* is considered to be the oldest advocate of this theory. In his work we read : " Heaven is beyond the earth, and water is beyond heaven.   The water floats heaven and carries the earth " (*l*).   This *dictum* can hardly refer to the Hun-t'ien theory and agrees much better with the Kai-t'ien : The celestial hemisphere and the disk of the earth both swim on the ocean encircling the earth and extending beyond the sky.   If heaven floats upon the ocean it could not well move through it in its rotation.

Chang Hêng, whose uranosphere we have noticed, also upheld the Hun-t'ien system.   Further details are unknown to us, but the *Chin-shu* records the following epitaph composed for *Chang Hêng* by *Ts'ui Tse-yü* : " With his calculations he fathomed heaven and earth and with his constructions he imitated creation.   By his extraordinary

---

(*k*) Sui-shu, XIX. 2 v. 天文志。其後桓譚鄭玄蔡邕陸績各陳周髀考驗天狀多有所違逮梁武帝於長春殿講義別擬天體全同周髀之文盍立新義以排渾天之論而已.

(*l*) 黃帝書曰天在地外水在天外水浮天而載地者也.   Chin-shu, XI. 3 r.

talents and marvellous ability he equalled the spirits,"
and by way of comment adds " so correct were his uranosphere and his apparatus of the moving earth " (*m*). It
would appear as though Chang Hêng had thought of the
earth as moving, but such is not the case. From his
biography in the *Hou Han-shu* we learn that an apparatus
is meant which Chang Hêng had devised with a view to
observing *earthquakes* (*n*).

(*m*) 崔子玉爲其碑銘曰數術窮天地制作侔造
化高才偉藝與神合契蓋由於平子渾儀及地動
儀之有驗故也. *eod.*

(*n*) Hou Han-shu 89, 4 v.: 張衡傳, 陽嘉元年復造候
風地動儀以精銅鑄成員徑八尺合蓋隆起形似
酒尊飾以篆文山龜鳥獸之形中有都柱傍行八
道施關發機外有八龍首銜銅丸下有蟾蜍張口
承之其牙機巧制皆隱在尊中覆蓋周密無際如
有地動尊則振龍機發吐丸而蟾蜍銜之振聲激
揚伺者因此覺知雖一龍發機而七首不動尋其
方面乃知震之所在驗之以事合契若神自書典
所記未之有也嘗一龍機發而地不覺動京師學
者咸怪其無徵後數日驛至果地震隴西於是皆
服其妙自此以後乃令史官記地動所從方起.

" In A.D. 132 Chang Hêng again constructed an instrument to indicate
the weather and earthquakes, cast from fine copper, with eight feet
diameter, which, with its cover, stood up like a wine amphora. It was
adorned with seal characters, mountains, turtles, birds, and animals,
had a main prop in the centre and eight groves at the sides. Bolts
could be opened and a mechanism set in motion. Outside there were
eight dragon heads with copper balls in their mouths and, below,
toads which could receive these balls in their open mouths. The cogged
wheels were very elaborate, but all concealed in the amphora, the lid of
which was tightly closed, leaving no fissure. When there was an earthquake, the amphora shook the dragons, the mechanism became stirred,
and they vomited the balls, which were caught by the toads. The
sound of the concussion was the signal to rouse the observer. Even
if only one dragon was set in motion and seven heads were not stirred,
upon investigating the environs the place of the earthquake was

Wang Fan (*o*) (third century A.D.), who also had constructed a sphere and written an astronomical work, states that according to the views of former scholars the universe was shaped like the egg of a bird. Heaven encloses the earth from without as the shell does the yolk of the egg, its curve being without beginning or end, having a perfectly round shape, not that of a hemisphere, as the Kai-t'ien hypothesis assumes. Hence the name *Hun-t'ien.* Wang Fan goes on to speak about the hemisphere enclosing the upper part and the one surrounding the lower part of the earth and on the two limits, the northern and southern poles (*p*). The parallel between the *cosmos* and an *egg* recurs very often; *Ko Hung* and later writers all use it. It is an idea common to many different nations. According to an *Egyptian* legend *Khnum* made the cosmic egg from the mud of the Nile. From it was born *Re*, the god of light who created the world. From the *Śatapatha Brāhmaṇa* and the *Chāndogya Upanishad* we learn that the world proceeded from a golden egg created by *Brāhma* or *Prajāpati* (*q*). *Damasius* relates that *Chronos-Herakles* generated an enormous egg, which burst in the middle (*r*). The upper part became heaven, the lower earth. The

---

discovered. There was the most wonderful agreement with facts, and nothing similar had happened since records were kept. Once the mechanism of one dragon moved, but no earthquake was felt. All the scholars in the capital were surprised at this inaccuracy, but several days later a courier brought the news that in fact there had been an earthquake in Shênsi. Then all believed in this wonderful invention, and an astronomer was ordered to record all the places from where earthquakes started."

(*o*) 王蕃.

(*p*) Sung-shu 23, 1 r : 制渾儀立論考度曰前儒舊說天地之體狀如鳥卵天包地外猶殼之裹黃也周旋無端其形渾渾然故曰渾天也.

(*q*) *Hastings*, Encyclopædia of Religion and Ethics, Vol. IV. (*Cosmology*, art. by L. H. Gray, p. 126).

(*r*) *Zeller*, Philosophie der Griechen, Vol. I. p. 81.

Persians had the same comparison, making the shell represent the outer heaven and the yolk the earth (*s*). We find the cosmic egg with the *Phenicians, Finns, Fijians.* In *Hawaii*, the *Society Islands*, and *Tahiti, Tangalva* lived for many years as a bird in a gigantic egg. When it burst, both halves became heaven and earth (*t*).

Ko Hung maintains that "heaven is like a hen's egg and earth like the yellow in the egg, suspended lonely in the midst of heaven. Heaven is great, and earth is small, heaven is outside and water inside. Both heaven and earth rest on the air and move, carried by the water. . . . One celestial hemisphere covers the earth, the other spreads around it underneath. Consequently only half of the twenty-eight solar mansions are visible, the other half are invisible. Heaven turns round like the nave of a wheel" (*u*). It is difficult to know for certain how Ko Hung conceived heaven and earth both resting on the air and on water. He may have considered both as reposing on the atmosphere underneath, but it is possible also that he imagined the entire cosmos, *i.e.*, the uranosphere with the earth in its centre suspended in the air without. The earth swims on the ocean, but the circling sky cannot well do that. Ko Hung may have regarded the ocean as something steady like the earth and the sky as hanging about it. It is hardly permissible to conceive of the motion of the earth as a rotation, an idea quite alien to the Chinese

(*s*) *Spiegel*, Eranische Altertumskunde, Vol. I. p. 189. Of different opinion, *Casartelli* (Hastings, p. 162).

(*t*) *Hastings*, Vol. IV. p. 174.

(*u*) Chin-shu XI. 2 v.: 葛洪釋之曰渾天儀注云天如雞子地如雞中黃孤居於天內天大而地小天表裏有水天地各乘氣而立載水而行周天三百六十五度……則半覆地上半繞地下故二十八宿半見半隱天轉如車轂之運也.

mind (*x*). Most likely a movement in horizontal and vertical direction is meant, on which we shall touch further.

Wang Ch'ung informs us that by some heaven was supposed to move round below the earth. This he thinks impossible, for ten feet deep one finds water in the earth, consequently heaven would have to move through water. (*y*). Wang Ch'ung would seem to assume that there is water below the earth. The counter-arguments of *Ko Hung*, who, apart from the cited passage of the *Huang-ti shu*, relies on the *Yiking*, are very naïve and futile analogies. Because the dragon, the representative of the Yang, lived in the water, heaven, belonging to the same category, must be able to move through water as well. This is further inferred from several hexagrams of the Yiking (*z*).

Theoretically, according to this hypothesis, heaven is round like a ball. Thus *Chêng Hsüan* says that heaven has the shape of a ball, and that the earth is in its centre (*a*). The *Sung-shu* points out that in spite of this *Lu Chi* and others give to their sphere the form of an egg, thus making it elliptic (*b*).

In the conflict between the two world-conceptions *Kai-t'ien* and *Hun-t'ien*, the latter ultimately was victorious.

(*x*) *Gaubil*, Astron. chin. p. 241, says that *Chêng Hsüan* spoke about the rotation of the earth, but in a very confused way. I doubt whether this statement is correct. In Greece *Aristarchus of Samos*, about 300 B.C., was the first to teach the rotation of the earth round the sun and its own axis, while the firmament of the fixed stars remained motionless. This doctrine overthrowing the cherished ideas about the importance of our earth and its inhabitants could not overcome the common prejudices, and fell into oblivion. *Copernicus* did not know about this theory, and had to discover it again.

(*y*) Lun Hêng, XI. 6 r.

(*z*) Chin-shu, XI. 3 r.

(*a*) Sung-shu 23, 2 r.: 鄭 玄 云。天 體 圓 如 彈 丸 地 處 天 之 半.

(*b*) Sung-shu, 23, 2 v.

The official histories from the *Chin-shu* on declare it to be the only true conception.

(3) *Hsüan-yeh System.*

T'sai Yung states about this system that it had faded from the memory. It is believed to have originated in the *Shang* epoch (c). *Wylie* remarks that it has not been handed down, and that in the opinion of native authors it has a close resemblance to the system of the Europeans (d). To some extent this is true, for *Hsi Mêng* of the *Han* time, basing himself on older sources, gives us the following outline (e):

"Heaven has no solid substance. When looking up to it, it appears to us of immense height; the eyes become dazed, and the sight obscured, whence the dark blue colour. It is like seeing from the side yellow mountains in a great distance, for then they appear blue. Or, when we gaze down into a valley a thousand fathoms deep, it is of a sombre black. Blue is not the real colour, and the blackness is not substantial either (f). The sun, the moon, and

---

(c) *Erh-ya su.*

(d) A. *Wylie*, Notes on Chinese Literature, p. 86.

(e) Chin-shu XI. 2 r. : 漢秘書郎郗萌記先師相傳云天了無質仰而瞻之高遠無極眼贅瞀精絕故蒼蒼然也·譬之旁望遠道之黃山皆青俯察千仞之深谷而窈黑夫青非眞色而黑非有體也·日月衆星自然浮生虛空之中其行其止皆須氣焉是以七躍或逝或住或順或逆伏見無常進退不同由乎無所根繫故各異也·故辰極常居其所而北斗不與衆星同沒也·攝提塡星皆東行日行一度月行十三度遲疾任情其無所繫著可知矣若綴附天體不得爾也·

(f) Perhaps the term 宣夜 means the "all-pervading night," the empty space which has no colour and is as dark as night.

all the stars float and live free in the empty space. Their movements and their rest must be caused by air (*g*). Thus the seven luminaries proceed and stop, following sometimes a natural course, sometimes reversing it. We do not observe any regularity, their progress and their backward course are not alike (*h*). Because they are not attached to any basis, they vary so much. The pole star always keeps its place and the ' northern bushel ' does not go down along with the other stars. Jupiter and Saturn both move eastward; when the sun passes one degree, the moon passes thirteen. Their speed depends on circumstances, which shows that these stars are not attached to anything (*i*), for if they were fastened to the body of heaven, this could not be so."

Whereas by the *Kai-t'ien* doctrine heaven is likened to a hemisphere and by the *Hun-t'ien* theory to a full sphere, the *Hsüan-yeh* system claims that it has no shape at all, being deprived of substance which is indispensable to produce shape. We merely have an infinite void in which the stars, balanced and moved by air, are suspended. This view cannot have found many advocates, for we do not hear anything more about it. Only *Chêng Hsüan* is recorded to have asserted that heaven is the pure Yang fluid and has no shape (*Erh-ya su*).

(4) *Hsin-t'ien System.*

Yao Hsin (*k*) (third century A.D.) is considered the inventor of this theory. It contends that heaven is shaped

---

(*g*) *Anaximander* maintains that the movement of all celestial bodies is caused by currents of air : Zeller, I. p. 208.

(*h*) This irregularity applies particularly to the vagrant stars, the planets, whose alternating forward and backward movements *Ptolemy* endeavoured to explain by his epicycles.

(*i*) *Kai-t'ien* and *Hun-t'ien* suppose some close connection between the stars and the solid heavenly sphere.

(*k*) 姚 信.

like the hood of a carriage (*l*), viz., high in the north and
low in the south, where it even enters into earth while
revolving. The reasons adduced are exceedingly queer :
Man resembles heaven most of all creatures, consequently
what is true of man must hold good for heaven as well.
Man may bend down his chin on his breast, but he
cannot press down his neck upon his back, ergo heaven is
depressed in the south and elevated in the north (*m*).
It is hardly possible to carry wrong analogies any further.
This form of heaven, however, Yao Hsin regards as
changeable and dependent upon the lowering and rising
of the axis of heaven and the pole in the different seasons.
" At the time of the winter solstice the pole is low
and heaven in its gyration is near the south, consequently
the sun is far away from man and the ' bushel ' near
him. Then the air of the northern sky arrives, and it
freezes. At the time of the summer solstice the pole
rises, heaven in its motion approaches the north, and
the ' bushel ' is far distant from man, while the sun
comes near him. Then the air of the southern sky super-
venes, and heat ensues. The pole being raised, the sun in
its course enters the earth but slightly, whence the nights
are short. Heaven is high above the earth, and the days
are long. The pole being lowered, the sun proceeding
enters very deeply into the earth, therefore the nights are
long, and heaven rising but slightly above the earth, the
days are short " (*n*).

(*l*) 軒.

(*m*) 人 爲 靈 蟲 形 最 似 天 今 人 頤 前 多 臨 胷 而 項
不 能 覆 背 近 取 諸 身 故 知 天 之 體 南 低 入 地 北 則
偏 高.

(*n*) Chin-shu XI. 2 v. and Sung-shu XXIII. 4 r. 又 冬 至 極 低
而 天 運 近 南 故 日 去 人 遠 而 斗 去 人 近 北 天 氣 至

The notion of the lifting and sinking of heaven was known in the Han time already, for Wang Ch'ung, while challenging it, gives a plausible reason : " Some people hold that in summer, when the Yang fluid abounds, it is in the south, and that in consequence heaven rises and becomes high.   In winter the Yang fluid decays, and heaven sinks down and becomes depressed.   When heaven is high, the course of the sun increases in length, and the days are lengthened; when heaven is low, the solar curve decreases, and the days are short " (*o*).

The *Sung-shu* opines that this theory should be termed 軒 天 *Hsien-t'ien*, hsien= 軒 昂 *hsien-ang*, " high," 昕 being past comprehension (*p*).

Generally speaking, this hypothesis is nothing more than a modification of the *Kai-t'ien* system.   The celestial dome does not enclose the earth from below also, but merely enters more or less deeply into the earth forming the foundation, as it were.   The mobility of the axis of the universe through which the entire heavenly vault is raised in summer and depressed in winter, is different.   We can conceive it as an umbrella, sometimes inclined sideways, sometimes lifted up, the outer rim of which is represented by the orbit of the sun.   According to the *Kai-t'ien* system heaven is perpetually higher in the south than in the north. In the *Hsin-t'ien* system this is reversed.

This theory did not attain any importance.   The historical works deem it extravagant and as little founded

---

故 冰 寒 也 夏 至 極 起 而 天 運 近 北 而 斗 去 人 遠 日
去 人 近 南 天 氣 至 故 蒸 熱 也 極 之 立 時 日 行 地 中
淺 故 夜 短 天 去 地 高 故 晝 長 也 極 之 低 時 日 行 地
中 深 故 夜 長 天 去 地 下 淺 故 晝 短 也.

(*o*) Lun-hêng transl. Vol. I., p. 259.
(*p*) Sung-shu, *loc. cit.*

scientifically as the two others which still remain to be discussed.

(5) *Chiung-t'ien System.*

An ancestor of *Yü Hsi* (fourth century A.D.), *Yü Sung*, is credited with having evolved this theory, which gives to heaven the form of the shell of a hen's egg swimming with its edge on the ocean surrounding the earth, and simultaneously carried by the original vapours. It may be compared with an upturned little basket swimming on water without going down, since it is filled with air which presses on the water. The sun turns round the northern heavenly pole, sinks down in the west, and reappears in the east without penetrating into the earth (*q*). Where it stays in the meantime we are not told. Presumably it takes its course through the ocean which then must flow beneath the earth. *Yü Sung* undoubtedly considers heaven to be a hemisphere swimming on the ocean. The idea to support heaven by the pressure of the air at the same time is original, and bespeaks some power of observation. Otherwise, this theory, too, may be regarded as a modification of the *Kai-t'ien* system.

(6) *An-t'ien System.*

This hypothesis is held to be merely an amplification of the *Hsüan-yeh* theory on the unsubstantial sky, and is connected with the name of *Yü Hsi*, who, born in Kuei-chi, lived under the régime *Hsien-k'ang*, 355-343 A.D., of the *Chin* emperor *Ch'êng-ti*. He claims that heaven is im-

---

(*q*) Chin-shu, XI. 2 r., and Sui-shu, XIX. 3 r. 虞喜族祖河
間相聳又立穹天論云天形穹隆如雞子幕其際
周接四海之表浮於元氣之上譬如覆匼以抑水
而不沒者氣充其中故也日繞辰極沒西而還東
不出入地中.

measurably high and earth unfathomably deep. Heaven above is in a state of permanent rest, and the mass of the earth below is likewise immovable. Both cover each other and tightly fit together. Should one part be square, both must be square, and if one be round, both must be circular. It is impossible to assume that one is square, the other round. Their luminaries are distributed, each pursuing its own course like the low and high tides of the ocean and its rivers, or things sometimes moving, sometimes vanishing. *Ko Hung* assails this theory, objecting that, if the fixed stars were not attached to heaven, the latter would be useless. One might say that there is no heaven, but not that heaven is motionless, an apophthegm lauded by *Sse-ma Piao* as a piece of deep wisdom (r).

Albeit yet this theory seems to be different from the *Hsüan-yeh* hypothesis in that it does not contend that heaven is nothing but air, and supposes it to have some shape and to fit exactly together with the earth at its edge, being either square or round. It is true that the immeasurableness must be taken as immensely great, not as infinite, for under such a condition no shape could be possible. The supposition of freely moving stars, not fixed to the empyrean, is again in keeping with the *Hsüan-yeh* theory. The motionlessness of heaven is the characteristic feature

---

(r) Chin-shu, XI. 2 r., and Sui-shu, XIX 3 r.

成帝咸康中
會稽虞喜因宣夜之說作安天論以爲天高窮於
無窮地深測於不測天確乎在上有常安之形地
塊焉在下有居靜之體當相覆冒方則俱方圓則
俱圓無方圓不同之義也其光曜布列各自運行
猶江海之有潮汐萬品之有行藏也葛洪聞而譏
之曰苟辰宿不麗於天天爲無用便可言無何必
復云有之而不動乎由此而談稚川可謂知言之
選也.

of this system. Perhaps it may be considered as a transformation of the *Kai-t'ien* doctrine : We have a hemisphere
or a square surface with a dome rising above it, but this
dome does not move.

To summarise we may divide the various systems into
four types according to the form of the universe :

(1) Heaven a dome, a hemisphere : *Kai-t'ien*; elliptic :
   Ch'iung-t'ien; irregularly shaped : *Hsin-t'ien*; of
   immeasurable height : *An-t'ien*.

(2) Heaven a flat disk parallel to earth : *Wang Ch'ung*.

(3) Heaven a sphere, ovoid : *Hun-t'ien*.

(4) Heaven without form or substance : *Hsüan-yeh*.

III. Similar Theories of Other Nations.

For the primitive mind the assumption that heaven is a
vault stretched over the earth, which is more or less flat,
would appear the most natural, for indeed heaven looks
like a blue dome or a vault. Thus we meet with the *Kai-
t'ien* system among most of the ancient nations—the
Chaldeans (*Babylonians*), *Jews*, *Persians*, *Egyptians*,
Greeks, and some of our modern *primitives*.

It is peculiar to the *Semitic* peoples and the *Persians* to
assume two celestial vaults. This notion most likely was
derived from the Chaldeans, who, in astronomy, became the
teachers of all the other countries. The Chaldeans held
that the demiurgos *Bel-Marduk* created two superimposed
vaults. The inner one was closed by a circular dam preventing the ocean surrounding the earth from flowing in.
Heaven and earth were both motionless. The stars were
regarded as fireballs penetrating into the exterior vault
and passing out again (*a*).

In the *Old Testament* heaven has the form of a vast
vault leaning on earth all round. Under the surface of the

(*a*) *A. Bouché-Leclercq*, L'astrologie grecque, Paris, 1899, p. 40.

earth there is not only earth, but also the profundity of the
ocean forming the dark nether part of the world. The
ocean washes the " Pillars of Heaven," the foundation of
the great vault. The low meteorological heaven is looked
upon by the Jews as firmament, $rājia^{\iota} = \sigma\tau\epsilon\rho\acute{\epsilon}\omega\mu\alpha$, the
firmamentum of the *Vulgata*, a vault of great solidity which
is transparent, so that the light of the stars can pass
through. It carries the " upper water," the rain collected
between the lower and the upper vault, the astronomica¹
heaven. This is also the storehouse for hail and snow, and
on the sides lower down there are the rooms of the winds.
The starry sky is often described as soft and flexible like a
cloth, on which the stars are fastened (*b*). In *Genesis* I.,
14, 15 and 17, on the other hand, it is said that God
placed the lights in the firmament of heaven. Among the
Jews, also, the astronomical views have undergone many
changes (*c*).

The *Iranians* had two heavens, one exterior (twâsha)
in constant motion, to which the stars, notably the planets
and the zodiac, were attached, and an interior (âsmân) of
blue, pellucid stones, the firmament of the Bible (*d*).

The *Greeks* started from the Babylonian world-conception, but did not recognise two skies. In their imagination
the world was an enormous hall with heaven above as a
ceiling. Below the crust of the earth there was a dark
cellar, the nether world. Round about flowed the ocean.
When the sun had set in the west, in the course of the
night it would sail back on the ocean, and on the next
morning rise again in the east cleanly washed (*e*).

(*b*) Ps. CIV., 2 : " God stretcheth out the heaven like a *curtain* "—
Isa. XL., 22 : " He stretcheth out the heaven like a *veil*, and spreadeth
it out like a *tent* to dwell in."

(*c*) G. *Schiaparelli*, Astronomy of the Old Testament, Oxford, 1903
(transl.), pp. 22, 26, 31, 33, 39, 43, 50.

(*d*) *Spiegel*, Eran. Altertumsk. I., 188, and II., 14.

(*e*) *Troels-Lund*, Himmelsbild und Weltanschauung, transl. by L.
Bloch, 3rd ed., 1908, p. 92.

The *Egyptians* still endeavour to account for the strange disappearance of the sun mythologically : the sun dies in the evening, and during the night his place is taken by his consort, the moon. The new sun on the following day is the son of both. Since the sun is held to be a god, we here have the triad : God the father, God the mother, and God the son. According to another religious explanation the sun, during the night, travels back to the east on dark paths through the lower world (*f*).

The *North American Indians* and the *South Sea Islanders* maintain that the earth is flat and arched over by the solid vault of heaven (*g*).

To the view of *Wang Ch'ung* that heaven and earth are flat planes, of which the upper one turns round, which gives the illusion of the disappearance of the sun, we have an interesting parallel in *Xenophanes*, born in 570 B.C., who took the sun, the moon, and the stars for masses of fiery vapour, which do not gyrate round the earth, but in an endless straight plane fly above it. The circular orbit is said to be nothing but an optical illusion (*h*).

Wang Ch'ung regards the sun as fire, the moon as water and assigns to the stars the same substance as that of the sun and the moon, *i.e.*, they most likely consist of a mixture of fire and water or of fiery vapours. Insomuch as *Xenophanes* declares the earth to be immeasurably deep

---

(*f*) *Troels-Lund*, p. 66.

(*g*) *Tylor*, Primitive Culture, II., p. 71.

(*h*) *Zeller*, I., p. 500, Stob. I., 534 (Plac. II., 24, 7): ὁ τ'αὐτὸς τὸν ἥλιον εἰς ἄπειρον μὲν προϊέναι δοκεῖν δὲ κυκλεῖσθαι διὰ τὴν ἀπόστασιν. The *Egyptians* fancied heaven to be an ocean parallel to earth, on which the stars travel in ships. There is another ocean beneath the earth, on which the sun sails during the night. (*Hastings*, IV., 145, art. by *Flinders Petrie*.) Similarly the *Tewa Indians* make the sun and the moon pass daily over trails above the great waters of the sky. At night they pass through a lake to the under-world and emerge again through a lake in the east. (*I. P. Harrington*, The Ethnography of the Tewa Indians, Washington, 1916, in the 29th Annual Report of the Bureau of American Ethnology, p. 46.)

and the air immeasurably high (*i*), he agrees with the *An-t'ien* system. The *Jews* likewise presumed the distance between heaven and earth to be infinite.

Thales seems still to have held to the *Kai-t'ien* system, for he is believed to have represented the earth as swimming on water (*k*), the same conception which we found in the *Huang-ti shu*. *Anaximander*, born 611 B.C., was perhaps the first who assumed a celestial sphere and thus passed over to the *Hun-t'ien* system, which from that time on became dominating in Greece and found its most perfect expression through *Ptolemy*. Any influence of Chinese astronomy on the Greek or *vice versâ* is out of the question of course. The difficulties to explain in a satisfactory manner the motions of the stars by the *Kai-t'ien* theory were calculated to conduce sooner or later to the spherical hypothesis in Greece not less than in China.

The Greeks like the Chinese imagined the stars as attached to the sky and turning round with it. Many of the old meteorologists and philosophers, however, were of opinion that this motion did not pass over the earth, but sideways around it (*l*). *Anaximenes* explains the disappearance of the sun during the night by the conjecture that the earth is higher in the north than in the south, and that in the north the sun is covered by high mountains (*m*).

(*i*) *Ueberweg*, Grundriss der Philosophie, Berlin, 1894, I., at p. 72 *seq.* Arist. De Xenoph. Zen. Gorg. c. 2, 976a, 32 : ὡς καὶ Ξενοφάνης ἄπειρον τό τε βάθος τῆς γῆς καὶ τοῦ ἀέρος φησὶν εἶναι.

(*k*) *E. Hoppe*, Mathematik und Asronomie im Klassischen Altertum, 1911, p. 64.   *Zeller*, Bd. I., p. 182.   *Arist.* Met. I., 3, 983, b. 21 : ἀλλὰ Θαλῆς μὲν ὁ τῆς τοιαύτης ἀρχηγὸς φιλοσοφίας ὕδωρ εἶναί φησιν (διὸ καὶ τὴν γῆν ἐφ' ὕδατος ἀπεφήνατο εἶναι) Arist. De Caelo II., 13, 294a, 29 : Τοῖτον γὰρ ἀρχαιότατον παρειλήφαμεν τὸν λόγον, ὅν φασιν εἰπεῖν Θαλῆν τὸν Μιλήσιον, ὡς διὰ τὸ πλωτὴν εἶναι [γῆν] μένουσαν ὥσπερ ξύλον ἤ τι τοιοῦτον ἕτερον.

(*l*) *Zeller* I., 227.   Arist. Meteor. II., 1, 354a, 28 : τὸ πολλοὺς πεισθῆναι τῶν ἀρχαίων μετεωρολόγων τὸν ἥλιον μὴ φέρεσθαι ὑπὸ γῆν, ἀλλὰ περὶ γῆν καὶ τὸν τόπον τοῦτον, ἀφανίζεσθαι δὲ καὶ ποιεῖν νύκτα διὰ τὸ ὑψηλὴν εἶναι πρὸς ἄρκτον τὴν γῆν.

(*m*) *Hippolyt*, Refut. haer. οὐ κινεῖσθαι δὲ ὑπὸ γῆν τὰ ἄστρα λέγει καθὼς ἕτεροι ὑπειλήφασιν, ἀλλὰ περὶ γῆν, ὡσπερεὶ περὶ τὴν ἡμετέραν κεφαλὴν

This was also the view of *Leucippus* and *Democritus*, of *Anaxagoras*, and *Diogenes* of *Apollonia* (*n*). This is the much debated lateral millstone movement of the *Kai-t'ien* theory. The Greek philosophers like the Chinese comparing the sky with a reclining umbrella noticed that this lateral movement parallel to the surface of the earth was not conformable to reality and therefore made a similar conjecture to the effect that the axis of the world originally stood vertically on the earth, but later by some unknown cause became inclined to the south. Consequently the stars which at the outset moved but from east to west around the disk of the earth then sank down below the horizon, their orbit intersecting the horizon, which also became the cause of day and night (*o*).

Leucippus and *Democritus* tried to explain the inclination of the axis by the surmise that the earth had inclined towards the south not being able to withstand the pressure of the cosmos owing to its lesser density in the hot regions (*p*). Whereas these philosophers were satisfied with one single inclination of the axis, the *Hsin-t'ien* system, as we saw, supposes a constant rising and sinking caused by the extension and contraction of heaven in the south, the region of the hot fluid, which in summer and winter reaches a maximum.

στρέφεται τὸ πιλίον, κρύπτεσθαί τε τὸν ἥλιον οὐχ ὑπὸ γῆν γενόμενον, ἀλλ' ὑπὸ τῶν τῆς γῆς ὑψηλοτέρων μερῶν σκεπόμενον, καὶ διὰ τὴν πλείονα ἡμῶν αὐτοῦ γενομένην ἀπόστασιν.

(*n*) *Zeller*, I., 243 and 802.

(*o*) *Zeller*, I., 243. *Diogenes* and *Anaxagoras* said according to *Plac.* II., 8, 1. μετὰ τὸ συστῆναι τὸν κόσμον καὶ τὰ ζῷα ἐκ τῆς γῆς ἐξαγαγεῖν ἐγκλιθῆναι πως τὸν κόσμον ἐκ τοῦ αὐτομάτου εἰς τὸ μεσημβρινὸν αὐτοῦ μέρος, and in *Diog.* II., 9 *Anaxagoras* stated: τὰ δ' ἄστρα κατ' ἀρχὰς μὲν θολοειδῶς ἐνεχθῆναι ὥστε κατὰ κορυφὴν τῆς γῆς, τὸν ἀεὶ φαινόμενον εἶναι πόλον, ὕστερον δὲ τὴν ἔγκλισιν λαβεῖν.

(*p*) *Zeller*, I., 802.

IV. Creation.

In contrast to other nations the Chinese have no mytho-logical cosmogony; the oldest sources already attempt to account for creation in a scientific way. We find the most elaborate attempts of this kind in the works of Taoist philosophers who took a greater interest in nature than the Confucianists. The oldest author who proposes a theory of creation is *Lieh-tse*, about 400 B.C. He starts from chaos, in which the three primary elements of the universe—force, form and substance—were still undivided. He connotes this state as the great evolution, when all things are still in a great medley, brewing, surging and floating, and nothing in particular can be distinguished. This first stage is followed by a second, the great inception, when force becomes separated, then by a third, the great beginning, when forms appear, and a fourth, the great homogeneity, when substances become visible. Then the light and pure substances rise above and form heaven, the heavier and coarser sink down and produce the earth : " The teacher *Lieh-tse* said : The sages of old held that the *Yin* and *Yang* govern heaven and earth. Now, form being born out of the formless, from what do heaven and earth take their origin ? It is said : There was a great evolution, a great inception, a great beginning, and a great homogeneity. During the great evolution, force was still imperceptible, in the great inception force begins to work, in the great beginning forms appear, and during the great homogeneity substances are produced. The state when force, forms and substances, though existing, were still undivided is called chaos. Chaos designates the conglomeration and insepar-ability of things. ' They could not be seen though looked at, not be heard though listened to, not be attained though grasped at,' therefore one speaks of incessant evolution. Evolution is not bound to any forms or limits. Evolution in its transformations produces one, the changes of one produce seven, the changes of seven produce nine. Nine is the climax, it changes again and becomes one. With one forms begin to change (*a*). The pure and light matter becomes the heaven above, the turbid and heavy matter forms the earth below. Their aggregation gives birth to man, and the vitalising principle of heaven and earth creates all beings " (*b*).

Ch'ü Yuan (fourth century B.C.) in his " *Questions about Heaven* " takes a much more sceptical standpoint than *Lieh-tse*. But from these it is evident that he was perfectly conversant with the notions of chaos. He inquires, " Who could transmit something to us about the inception of time ? And before things above and below had any form, what could we use as a starting-point for our investigations ? " (*c*). At that time heaven and earth were

---

(*a*) This queer assertion that 1 changes into 7, 7 into 9, and 9 again into 1, which I once compared with the calculation of the witch in Faust (cf. my art. on *Yang Chu* in Journ. Peking Orient. Soc., Vol. III., 1893, p. 211), may have a meaning after all, to wit, from the original unity, the Monad=1 proceed the Yin and Yang and the Five Elements=7. From these elements are evolved heaven and earth, $2+7=9$, and these 9 may again be regarded as a unit, the universe=1. The forms of the universe undergo continual changes.

(*b*) *Lieh-tse*, I., p. 2 r. 子列子曰昔者聖人因陰陽以統天地夫有形者生於無形則天地安從生故曰有太易有太初有太始有太素太易者未見氣也太初者氣之始也太始者形之始也太素者質之始也氣形質具而未相離故曰渾淪渾淪者言萬物相渾淪而未相離也視之不見聽之不聞循之不得故曰易也易無形埒易變而爲一一變而爲七七變而爲九九變者究也乃復變爲一一者形變之始也清輕者上爲天濁重者下爲地沖和氣者爲人故天地含精萬物化生.

(*c*) *Ch'u-tse*, III., 1 : 屈原天問曰遂古之初誰傳道之上下未形何繇考之.

not yet separated and there were no men, consequently no coeval testimony was available. " When the difference between light and darkness was still blurred, who could fully realise this state of affairs, and as long as all forms were still in a chaotic motion, how could one recognise anything ? " " Bright light and deep darkness, who produced them ? And which of the Yin, the Yang, and the third is the origin and which the transformation ? " (d). This third according to *Chu Hsi's* comment is heaven, but heaven conceived as a higher, intellectual power or principle, not materially. In support of this view a saying of *Ku Liang* (fifth century B.C.) is adduced : " The Yin alone cannot exist, nor the Yang alone, nor heaven either. Only when the three are combined, they come into being " (e). From all these questions it results no doubt that *Ch'ü Yuan* assumed a time when heaven and earth were not yet formed, light and darkness not yet separated, all forms still flowing, and that he owned a superior, immaterial principle in addition to Yin and Yang.

Lü Pu-wei, of the third century B.C., begins with the *Great Unity* (Monad), from which proceed the two modes (heaven and earth), which again give rise to the Yin and Yang. The one ascends, the other goes down. First in a state of complete confusion (chaos) they separate, but reunite later. Their union and separation change continually, which no doubt refers to the production of the organic world. All things are created by the Monad, and transformed by Yin and Yang (f).

(d) *Loc. cit.* 冥昭瞢闇誰能極之馮翼惟象何以識之。明明闇闇惟時何爲陰陽三合何本何化.

(e) 穀梁子曰獨陰不生獨陽不生獨天不生三合然後生.

(f) *Lü-shih ch'un-ch'iu*, V., 4 r. seq. 呂子大樂篇。太一出兩儀兩儀出陰陽陰陽變化一上一下合而成章

In opposition to *Ch'ü Yuan's* sceptical view the Taoist philosopher *Huai-nan-tse* (second century B.C.) holds a strongly dogmatical one, and fancies to be able to make positive statements on the primogenial condition of the universe, but barely enunciates utterly vague phrases, which, in spite of a profusion of queer and rare words, do not convey more meaning than the less pretentious assertions of *Lieh-tse*. He distinguishes a beginning, a time before this beginning, and a time still preceding this time before the beginning. And likewise he speaks of a state of non-existence, a state preceding this, and a state still further before the state when non-existence did not yet exist. Of course, he does not take these notions in an absolute sense referring to the beginning of existence, but understands by them the inception of the existence of our universe in its actual form (*g*).

With more consistency than *Lieh-tse Huai-nan-tse* makes the world begin with *Tao* : " Tao begins in the Great Void, which engenders the universe, which produces the fluid. In this a separation takes place. The purer and brighter particles are thinner and finer and form heaven. The coarser and more turbid accumulate and become earth. The blending of the purer and finer parts is easy, the condensation of the heavier and turbid parts more troublesome and difficult, therefore heaven is created prior to earth. The combined essence of heaven and earth is Yin and Yang, the activity of Yin and Yang produces the four seasons, and the dispersion of the essence of the four seasons produces the ten thousand things. From the hot Yang fluid comes fire, and the essence of fire becomes

---

渾渾沌沌離則復合合則復離是謂天常 …… 萬物所出造於太一化於陰陽.

(*g*) It seems to be the common view of Taoist philosophers that existence sprang from non-existence, see *Lao-tse Tao-tě-king*, chap. 40, and *Chuang-tse*, VIII., 8 v.

the sun. From the cold Yin fluid comes water, and the essence of water forms the moon. The sexual intercourse between the sun and the moon gives birth to the stars. Heaven harbours the sun, the moon and the stars; earth comprises water, the rivers, the soil and dust " (*h*).

Chang Hêng pursuant to his *Hun-t'ien* theory holds that heaven is produced not above, but outside, and earth not below, but in the centre. About creation he says *inter alia* " When the original fluid became divided, the hard and soft were first separated, and the pure and turbid particles differently treated. Heaven was produced without, and earth was fixed in the centre. Heaven received its substance from Yang, therefore it became round and moved, earth was made of Yin, whence it became flat and motionless. Motion acts and generates, motionlessness enfolds and transforms " (*i*).

In the writings of *Confucius* and *Mencius* there is no reference to creation, for such questions were foreign to the two philosophers whose interest centred in ethics and political economy. But we have a reference in the Great Commentary of the *Yiking*, probably a work of a disciple

---

(*h*) Huai-nan-tse, III., 1. 淮南子天文訓。道始於虛霩 虛霩生宇宙宇宙生氣氣有涯垠清陽者薄靡而 爲天重濁者凝滯而爲地清妙之合專易重濁之 凝竭難故天先成而地後定天地之襲精爲陰陽 陰陽之專精爲四時四時之散精爲萬物積陽之 熱氣生火火氣之精者爲日積陰之寒氣爲水水 氣之精者爲月日月之淫爲精者爲星辰天受日 月星辰地受水潦塵埃.

(*i*) T'u-shu chi-ch'êng 乾象典 chap. VII., 天地總部雜錄 p. 6 v. 元氣剖判剛柔始分清濁異位天成於外地 定於內天體於陽故圓以動地體於陰故平以靜 動以行施靜以合化.

of Confucius, and another in the *Liki*. We read in the Great Appendix that in the Yiking it is the *Absolute* = *T'ai-chi* which produced the two modes, which again originated the four forms (hsiang) (*k*). In the opinion of most Chinese commentators, shared by many sinologues, these words refer to cosmogony, an idea which is assailed by Legge (*l*). It is true that the words may be referred to the symbols of the Yiking, but physical phenomena correspond to them. The two words, *ch'ien* and *k'un*, represent heaven and earth, and the four hsiang various modifications of Yin and Yang. Legge (p. 12) presumes that the word T'ai-chi, the Absolute, was introduced into the text from a Taoist source. Such an assumption is not imperative. The cosmogony in itself is not Taoist, although it is discussed most fully by Taoist writers. Since we do not meet with any other cosmological theories, the cosmogony under review must have been generally accepted, by Confucianists no less than by Taoists.

In the *Liki* the place of the Absolute is taken by the Great Unity (Monad) as with *Lü Pu-wei*. " It splits and becomes heaven and earth, it changes and becomes Yin and Yang, it alternates, and becomes the four seasons " (*m*). *K'ung Ying-ta* (*n*), a Confucianist of the seventh century A.D., makes the comment that the Monad is the original fluid still in its chaotic state before the separation of heaven and earth, a view not challenged by other commentators.

In spite of some divergence in details there is a considerable consensus of opinions about the process of

---

(*k*) *Legge*, Yiking (Sacred Books of the East, Vol. XVI.), p. 373.

繫 辭 上 傳。易 有 太 極 是 生 兩 儀 兩 儀 生 四 象 四 象 生 八 卦.

(*l*) *Legge*, Yiking, p. 44.

(*m*) Liki (Sacred Books of the East, Vols. XXVII.-XXVIII.), translation by *Legge*, Vol. I., p. 287.

(*n*) 孔 穎 達.

creation. A creator is nowhere mentioned, only a chaos in which the future world was already virtually contained. From this primary state were evolved two principles or forces, Yin and Yang, from which at the same time heaven and earth were produced. The ultimate cause of the world is variously designated as Tao, Monad, the Absolute, or as Heaven in the sense of a spiritual principle.

The Greek philosophers agree with the Chinese views of creation in many respects. The *Pythagoreans* call the One or the Monas the mother of the gods, it being the first cosmic body from which the formation of the universe proceeds. The *Orphic Cosmogony* according to *Eudemus* does not assume Chaos to be the first thing, but *night*, from which heaven and earth are evolved. To *Diogenes of Apollonia* the primary matter is air, which being warmed and cooled down becomes either rarefied or condensed. The heavier matter sinks down and forms the earth, the lighter moves upwards and forms the sun and the stars (*o*). *Anaxagoras* claims that by the motion of Chaos the thick and thin, cold and warm, dark and bright, moist and dry particles, just what the Chinese term Yin and Yang, are divided into two masses. That which is heavy, thick, and moist is driven into the centre, the remainder to the periphery. From the vapour mass in the centre water became disassociated, from the water earth, and by cold earth was changed into stones (*p*). In a similar manner *Democritus* and the *Atomists* believed that from the mass of atoms the lighter ones were uplifted and above formed heaven, fire and air, whereas the heavier ones subsided in the centre and there became earth (*q*). The *Epicurean*

(*o*) *Zeller*, I., pp. 381, 80, 241 seq.

(*p*) *Zeller*, I., 897, Fragm. Schaubach 20 (9): ἀπὸ τουτέων ἀποκρινομένων συμπήγνυται γῆ· ἐκ μὲν γὰρ τῶν νεφελῶν ὕδωρ ἀποκρίνεται, ἐκ δὲ τοῦ ὕδατος γῆ· ἐκ δὲ τῆς γῆς λίθοι συμπήγνυνται ὑπὸ τοῦ ψυχροῦ.

(*q*) *Zeller*, I., 798-799.

cosmogony has quite a similar conceit. One of its principal advocates, *Lucretius*, says in his didactic poem :

> " Quippe etenim primum terrai corpora quaeque,
> propterea quod erant gravia et perplexa coibant
> in medio atque imas capiebant omnia sedes;
> quae quanto magis inter se perplexa coibant,
> tam magis expressere ea quae mare, sidera, solem
> lunamque efficerent et magni moenia mundi " (r).

It is a common misstatement that in Chinese cosmogony *P'an Ku*, the first living being or the first man, often styled the Chinese Adam, plays the chief part (s). The legend of P'an Ku is unknown in earlier Chinese literature and not mentioned by any author of higher standing. It does not make its appearance prior to the first centuries of our era. According to one tradition P'an Ku came into being in the midst of the cosmic egg : while the pure elements coagulated and became heaven, and the turbid ones earth, P'an Ku was created in the middle between them. Heaven grew daily ten feet higher, earth ten feet deeper, and P'an Ku ten feet taller. So he grew to be a giant and lived 18,000 years (t). In another myth P'an Ku is the product of the Yin and Yang forces and acts as Demiurgus, wherefore he is often depicted with an axe with which he cut out the mountains. When he died, his breath became wind, his voice thunder, his four limbs the four directions, his five extremities the five sacred mountains, his left eye the sun, his right eye the moon, his blood rivers, his beard stars, his hair trees and plants, his flesh the soil,

---

(r) *Lucretius*, V., 439-444.

(s) Cf. *Enciclopedia Universal Europeo-Americana*, Vol. XV., p. 1152, art. '' Cosmogonia.''

(t) *P'ei-wên yün-fu* under P'an Ku, where a quotation from *Hsü Chêng* 徐整, 3rd cent. A.D. and two poets of the 8th and 9th centuries is given.

his teeth, bones and marrow metals, precious stones and pearls, his perspiration rain, and his parasites men (*u*).

One might be inclined to regard this myth as a later Chinese invention, were it not so very crude and primitive and common to so many people. The *Egyptians* and *Chaldeans* fancied the body of a giant stretched over the celestial vault, so that the twelve signs of the zodiac corresponded to the parts of his body. In the *Rigveda* the world is formed of the various parts of the body of *Puruṣa* representing the male principle (*x*). The old *Iranians* thought of earth as a sort of human body in which the mountains correspond to the bones, the rivers to the blood and the earth to the flesh. This description is given by the *Bundehesh*, which though later than the time of the *Sassanides* is said to be in consonance with the *Avesta* (*y*). In the oldest *Scandinavian* sagas *Odin* and his brothers killed the giant *Ymir*. With his body they filled the horrible deep abyss *Ginnungagap* and there made the world. From his flesh they formed the earth, from his blood streams, lakes and the ocean, from his teeth and smaller bones rocks and pebbles, from the larger bones the mountains. With his eyebrows they encompassed the earth and named her *Midhgardh*. Heaven was shaped

---

(*u*) Cf. *Mayers*, Reader's Manual, *Giles*, Biogr. Dict., and *W. Williams*, Middle Kingdom, Vol. II., p. 138.

(*x*) *Hastings*, Vol. IV., p. 156, art. by *H. Jacobi*. Puruṣa had been sacrificed by the gods and was cut into pieces. " When they divided Puruṣa, into how many parts did they distribute him? What was his mouth? What was his arms? What were called his thighs and feet? The Brāhmaṇa was his mouth; the Rājanya became his arms; the Vaishya his thighs; the Sūdra sprang from his feet. The moon was produced from his soul; the sun from his eye; Indra and Agni from his mouth; and Vāyu from his breath. From his navel came the atmosphere; from his head arose the sky; from his feet came the earth; from his ear the four quarters; so they formed the worlds " (*Rigveda*, X., 9, translated by *Muir*).

(*y*) *Spiegel*, Eran. Altert. I., 190.

from Ymir's skull, and the brains of the giant were transformed into floating clouds and fogs (z).

Opa, " the world, the universe," is looked upon by the *Tewa Indians* as a living being and worshipped as " Universal Man," whose backbone is the Milky Way (a). The Polynesians have an analogous conception. In the western *Society Islands* the earth is supposed to be the external body of *Tangalva,* the god of heaven (b).

A very old cosmological myth which can be traced much farther back than that of *P'an Ku* is the story of *Kung Kung* and *Nü Wa. Wang Ch'ung* already calls it a very old tradition (c). Kung Kung, a legendary person of prehistoric time, in his anger ran against Mount *Pu-chou,* the " Pillar of Heaven," so that heaven collapsed. Nü Wa, the putative sister of *Fu Hsi,* melted multicoloured stones and therewith repaired the vault of heaven, and she cut off the legs of a sea-turtle and placed them as columns at the four extremities of the world. But heaven was not quite complete in the North-west, wherefore the sun and the moon moved in this direction, and the earth was short of a piece in the South-east, whence all the rivers flowed toward this point (d). The notion of heaven as a massive vault which can be repaired with masonry and moreover is supported by a pillar, the *K'un-lun* Mountain, is very characteristic. Later Nü Wa made four corner-pillars as a safeguard (e). The assumption that in the North-west

(z) *Hastings,* Vol. IV., p. 178, art. by *S. G. Youngert.*
(a) *T. P. Harrington,* Tewa Indians, p. 41.
(b) *Hastings,* Vol. IV., p. 174, art. by *L. H. Gray.*
(c) *Lieh-tse,* V., 5 v.
(d) *Lun Hêng,* transl., Vol. I., p. 250.
(e) Pillars of heaven is a conception very frequent among ancient and primitive people. We met them with the *Jews.* The *Babylonians* likewise made heaven repose on the " world mountain." In Egypt *Horus,* Heaven, was supported by four pillars, his sons (*Hastings,* Vol. IV., p 145, art by *Flinders-Petrie*). The *Indian Buddhists* have their many heavens all piled up above Mount *Meru.* In the *Celtic* hymns of *Uttar* two pillars of heaven are mentioned (*Hastings,* IV., p. 138). In *Teutonic*

a piece of heaven is wanting is meant to account for the setting of the stars at this place like the hypothesis of the *Kai-t'ien*, supporters claiming that heaven is high in the south and low in the north, and the wanting piece of earth in the South-east is believed to be the cause why most Chinese rivers, the Yangtse and Huang-ho included, take their course to the ocean in a south-easterly direction.

V. DESTRUCTION OF THE WORLD.

That the ancient Chinese already have raised the question as to the duration of the world we gather again from *Lieh-tse*, one of our principal sources for the intellectual life of the *Chou* dynasty : A man of the State of *Ch'i* was afraid that heaven and earth might collapse. Another set himself to correct his error, pointing out that heaven and earth are air and therefore cannot fall down. The objection that the sun, the moon, and the stars might come down he met by the remark that they were merely lights in the atmosphere and that even falling down they could not injure anybody. The earth on the other side was a solid mass, which no trampling or pounding could shake. Against both a certain *Ch'ang Lu-tse* contends that there is no reason for inferring an imminent annihilation of the biggest accumulation of matter in empty space. Yet once it must come to this, for all accumulations of air and matter were bound to disperse again. In contrast to this theory *Lieh-tse* himself takes the position of a sceptic favouring neither the one nor the other alternative, as nothing was

---

cosmology the sons of *Bör* lifted the vault of heaven (*eod.* p. 177), and the same is done by the *Bacabs*, the *Maya* gods of the four quarters, who support heaven lest it fall down (*H. Beuchat*, Manuel d'Archéologie Américaine, Paris, 1912, p. 443). *Ch'ü Yuan*, T'ien-wên, *Ch'u-tse*, III., 1, speaks of eight pillars instead of four : " How is the celestial pole fixed? On what repose the Eight Pillars? Why is the south-east deficient? " 天 極 焉 加 八 柱 何 當 東 南 何 虧.

positively known (*f*). We thus have three different views :
the world can be annihilated, it cannot be destroyed, and
finally the *Ignoramus*.

From *Chuang-tse* also we learn that some eccentric
man of the name of *Huang Liao* raised the question why
heaven did not collapse or earth sink down, which was
answered by the famous sophist *Hui-tse*, but unfortunately
we are not told what his reply was (*g*).

In a much later source, the *Lang-huanchi* (*h*), the
destruction of the world and the creation of new worlds is
averred. Being questioned by a young woman whether
the world could perish, the " Teacher of the Nine Heavens "
replied that, if other things perished, the world which was
nothing but a thing could not but perish. Just as a man
after death could be resuscitated in some other place, the
world after perishing here might be created again some-
where else. As little as a tape-worm could know that outside the man in whom it is living there are still other men,
so we little knew but that beyond our world there might
exist others. Therefore the sage looked upon the growing
and decaying of the world with the same equanimity as
on the blossoming and fading of flowers.

The idea that the sky may collapse and the world perish
is rather familiar to primitive people. So we are informed
by *Strabo* that the *Celts* said to *Alexander*, " We fear but
one thing, namely, that heaven may fall down upon us " (*i*).
The modern *Tarahumare* in *Mexico* believe that many
worlds preceded ours which all were destroyed (*k*). In
Greek philosophy this problem is discussed scientifically.

(*f*) *Lieh-tse*, I., 10 r.

(*g*) *Chuang-tse*, translated by *H. Giles*, p. 453.

(*h*) 瑯 嬛 記 in T'u-shu chi ch'êng 乾 象 典 chap. 7, 天 地 總
部 雜 錄 p. 9 v.

(*i*) *Strabo*, VII., 3, 8.

(*k*) *Hastings*, IV., p. 169, art. by *R. L. Lowie*.

Anaximenes, Anaximander and *Diogenes of Apollonia* are reported to have assumed a destruction of the world with a subsequent new creation (*l*). *Heraclitus* believed in world periods of 10,800 years in which the world by combustion returned to its primary substance (*m*). The world periods = *Kalpas* of the *Buddhists* are well known. The time from the origin of a world to the production of a new world, after the destruction of the old one, is said to last 1,344,000,000 years, a *Mahākalpa*. The destruction = *samvartta* is due to fire, water and wind (*n*).

VI. INFINITY OF TIME AND SPACE.

The Taoists are universally convinced of the infinity of time and space. *Lieh-tse* tries to prove it in the following manner (*a*) :

" The *Yin* emperor *T'ang* asked *Hsia Kê* saying, ' Were there already things at the first beginning of the world? ' Hsia Kê replied, ' If there had been no things at the first origin, where should they come from now? Should later generations pretend that there were no things now, would they be right? ' T'ang said, ' Have then things *no* before

---

(*l*) *Zeller*, I., p. 214.

(*m*) *E. Hoppe*, Mathematik und Astronomie im Klassischen Altertum, 1911, p. 125.

(*n*) *Eitel*, Handbook of Chinese Buddhism.

(*a*) *Lieh-tse*, V., 1 r. 殷湯問於夏革曰古初有物乎
夏革曰古初無物今惡得物後之人將謂今之無
物可乎殷湯曰然則物無先後乎夏革曰物之終
始初無極已始或爲終終或爲始惡知其紀然自
物之外自事之先朕所不知也殷湯曰然則上下
八方有極盡乎革曰不知也湯固問革曰無則無
極有則有盡朕何以知之然無極之外復無無極
無盡之中復無無盡無極復無無極無盡復無無
盡朕以是知其無極無盡也而不知其有極有盡也·

and *no* after?' Hsia Kê replied, 'The end and the origin of things are boundless from the beginning. The origin might also be taken for the end and the end for the origin. Who can draw an accurate distinction between them? Yet, what lies beyond things and is anterior to all occurrences I cannot know.'

T'ang continued : 'Have the top and the bottom and the eight regions of heaven an end and a limit?' Hsia Kê said, 'I do not know.' T'ang entreated more earnestly, and Hsia Kê replied, 'If they have none, then there is infinity, and if they have, there is limitedness. How shall I know it? Yet, provided that beyond infinity there exists a non-infinity, or that within the unlimitedness there exists again a limit, then infinity would be no infinity, and unlimitedness no unlimitedness. Therefore I can understand infinity and unlimitedness, but I cannot understand an end and a limit.' "

The proof for the infinity of time is not bad. The premise that the world was created at a certain time compels us to assume that previous to creation there was nothing, and that the world issued from non-existence, or naught, against which conclusion our intellect rebels, for we are convinced that from nothing nothing can be produced. The proof for the infinity of space contains a *petitio principii.* Of course, the unlimited cannot be limited without or within, but why must we suppose such limitations?

In India the sect of the *Jains* regarded the world as eternal, without beginning or end (*b*). By the *Greek* philosophers the question of infinity is often ventilated.

VII. Heaven and Earth.

These are the two corner-stones of the cosmic system and the natural philosophy of the Chinese, and for this

---

(*b*) *Hastings*, IV., p. 160, art. by *H. Jacobi.*

reason are worthy of our special consideration. In this we must make a clear discrimination which is not to be found in Chinese texts. We can first look upon heaven and earth as natural objects and then as raised into the higher sphere, of mythology and religion. Both points of view are blended by the Chinese : sometimes they will speak of heaven as a part of nature, sometimes as a superior being. It is better to keep both points of view, the scientific and the religious one, separated, and to investigate how the one was evolved from the other.

A. THE PHYSICAL VIEWPOINT.

(a) *Substance.*

According to the various theories heaven has the shape of a hemisphere, a sphere, or an egg, and earth is a sort of plate or the centre of a ball or of an egg. Consequently one ought to surmise that both are formed from some solid substance. Of earth this is self-evident, but it is not the same with heaven. That heaven was conceived of as being a solid substance would appear from the attributes " hard and strong " with which heaven or its emblem *Ch'ien* is endowed in the *Yiking* saying : " How great is Ch'ien ! hard, strong, well-balanced, correct, pure, unalloyed, excellent ! " (*a*). At any rate at the time of the origin of the Nü Wa myth heaven was taken for a solid cupola, for otherwise it could not have reposed on a mountain, Nü Wa could not have repaired it with masonry, nor set up four pillars to support it. In accordance with the *Kai-t'ien* theory the sky revolves with all the stars attached to it. Such being the case, it cannot consist of air, but must be massive.

(*a*) *Yiking*, translated by *Legge*, App. IV., p. 415. 大 哉 乾 乎 剛 健 中 正 純 粹 精 也.

However, we also encounter the view that heaven is nothing but air and the stars the lights therein. At the above-mentioned discussion on the collapse of heaven in *Lieh-tse*, *Ch'ang Lu-tse* says, " Rainbows, clouds and fogs, wind and rain as well as the four seasons—we would say the atmosphere—are accumulations of air and form heaven. Mountains and hills, rivers and seas, metals and stones, fire and wood are accumulations of what has shape and form earth " (*b*). The unsubstantiality of heaven is the pivot of the *Hs'üan-yeh* hypothesis, which is believed to go back to remotest antiquity.

Wang Ch'ung impugns this view of the literati of his time that heaven is but air, pointing out that, if heaven were not material as earth is, then the distance from the earth up to heaven could not measure 60,000 Li, and its circumference not be 365 degrees. Nor could the star mansions corresponding to the post-stations on earth and serving as resting-places for the sun and the moon, be fastened to an unsubstantial heaven (*c*).

The conception of heaven as a solid vault is quite usual among ancient nations. That of the *Jews* is transparent at the same time, as we saw, and allows free passage to the light of the stars. Similarly the *Iranians* assumed the inner sky *âsmân* to consist of blue pellucid stones. Another tradition describes it as made of shining bronze, and conformably to later views it is of steel (*d*). It is well known that *Homer* thought of the celestial vault as solid and made of bronze. In the *Finnish* poem *Kalewala*, *Ilmarinen* forges the firmament out of the finest steel (*e*). The spheres which

---

(*b*) *Lieh-tse*, I., 12 v. 長盧子聞而笑之曰虹蜺也雲霧也風雨也四時也此積氣之成乎天者也山岳也河海也金石也火木也此積形之成乎地者也.
(*c*) *Lun Hêng*, translated, Vol. I., pp. 257, 509.
(*d*) *F. Spiegel*, II., 109.
(*e*) *Tylor*, Primitive Culture, II., 71.

the *Greek* philosophers and astronomers invented with a view to explain the irregular motions of the planets are simply repetitions of the solid heavenly sphere. They assumed it to be transparent, for otherwise the outer spheres would not have been visible. Such pellucid hollow globes are the spheres of the *Pythagoreans* and *Aristotle* (*f*).

Chuang-tse calls heaven and earth the two largest bodies, and the Yin and Yang the two greatest forces of nature (*g*). *Wu-nêng-tse* of the T'*ang* epoch states that heaven and earth are the two greatest things in the two fluids, Yin and Yang. The naked creatures, those covered with scales, feathers, skin, and crusts are things within these greatest things, produced by their harmonious fluid. They are contained therein just like fish and turtles in rivers and seas or plants and trees on mountains and hills (*h*).

(b) *Colour.*

The colour of heaven is *blue*, that of earth *yellow*. In the *Chou-pi* (*i*) we read that heaven is dark blue and earth of a yellowish brown. Contrariwise, the *Yiking* characterises both colours simply as the blue and yellow (*k*). The blue colour of heaven is not open to criticism, for the clear sky appears to us blue indeed, but exception may perhaps be taken to the colour of earth being described

---

(*f*) *Zeller*, I., 384; *Troels-Lund*, Himmelsbild, p. 99.

(*g*) *Chuang-tse*, XXV., p. 35. 天 地 者 形 之 大 者 也 陰 陽 者 氣 之 大 者 也.

(*h*) 無 能 子 I., 1 v. 聖 過 篇。天 與 地 陰 陽 氣 中 之 巨 物 爾 裸 鱗 羽 毛 甲 五 靈 因 巨 物 合 和 之 炁 又 物 於 巨 物 之 內 亦 猶 江 海 之 含 魚 鼈 山 陵 之 包 草 木 爾.

(*i*) *Chou-pi*, I., 4 r. 天 青 黑 地 黃 赤.

(*k*) *Legge*, *Yiking*, App. IV., p. 421.

as yellow or yellowish brown. Earth is always yellow to
the Chinese. The original home of the Chinese people was
on yellow earth, viz., in the loess countries of northern
China.

Chuang-tse already has misgivings as to whether blue
is really the colour of heaven, or rather, whether it merely
appears so to us owing to the distance (*l*). This idea was
expanded by *Hsi Mêng* of the Han time, the votary of the
Hsüan-yeh hypothesis, and declared to be an optical
illusion. (See above, p. 23.)

Blue is also considered the colour of heaven in other
countries, sometimes they speak of a transparent blue or
even of transparent crystal. When heaven is conceived of
as made of steel (*Iranians*), the blue colour is involved of
course. As to the bronze heaven of *Homer*, one had solely
the effulgence of heaven in view and not so much its
colour.

(c) *Form.*

In accordance with the *Kai-t'ien* hypothesis heaven is
shaped like an umbrella and earth like an upturned bowl.
That would give heaven the form of a hemisphere and earth
that of a rounded plate. The *Hun-t'ien* theory assumes
that heaven is formed like an eggshell and earth like the
yolk in the egg. Then we would have two ellipsoids.
However, *Chang Hêng*, a chief exponent of this theory,
informs us that heaven is round and earth flat. (See
above, p. 13.) For the adherents of the *Hsüan-yeh*
hypothesis heaven has no shape at all, because it is nothing
but air. *Lü Pu-wei* already gives utterance to this view

(*l*) *Chuang-tse*, I., 2 r. 天之蒼蒼其正色邪其遠而無
所至極邪.

remarking that heaven is without shape and nevertheless produces all things (*m*).

The notion that heaven is *round* and earth *square* dates from very old time. We found it clearly expressed in the *Chou-pi*. How did the Chinese come to regard earth as square? The circle and the square are designated in the Chou-pi as the foundations of all geometrical and trigonometric measurements. Heaven being analogous to the circle, the counterpart of heaven, earth, must of necessity be analogous to the square, and this wrong analogy later on became an equation. Heaven and earth are considered opposites just as the square is the opposite of the circle. The later representatives of the *Kai-t'ien* theory say directly that earth is square like a chess-board. But already the commentators of the Chou-pi were baulked at this and they attempted to explain away this dictum, asserting that heaven and earth are unmeasurable and, as a matter of fact, neither round nor square. Round and square referred to the Yin and Yang, the elements of heaven and earth, which were represented by an odd and an even number. These numbers according to *Gaubil* (*n*) are 3 for the circle, because it contains the diameter thrice, and 4 for the square. According to Chinese ideas the number 3 also represents heaven and 4 earth. This explanation is as unsatisfactory as that given by *Huai-nan-tse*: "The principle of heaven is round, that of earth square. The square governs darkness, the circle brightness" (*o*). Darkness and brightness refer to the Yin and Yang principles embodied in heaven and earth. How can a principle

---

(*m*) *Lü-shih ch'un-ch'iu* XVII., 5 v. 呂子君守篇. 天無形 而萬物以成.

(*n*) *Biot*, Chou-pi, p. 602, note 1.

(*o*) *Huai-nan-tse* III., 1 v. 天文訓. 天道曰圓地道曰 方方者主幽圓者主明.

be square, and what has geometrical form to do with light or darkness? In the *Ta-tai li Tsêng-tse* replies to an inquiry of *Tan Chü-li* whether heaven was really round and earth square : " That which heaven produces is above, and that which earth does is below. What is above is always considered as round, and what is below as square. If really heaven were round and earth square, then the four corners would not cover the circle " (*p*). And Tsêng-tse goes on saying that he heard from the master (Confucius) that the principle of heaven was round and that of earth square, exactly what *Huai-nan-tse* said, whose further arguments are almost literally reproduced by Tsêng-tse, who does not know what to say either, for why is the lower part regarded as square?

Lü Pu-wei likewise speaks about the principle of heaven and earth and holds that the principle of heaven is round, because the movement of the heavenly fluid upwards and downwards is in a circle. On the other hand, all things on earth had their special functions, which could not be interchanged; therefore the nature of earth is 方 *fang*, which means " place, position," but also " square," *i.e.*, everything on earth has its proper place (*q*). This is nothing but a *galimatias*, a play on words.

The incongruity of circle and square seems to have disturbed *Ch'ü Yuan* already, for he inquires, " On what does the edge of the nine heavens repose, and on what does it depend? It has many corners and sinuosities; who

---

(*p*) *T'u-shu chi-ch'êng* 乾 象 典 chap. 1, 天 地 總 部 彙 考 I., 2 r. 大 戴 禮 曾 子 天 圓. 天 之 所 生 上 首 地 之 所 生 下 首 上 首 之 謂 圓 下 首 之 謂 方 如 誠 天 圓 而 地 方 則 是 四 角 之 不 揜 也.

(*q*) *Lü-shih ch'un-ch'iu* III., 12. 呂 子 圓 道 篇.

knows their number?" (*r*). The difficulty, however, is not so very great. If earth is a square swimming on the ocean, the celestial dome may repose on the ocean and at the same time touch the four corners of earth. Or the dome may rise directly on the four sides like the cupola of a house, which is square below and round above. This appears to have been the view of the *Chou-li* in which there is a passage to the effect that earth is square like the *box* and heaven round like the *awning of a carriage* (*s*). The same idea underlies the expression 堪 輿 *kan-yü* " Heaven and Earth," literally a " *carriage with a canopy.*"

The opinion of the different shape of heaven and earth is most strongly opposed by the *An-t'ien* hypothesis, which maintains that heaven and earth exactly fit together and therefore must have the same form, being both either round or square.

To us the notion of the earth as a ball or at least as a round plate appears so natural, that we feel prompted to assume that other nations must have the same conception, but that is far from being the case. In a *Peruvian* model of the world by *Salcamayhua* the earth is square (*t*), conformably to the ancient Chinese idea. Also in a book of the *Maya* the earth is represented as a cube overhung by a tree (*u*). Among the Greeks *Parmenides* was the first who conceived the idea of earth as a sphere (*x*), a view shared by the Pythagoreans (*y*). In olden days the Greeks did not yet look upon the earth as a sphere, nor as a cube

---

(*r*) *Ch'ü Yuan T'ien-wên, Ch'u-tse* III., 1 r. 九 天 之 際 安 放 安 屬 隅 隈 多 有 誰 知 其 數.

(*s*) *Chou-li* XL., 5 r. 冬 官 輈 人. 軫 之 方 也 以 象 地 也 蓋 之 圜 也 以 象 天 也.

(*t*) *H. Beuchat*, Manuel d'Archéologie américaine, p. 630.

(*u*) *Loc. cit.*, p. 443.

(*x*) *Zeller* I., 525.

(*y*) *Zeller* I., 383.

either, but as a compromise between the two, viz., a roller
or a cylinder. According to *Anaximander* it was a roller
suspended in the air and the centre of the world, its height
being a third of its diameter (*z*). *Anaxagoras* as well
regarded it as such a flat roller or a thin cylinder (*a*), and
Anaximenes as a cylindric plate (*b*).

(d) *Yin and Yang the two substances of heaven and earth.*

When the world issued from chaos the lighter and
purer substances ascended and formed heaven, whereas the
heavier and more turbid ones descended and became earth.
These lighter substances are the *Yang*, the heavier
substances the *Yin* fluid. Yang is the primogenial matter
of heaven, Yin the primary matter of earth, ergo we have
two kinds of matter. Yin and Yang are often used by old
writers as direct synonyms of the fluids of heaven and
earth. Thus *Wên-tse* (4th cent. B.C.) says, " The fluid of
heaven comes down, and the fluid of earth ascends, Yin
and Yang unite, and the ten thousand things are
together (*c*). The union of Yin and Yang is the interaction of the celestial and the terrestrial fluids, without
which no things can be produced. If the fluid of heaven
does not come down, nor the fluid of earth ascend, Yin
and Yang cannot be blended, then the ten thousand things
do not develop " (*d*).

The *Liki* expresses itself in a similar way : " The fluid
of earth rises, and the fluid of heaven sinks down, Yin
and Yang grind each other, and heaven and earth affect

(*z*) *Hoppe*, p. 71.
(*a*) *Überweg*, Grundriss I., 88; *Troels-Lund*, p. 103.
(*b*) *Überweg* I., 48.
(*c*) *Wên-tse* VI., 25 r. 文子上德篇. 天氣下地氣上陰
陽交通萬物齊同.
(*d*) *Eod.* 天氣不下地氣不上陰陽不通萬物不昌.

one another " (*e*).   In another passage of the Liki it is
said, " Heaven holds the Yang and hangs .out the sun and
the stars, earth holds the Yin and sinks down in mountains
and rivers " (*f*).   This means, according to the commentary, that heaven by its purity holds fast the Yang
and forms from it the heavenly signs, the sun and the
stars, while earth by her impurity holds fast the Yin
from which it produces its forms, mountains and rivers.

Huai-nan-tse states that the purer and brighter particles
or Yang are thinner and finer and form heaven, while the
coarser and more turbid accumulate and become earth.
This refers to creation.   With regard to the later co-
operation of heaven and earth he says : " The combined
essence of heaven and earth is Yin and Yang, the activity
of Yin and Yang produces the four seasons, and the dispersion of the essence of the four seasons produces the
ten thousand things."   The same idea is expressed still
clearer by *Chang Hêng* saying : " Heaven received its
substance from Yang, therefore it became round and it
moved, earth was made of Yin, whence it became flat and
motionless " (*g*).

The simplest outline is given by *Wu-nêng-tse* (T'ang
time) as follows :

" Anterior to the separation of heaven and earth
there was a single, chaotic fluid.   This ran over
and was divided into two modes, there were pure and
muddy, light and heavy parts.   The light and pure ones
went up and formed *Yang and heaven*, the heavy and
muddy ones sank down and became *Yin and earth*.

(*e*) *Liki* II., 104. 禮 記 樂 記. 地 氣 上 齊 天 氣 下 降 陰
陽 相 摩 天 地 相 蕩.

(*f*) *Liki* I., 381. 禮 記 禮 運. 天 秉 陽 垂 日 星 地 秉 陰
竅 於 山 川.

(*g*) Cf. above, pp. 37 and 38.

Heaven was hard and strong and in motion, earth was soft and yielding and in repose. This was the natural state of the fluids. After heaven and earth had taken up their positions, the Yin and Yang fluids mixed, and all animals with skin, scales, fur, feathers and shells were created thereby " (*h*).

Lieh-tse when stating that the principle of heaven and earth is if not Yin, then Yang (*i*), has probably nothing else in view than that Yin and Yang are the substances from which heaven and earth are formed and which they employ in producing all the organisms. The *Su-wên* does not hesitate to identify heaven and earth with their substances. " Heaven and earth," it says, " are considered as Yin and Yang " (*k*).

(e) *Dimensions.*

(1) *Distance between heaven and earth.*

In accordance with the mathematical calculations of the *Chou-pi* the distance between heaven and earth, both solid bodies, is 80,000 Li, this being the space between the celestial pole and earth (*l*). *Huai-nan-tse* substitutes for this number 5,000 million Li, presumably a mere imaginary figure (*m*). *Wang Ch'ung* goes back to 60,000 Li,

---

(*h*) *Wu-nêng-tse* I., 1 r. 聖過篇. 天地未分混沌一氣 一氣充溢分爲二儀有清濁焉有輕重焉輕清者 上爲陽爲天重濁者下爲陰爲地矣天則剛健而 動地則柔順而靜焉之自然也天地旣位陰陽焉 交於是裸蟲鱗蟲毛蟲羽蟲甲蟲生焉.

(*i*) *Lieh-tse* I., 3 v. 天瑞. 天地之道非陰則陽.

(*k*) *T'u-shu chi-ch'êng* 乾象典 chap. 17. 陰陽部雜錄 I., 6 r. 素問以天地爲之陰陽.

(*l*) *Biot*, Chou-pi, p. 620.

(*m*) *Huai-nan-tse* III., 3 r. 天文訓. 天 . . . . 去地五億 萬里.

which is said to be only the lower limit, the real distance being somewhat higher (*n*). According to the *Kuang-ya-shih* (third century A.D.) heaven is 116,787 Li distant from earth (*o*). *Tsu Hêng* (*p*) of the *Liang* epoch states that the figure 178,500 Li assumed by former scholars as the interstice between heaven and earth is too high, and he himself by means of the gnomon computes different heights for the solstices and equinoxes. His lowest figure is 42,658 Li, the highest 69,320 Li (*q*).

(2) *World diameter and circumference of heaven.*

The *Chou-pi* calculates the orbit of the sun for each month and the diameter belonging to the circle thus described. These orbits are the same for two months of the same year. At the summer solstice the diameter is 238,000 Li, the circumference of the solar orbit 714,000 Li. At the time of the equinoxes : diameter 357,000 Li, circumference 1,071,000 Li. At the winter solstice : diameter 476,000 Li, circumference 1,428,000 Li. The circle passing through the four cardinal points, *i.e.*, the horizon has 816,000 Li diameter and 2,430,000 Li circumference. This is the circumference of the celestial sphere. Dividing the horizon into degrees one obtains 6,652 Li 293 $\frac{327}{1481}$ Pu for each degree (*r*).

Wang Ch'ung holds that each degree measures 2,000 Li. By multiplication with 365 he then finds 730,000 Li as the circumference of heaven, which every day makes a complete revolution of 365 degrees. The sun is supposed to move

---

(*n*) *Lun Hêng*, translated, I., 257, 275.
(*o*) *T'u-shu chi-ch'êng* 乾 象 典 chap. 7, 天 地 總 部 雜 錄 7 r. 廣 雅 釋.
(*p*) 祖 晅.
(*q*) *T'u-shu chi-ch'êng*, *eod.*, chap. 1, 天 地 總 部 彙 考 I., 14 r.
(*r*) *Biot*, Chou-pi, p. 618.

forward independently but one degree daily, while the moon makes thirteen degrees (*s*).

Wang Fan (*t*) (third century A.D.) informs us that by his predecessors, *Lu Chi* for instance, the diameter of heaven was reckoned at 357,000 Li and the circumference at 1,071,000 Li, so that one degree would measure 2932 Li. These are the same figures adduced by the Chou-pi for the solar orbit at the time of the equinoxes, but not for the biggest orbit. Wang Fan himself corrects this figure of the world diameter to 329,401 Li by not employing the proposition that the circumference of a circle is three times as long as its diameter, and using instead the proportion 45 :142, implying, no doubt, that the horizon is not a precise circle (*u*).

Chêng Hsüan gives the diameter of heaven as 162,788 Li and its circumference as 512,687 Li (*x*). In the *Kuang-ya-shih Chang I* (230 A.D.) says that from north to south heaven measures 233,500 Li 75 Pu, from east to west 4 Pu less. Consequently the circumference must be 700,700 Li 25 Pu (*y*). These numbers almost tally with those of the Chou-pi for the summer solstice.

(3) *Size of the earth.*

With regard to the circumference of the earth in the *Chou-pi* a passage from *Lü Pu-wei* is quoted, which admittedly is a later interpolation. But even this carries us back to the third century B.C. In accordance with this passage the earth measures 28,000 Li from east to west,

---

(*s*) *Lun Hêng*, translated, I., 266.

(*t*) 王 蕃.

(*u*) *T'u-shu chi-ch'êng*, 乾 象 典 chap. 1, 天 地 總 部 彙 考 I., 7 r.

(*x*) *Eod.* I., 7 v.

(*y*) *T'u-shu chi-ch'êng*, *loc. cit.*, chap. 7. 天 地 總 部 雜 錄 7 r. The figure 610,700 Li 25 Pu given in the text must be a misprint.

but somewhat less from north to south, namely, 26,000 Li (z). The earth being quadrilateral we thus obtain a square which is not quite equilateral, but from east to west somewhat longer than in the direction from north to south. The total area of the earth would be 728 million square Li.

Wang Ch'ung assumes as a mere estimate that the earth stretches 100,000 Li from north to south and also 100,000 Li from east to west, which he says would give an area of 1,000,000 square Li. Wang Ch'ung is a bad arithmetician, for the square of 100,000 is 10,000 million. Still by another method he endeavours to solve the problem. After the view of Tsou Yen (fourth century B.C.) the earth has nine continents each as big as China. Now China is supposed to measure 5,000 Li, from north to south and likewise from east to west, ergo, says Wang Ch'ung, its area must be of 25,000 square Li, again a mistake, for it ought to be twenty-five million. This sum multiplied by nine gives 225 million square Li as the total area (a).

(4) *Sizes of the sun, the moon, and the stars.*

We have already seen that in the opinion of Ko Hung the sun has a diameter of 1,000 Li and a circumference of 3,000 Li (b). How Ko Hung arrived at this figure we are not told, most likely by a simple estimate comparing the size of the sun with one degree. According to Wang Ch'ung one degree precisely measured 2,000 Li, according to Wang Fan, Lu Chi and others nearly 3,000 Li, consequently he estimated the diameter of the sun as being $\frac{1}{2}$ or $\frac{1}{3}$ degree.

Pan Ku (Po-hu-t'ung) and Hsü Chêng (third century A.D.) held the view that the *moon* had the same size as the sun, i.e., 1,000 Li diameter and 3,000 Li circumference, in which appearances are on their side. Furthermore, Hsü

(z) *Biot*, Chou-pi, p. 616.
(a) *Lun Hêng*, translated, I., 256, 257.
(b) *See* p. 17.

Chêng contended that the sun and the moon were both 7,000 Li below heaven, consequently not attached to it (c).

Wang Ch'ung was of opinion that the *stars* were much bigger than they appeared to us and might measure 100 Li (d). *Hsü Chêng* adopts this figure as the diameter of the great stars, to the middle-sized he gives 50 Li, and to the small ones 30 Li (e).

Among the *Greeks Aristarchus of Samos* was the first to declare that the sun is seven times as big as the earth. Previous to him it passed for not bigger than the Peloponnesus (f).

(f) *Functions of heaven and earth.*

In the economy of the universe heaven and earth have definite functions, which they discharge either by their mere existence or by certain activities. Accordingly we may distinguish their functions into passive and active ones.

(1) *Passive Functions.*

We read in the *Liki* : "Heaven without selfishness *covers* the world, and earth without selfishness *carries* everything" (g). *Lieh-tse* combines the active and passive functions, saying : "It is the function of heaven to generate and to cover, and that of earth to form and to carry" (h). Earth is the basis, the foundation for all things, animated as well as inanimate; everything reposes on her, she carries everything. Heaven in turn forms an arch over every-

---

(c) *T'u-shu chi-ch'êng,* 乾 象 典 chap. 29, 明 部 彙 考 I., 4 v.

(d) *Lun Hêng* I., 275.

(e) *T'u-shu chi-ch'êng* 乾 象 典 chap. 55, 星 辰 部 彙 考 12, 6 v.

(f) *Troels-Lund,* p. 100.

(g) *Liki,* translated by *Legge,* II., 282. 孔 子 閒 居. 孔 子 曰 天 無 私 覆 地 無 私 載.

(h) *Lieh-tse,* I., 3 r., 天 瑞. 天 職 生 覆 地 職 形 載.

thing overspreading the earth and whatever is on her, encircling and protecting her, as it were. Heaven and earth, as conceived by the Chinese, have a certain purpose of course which primarily consists in affording to the myriads of beings, notably man, the possibility of existing. To this end a place is requisite where he may live in safety, and nowhere are the conditions more favourable than on the firm and steady earth, which is capable of carrying every weight and is protected from unfavourable influences from without by the vault of heaven. But with this the functions of the two chief supports of the cosmos are not yet exhausted. Both are active as well.

(2) *Active Functions.*

(α) While earth is firm and motionless, heaven is in constant rotation. Every day it makes a complete revolution, carrying along the sun, the moon, and the stars, which are attached to it. Thus it produces day and night. According to *Wang Ch'ung*, it moves faster than a potter's wheel or a flying arrow, making 730,000 Li a day, viz., the circumference of heaven (*i*). As long as the diurnal luminary is visible, there is day; when it vanishes and the nocturnal luminary takes its place, we have night.

(β) In this earth does not participate, remaining entirely inert, but she co-operates with heaven in producing the four seasons. From several utterances of ancient authors it might appear as if the seasons were produced by heaven alone. So we learn from the *Liki*, " Heaven produces the seasons, and earth creates her stores," and " Heaven has the four seasons, spring and autumn, winter and summer " (*j*). *Kuan-tse* also says, " Heaven discloses his

---

(*i*) *Lun Hêng*, I., 266.

(*j*) *Liki*, translated, I., 378, and II., 282, 禮 運. 天 生 時 而 地 生 財。孔 子 閒 居. 天 有 四 時 春 秋 冬 夏.

power in the four seasons and earth hers in her stores " (*k*), and asserts that, " Heaven produces the four seasons and earth the ten thousand stores " (*l*). However, when we investigate how the seasons are brought about, we discover that earth, too, has an important share in them. Heaven being spoken of as the cause of the seasons, this means that he is looked upon as the chief factor, which is quite correct, since the influences determining weather and temperature are celestial and meteorological. The universal view is that weather is the outgrowth of the action and reaction one upon the other of the fluid of heaven and the fluid of earth, the Yin and Yang. " The activity of Yin and Yang," says Huai-nan-tse, " produces the four seasons " (*m*). The *warm celestial fluid*, Yang, and the *cold terrestrial fluid*, Yin, are constantly co-operating, so that in regular turns, now the one, now the other, predominates, and thus gives its impress to the season. Both being of about equal strength, this mixture of heat and cold causes a moderate temperature, as we have in spring and autumn, the preponderance of heat brings summer, that of cold results in winter. A real mixture of the heavenly and earthly fluid, the Yin and Yang, properly speaking, takes place only in spring, autumn and summer, in so far as during these seasons the fluid of heaven comes down upon earth and the fluid of earth ascends. Conversely, in winter the fluid of heaven rises upward, and the fluid of earth descends. Therefore, cold prevails on earth then. The *Yüeh-ling* of the *Liki* teaches us that " in the first spring month the heavenly fluid comes down and the fluid of earth rises. Heaven and earth are united, and plants and trees begin

---

(*k*) *Kuan-tse* XXII., 14 v. 管 子 山 權 數 篇. 天 以 時 爲 權 地 以 財 爲 權.

(*l*) 形 勢 解. 天 生 四 時 地 生 萬 財. *Kuan-tse* XX., 11 v.

(*m*) *Vide*, p. 37.

to grow and to stir." In the first winter month, however, "the fluid of heaven ascends and the fluid of earth sinks down. Heaven and earth cannot come together. There is a deadlock from which winter develops" (*n*).

A passage of the *Shi-chi* says of the *Great Bear* (Bushel) : "It revolves in the centre, comes to regulate the four quarters, separates the Yin and Yang and establishes the four seasons" (*o*). *De Groot* remarks about this passage that the **Great Bear** once a year revolves round the pole of heaven, standing at the same hour of night, in each of the four seasons in a different quarter of the sphere, thus indicating the four seasons . . . "nay, it even compels the whole sphere to move round with it, in this way producing the four seasons, the rotation of which constitutes the course of Nature" (*p*). This being the case, as a matter of fact, it would be the Great Bear that produces the seasons. This is not the Chinese view. The Great Bear, by its position, indicates the four seasons, but does not produce them, especially being, as it is, quite unable to move the heavenly sphere. On the contrary, the Great Bear, like all other constellations, is moved by the sphere revolving of its own accord.

We were given another explication of the seasons by the *Hsin-t'ien* system, which reduced them to the sinking and rising of the axis of heaven. In consonance with this theory, in winter the sun would be far away, in summer near. In winter the cold fluid of the northern sky pours forth, in summer the warm fluid of the southern sky. The

---

(n) 月令. 孟春之月天氣下降地氣上騰天地和同草木萌動。孟冬之月. 天氣上騰地氣下降天地不通閉塞而成冬.

(o) *Shi-chi*, chap. 27, p. 2, 運于中央. 臨制四鄉. 分陰陽. 建四時.

(p) *De Groot*, Religious System I., 317.

length and shortness of the days is said to depend on it
likewise (*q*).

In a different manner warmth and cold are localised in
a passage of the *Liki* to the effect that cold always originates
in the south-west and reaches its climax in the north-west.
Conversely, warmth comes forth in the north-east and
attains its full development in the south-east. " The icy
cold fluid of heaven and earth starts in the south-west and
is fully developed in the north-west . . . the warm and
mild fluid of heaven and earth commences in the north-
east and is at its height in the south-east " (*r*). Here the
expression heaven and earth would seem to denote nothing
else than the universe, for otherwise we would be compelled
to assume that heat and cold are common to heaven and
earth, whereas the usual view sees in heaven the repository
of heat, and in earth the store-room of the cold Yin fluid.
We shall have some more details about the localisation of
the cold and warm fluids later.

As a particular attainment the regularity and continuity
of the motions of heaven and earth are spoken of, by which,
no doubt, the flowing forth of the said fluids is to be understood, for aside from this earth does not move. " The
course of heaven and earth", says the *Yiking*, " is permanent and everlasting . . . the sun and the moon joined
to heaven can ever shine. The four seasons change and
transform and can ever produce " (*s*); and further :
" Heaven and earth have their fixed periods, and the four

(*q*) Cf. p. 25.

(*r*) *Legge, Liki* II., 437. 鄉 飲 酒 義. 天 地 嚴 凝 之 氣 始
於 西 南 而 盛 於 西 北 . . . . 天 地 溫 厚 之 氣 始 於
東 北 而 盛 於 東 南.

(*s*) *Legge, Yiking*, p. 239 恒 卦. 天 地 之 道 恒 久 而 不
已 也 . . . 日 月 得 天 而 能 久. 照 四 時 變 化 而 能 久
成.

seasons are completed (*t*)," *i.e.*, at certain times changes and movements of the cosmic forces (fluids) take place in a regular turn, whence the seasons derive their origin and their completion.

(γ) In the same way as by their co-operation heaven and earth produce the seasons they also produce the organic world, flora and fauna. In order that things may grow, heaven and earth, so to speak, must meet and their fluids intermingle. The heavenly substance comes down, the earthly one rises, and the outgrowth of the mixture of both are the " ten thousand things." Heaven, as it were, gives the seed, which earth receives and in her bowels develops to some organism. Heaven is only fecundating, the development belongs to earth. The *Yiking* commentaries repeatedly give utterance to this idea : " When heaven and earth meet, the various kinds of things develop " (*u*). " When heaven and earth act and react on each other, all things are formed and created " (*x*). " It is the course of heaven to send down its beneficent forces where they act most splendidly and the way of earth to send up her forces so that they become active " (*y*). " Heaven gives away and earth produces, and the increase is without limit " (*z*). This last clause is paraphrased by the commentator *Ch'êng* as follows : " It is the principle of heaven to give the first impulse, and the principle of earth to

---

(*t*) *Yiking*, p. 262. 節 卦. 天 地 節 而 四 時 成.

(*u*) *Eod.* p. 250. 姤 卦. 天 地 相 遇 品 物 咸 章 也.

(*x*) *Eod.* p. 238. 咸 卦. 天 地 感 而 萬 物 化 生.

(*y*) *Yiking*, p. 226. 謙 卦. 象 曰 謙 亨 天 道 下 濟 而 光 明 地 道 卑 而 上 行.

(*z*) *Loc. cit.*, p. 247. 益 卦. 天 施 地 生 其 益 无 方.

produce things. Heaven pours forth, and earth produces, and all things are thus created " (*a*).

One has compared heaven and earth with a receptacle in which the most varied transformations and changes go on. *Kuan-tse* called it the " *bag of the ten thousand things* " enfolding everything, but heaven is not yet the utmost limit, heaven and earth being again enclosed by the universe (*b*). The comparison of the universe with a melting furnace is still more frequent. According to *Chuang-tse* the world is a big furnace and that which creates and transforms in it the great founder (*c*). *Chia I* (second century B.C.) worked out the analogy still further : " Heaven and earth are the furnace, the transforming power the workman, Yin and Yang the coal, and the ten thousand things the copper " (*d*). The comparison of Yin and Yang with coal and of living organisms with metal is not very happy, for organisms are of the same stuff as Yin and Yang, whereas coal can never be transformed into metal. It is more to the point to fill the furnace with water and fire, Yin and Yang, as *Wang Ch'ung* does (*e*). In the water earthy substances are dissolved, for the Yin is muddy. From earth, moisture and warmth actually all organisms are produced.

(*a*) 程傳. 天道資始地道生物天施地生化育萬物.

(*b*) *Kuan-tse* IV., 1 v. 宙合篇. 天地萬物之橐也宙合有橐天地.

(*c*) *Giles, Chuang-tse*, p. 82, not quite correct. 以天地爲大鑪以造化爲大冶.

(*d*) *Ch'ien Han-shu*, chap. 48, p. 2 v. 賈誼傳. 天地爲鑪造化爲工陰陽爲炭萬物爲銅.

(*e*) *Lun Hêng* I., pp. 103, 294.

B. *The Mythological-religious viewpoint.*

Heaven and earth produce the myriad things, they beget them. Under the myriad or ten thousand things the Chinese understand but organic beings : men, animals and plants, which are born, live and die. Inorganic substances such as earth, stones, metals, air and fire are parts of earth or of heaven and contained therein, they do not grow from the interaction of both and have no life of their own. This is the point where the mythologising. tendency seems to come in, which makes heaven and earth beings similar to man. Heaven and earth beget the myriad things, husband and wife beget their progeny, ergo heaven and earth act like husband and wife, and if this analogy is carried one step further, we arrive at the thesis : Heaven and earth are husband and wife.

I. HEAVEN AND EARTH AS HUSBAND AND WIFE.

This sexual intercourse is often emphasised in the *Yiking* commentaries : " The marriage of the younger sister shows us the important and virtuous relation between heaven and earth. If heaven and earth did not mix, all the manifold things would not be produced (*f*)." *Ch'êng-tse* enlarges on this passage as follows : " One Yin and one Yang, that is the fundamental principle. The passionate union of Yin and Yang and the copulation of husband and wife is the eternal rule of the universe. If heaven and earth did not mingle, whence would all the things receive life ? When the wife comes to the man, she bears children. Bearing children is the way of propagation. Man and wife cohabit and produce offspring " (*g*). Heaven, in the *Yiking*

(*f*) *Yiking*, App. I., p. 257.   歸 妹 卦. 象 曰 歸 妹 天 地 之 大 義 也 天 地 不 交 而 萬 物 不 興.

(*g*) 程 傳. 一 陰 一 陽 之 謂 道 陰 陽 交 感 男 女 配 合

termed *Ch'ien*, represents the male, earth = *K'un*, the female (*h*). Heaven is considered a *Yang* being, earth a *Yin* being (*i*). " By the generative power of heaven and earth things are created in profusion. The male and female mix their essence, and all things are thereby formed and produced " (*k*).

The giving of life is held to be the noblest quality of heaven and earth (*l*). In this heaven precisely plays the part of man. "Heaven governs the great beginning of things, earth gives them their completion " (*m*). The commentary adds the following explanatory note : " Generally the Yang precedes and the Yin follows, the Yang pours out and the Yin receives. The light and pure Yang is still formless, the heavy and turbid Yin leaves its traces " (*n*). Heaven but gives the impulse of life, the earth receives his seed and in her bowels develops the young creature until its birth. Thus the *Liki* says that heaven generates and earth develops (*o*), and *Lieh-tse* characterises the functions of heaven as generating and covering and those of earth as forming and carrying (*p*).

天 地 之 常 理 也 天 地 不 交 則 萬 物 何 從 而 生 女 之
歸 男 乃 生 生 相 續 之 道 男 女 交 而 後 有 生 息.

(*h*) *Loc. cit.*, App. III., p. 349. 繫 辭 上 傳. 乾 道 成 男 坤
道 成 女.

(*i*) *Eod.*, App. III., p. 395. 繫 辭 下 傳. 乾 陽 物 也 坤 陰
物 也.

(*k*) App. III., p. 393. 繫 辭 下 傳. 天 地 絪 縕 萬 物 化 醇
男 女 構 精 萬 物 化 生.

(*l*) App. III., p. 381, *eod.* 天 地 之 大 德 曰 生.

(*m*) App. III., p. 349. 繫 辭 上 傳. 乾 知 大 始 坤 作 成 物.

(*n*) 本 義. 大 抵 陽 先 陰 後 陽 施 陰 受 陽 之 輕 清 未
形 而 陰 之 重 濁 有 迹 也.

(*o*) *Legge, Liki* I., 394.　　　　(*p*) *Vide* above, p. 61.

In respect of the creatures of the world heaven is the father, earth the mother. "Ch'ien," says a *Yiking* commentary, "is heaven, therefore they call it father, K'un is earth, therefore they call it mother" (*q*), and already in the *Shuking* we read that "Heaven and earth are father and mother of the ten thousand things" (*r*). *Chuang-tse* (*s*) uses almost the same words, and *Huai-nan-tse* declares that the sage looks upon heaven as his father and earth as his mother (*t*).

The idea to conceive of heaven and earth as husband and wife and as the parents of all living beings suggests itself very easily and therefore is widespread, particularly the notion of mother earth is to be found in many countries. The *Maori* and *New Zealanders* narrate that *Rangi*, heaven, closely united with his spouse *Papa*, earth, begot numerous children. By these, who in consequence of the narrow embrace of their parents had always to live in darkness, they were forcibly parted, a legend said to prevail among the *Polynesians* (*u*). With the *Tewa* Indians of North America heaven is the husband of earth, and they speak of "Sky Old Man" and "Earth Old Woman." The *Zuñi* Indians likewise call earth mother (*x*). The *Inkas* styled earth *Pachamama* or "All mother" (*y*), and the *Carribes* and *Comanches* also worshipped mother-earth (*z*).

"The two great parents" of the *Rig Veda* are

(*q*) *Yiking*, App. V., p. 429. 說卦傳. 乾天也故稱乎父坤地也故稱乎母.

(*r*) *Legge, Shuking*, p. 283. 泰誓. 惟天地萬物父母.

(*s*) *Chuang-tse*, p. 230. 達生篇. 天地者萬物之父母.

(*t*) *Huai-nan-tse*, VII., 1 v. 精神訓. 聖人 . . . . 以天爲父以地爲母.

(*u*) *Hastings*, IV., 174, art. by *Grey*; *Tylor* I., 322 seq.
(*x*) *Harrington*, pp. 45, 59.
(*y*) *T. A. Joyce*, South American Archaeology, 1912, p. 154.
(*z*) *Tylor* I., 326.

Dyauspitar, the Heaven-father and *Pṛthivī mātar*, the Earth-mother. Still in our days at the marriage ceremony in *India* the bridegroom speaks to the bride the following words of the *Yajur Veda:* " I am heaven, you are earth, come, let us marry." With the *Greeks* these two old Vedic deities are paralleled by Ζεὺς πατήρ (Diespiter) and *De-meter* (Γῆ μήτηρ), who were worshipped as husband and wife, and clearly indicate the conjugal union of heaven and earth. *Ouranos* and *Gaia* are other names of the couple (*a*). The *Romans* transformed Diespiter in *Jupiter*. *Varro* also refers to *Caelum pater* (*b*).

II. ELEMENTARY QUALITIES OF HEAVEN AND EARTH.

From the physical conception of heaven and earth on the one side and from the sexual on the other, their chief characteristics result at once. At the same time the tendency to contrast these qualities is obvious. The fact that heaven and earth are regarded as opposites accounts for it.

Heaven is *noble*, earth is *common* (*c*). These qualities, of course, are derived from nature. Heaven forms a high and imposing vault above earth, which *vis-à-vis* of heaven takes a low position. As wife earth likewise is inferior to her husband, heaven. " The Yang is noble," says the *Ch'un-ch'iu fan-lu*, " the Yin common . . . the husband, though common, still is regarded as Yang, and the wife, even if noble, as Yin " (*d*).

Heaven, as we saw, is *male*, and earth *female*. In

(*a*) *Tylor* I., 327 seq.

(*b*) *Bouché-Leclercq*, p. 88.

(*c*) *Yiking*, App. III., 348. 繫 辭 上 傳. 天 尊 地 卑.

(*d*) *Ch'un-ch'iu fan-lu* XI., 4 v. 春 秋 繁 露. 陽 尊 陰 卑 以 此 見 之 貴 陽 而 賤 陰 也 · · · · 丈 夫 雖 賤 皆 爲 陽 婦 人 雖 貴 皆 爲 陰.

producing all organisms heaven starts and gives the first impulse of life, whereas earth develops the germ until its maturity. Finally heaven is thought of as *hard* and *strong*, earth as *yielding* and *soft* (*e*). These are qualities in keeping with the male and female character. Moreover heaven consists of a hard substance, compared with which earth may be considered soft.

III. MORAL QUALITIES OF HEAVEN AND EARTH.

The physical qualities of heaven and earth were further conceived as *virtues*. Heaven and earth treat all beings equally. " Heaven is just and without selfishness, therefore he overspreads the beautiful and the ugly. Similarly earth is just and unselfish, therefore she carries the great and the small " (*f*). Consequently, because heaven and earth discharge their functions equally and impartially, without undue preference for any being, they are credited with *justice* and *unselfishness*. *Wên-tse* draws a distinction between the virtue of heaven and that of earth : " Heaven pours forth his virtue overspreading all things and feeding them. He gives, but takes nothing, therefore the spirits revert to him, and his virtue is supreme. Earth carries all things and lets them grow, she gives, but takes as well *e.g.* when by death the body returns to her. Therefore her virtue is of a minor order. The virtue of heaven is the highest possible " (*g*). Why the returning of the body to

---

(*e*) *Yiking*, App. III., 381. 繫辭下傳. 夫乾確然示人易矣夫坤隤然示人簡矣.

(*f*) *Kuan-tse* XX., 10 v. 管子形勢解. 天公平而無私故美惡莫不覆地公平而無私故小大莫不載.

(*g*) *Wên-tse* VI., 27 r. 文子上德篇. 天覆萬物施其德而養之與而不取故精神歸焉與而不取者上德也是以有德高莫高於天也 . . . . 地載萬物而長之與而取之故骨骸歸焉與而取之者下德也.

earth is a *taking*, while the reverting of the spirit to heaven is no *taking*, is not apparent. The whole train of thought is strange. The *Liki* assigns to both heaven and earth *justice* and *benevolence*, simply identifying them with cold and hot air. The severe, icy air passes as the fluid of justice, the congenial, warm one as the fluid of benevolence (*h*). Analogies thus become identities. *Lao-tse* disowns that heaven and earth have any affection for their creatures, which they treat like " straw dogs " (*i*).

If heaven and earth are endowed with virtues like justice and benevolence, they must be spiritual, humanised beings, such as they appear already in their capacity of parents of the universe. In the *Chou* epoch already the anthropomorphosis went to such length. In the *Tso-chuan* the minister of *Chin* says to the Duke of *Ch'in*, " You walk on the princess Earth and have august Heaven above. August Heaven and the princess Earth are sure to hear your words " (*k*). Ergo, heaven and earth can *hear* and have sensations. The *Kuo-yü* speaks of the punishments of heaven and earth (*l*). Accordingly, heaven and earth must act as a kind of *providence*. Apart from this the anthropomorphosis of heaven is pushed much further, as we shall see later, and in this respect earth remains behind.

(*h*) *Liki* II., 437. 鄉飲酒義. 天地嚴凝之氣 . . . . 此天地之義氣也天地溫厚之氣 . . . . 此天地之仁氣也.

(*i*) *Lao-tse, Tao-tê-king*, chap. 5. 天地不仁以萬物爲芻狗.

(*k*) *Tso-chuan, Duke Hsi* 15th year : 晉大夫三拜稽首曰君履后土而戴皇天皇天后土實聞君之言.

(*l*) *T'u-shu chi-ch'êng* 乾象典 chap. 13 天部紀事 p. 5 r. 國語. 死生因天地之刑.

IV. The Relation of Man to Heaven and Earth.

The sage resembles heaven and earth in his course of action (*m*), for " the great man harmonises with heaven and earth in his virtue, with the sun and moon in his enlightenment, with the four seasons in his regularity, and with the spirits in his actions of lucky or unlucky augury. He may precede heaven, and heaven will not act contrary to him, or he may follow heaven and act just as heaven does at the time " (*n*). The virtues of heaven and earth are, as we saw, unselfishness, justice, and benevolence. These the sage must imitate. His knowledge is compared with the brightness of the stars, his activity, insomuch as it is subject to fixed rules, with the regularity of the seasons, and his actions, in so far as they may have good or bad consequences, with the working of good and evil spirits. The assertion that the great man, by his doings, may even become the prototype for heaven is peculiar. They explain it by pointing out that the sage is governed by exactly the same principles as heaven, so that their way of dealing must of necessity be in harmony, and it makes absolutely no difference which of the two sets to work first.

Kuan-tse teaches how an enlightened ruler has to model his activity on that of heaven and earth : " Heaven produces the seasons and earth the ten thousand substances for the development of the great variety of things, but do not demand anything in exchange. The enlightened sovereign conforms to heaven and earth, teaching his people the proper times (for agriculture), admonishing them to ploughing and weaving, in order to improve their economic conditions. On the other hand, he does not disturb their

---

(*m*) *Yiking*, App. III., p. 354.

(*n*) *Yiking*, App. IV., p. 417. 夫 大 人 者 與 天 地 合 其 德 與 日 月 合 其 明 與 四 時 合 其 序 與 鬼 神 合 其 吉 凶 先 天 而 天 弗 違 後 天 而 奉 天 時.

work, nor does he seek his own profit. Whence it is said that by giving without taking he conforms to heaven and earth " (*o*). The ruler thus should only have the welfare of his people at heart and not his own, and by such disinterestedness rise to the high standard of heaven and earth.

Yet it is not man as such, but only some select persons, sages and enlightened princes, that are placed on a par with heaven and earth. They may learn the principles of heaven and earth from the Yiking, where they are laid down (*p*). Heaven and earth are the *gates of the Yiking* (*q*). This statement needs to be restricted however. From the chief text of the Yiking nothing can be learned about the universe and its laws, but it can be done from the diverse amplifications and commentaries.

The relation of the sovereign to his subjects is said to be similar to that of heaven to earth, heaven being high and exalted and earth low and mean (*r*).

Not only are human virtues brought into connection with heaven and earth, but even *music* and *rites* are said to serve as models to both. It is hard to understand how that is possible, for the explanations given by the *Liki* are rather vague and indefinite. " Music," says the Liki, " is the harmony of heaven and earth, and ceremonies are their regular course " (*s*). This probably does not mean any-

---

(*o*) *Kuan-tse* XX., 11 v. 形 勢 解. 天 生 四 時 地 生 萬 財 以 養 萬 物 而 無 取 焉 明 主 配 天 地 者 也. 敎 民 以 時 勸 之 以 耕 織 以 厚 民 養 而 不 伐 其 功 不 私 其 利 故 曰 能 予 而 無 取 者 天 地 之 配 也.

(*p*) *Yiking*, App. III., p. 353, and *Liki* II., p. 233.

(*q*) *Yiking*, App. III., p. 395. 繫 辭 下 傳. 子 曰 乾 坤 其 易 之 門 耶.

(*r*) *Liki* II., 103.

(*s*) *Liki* II., 100. 樂 記. 樂 者 天 地 之 和 也 禮 者 天 地 之 序 也.

thing else but that harmony, which is the basis of all music, is analogous to the harmony between heaven and earth, both working together harmoniously, and that rites and ceremonies, in their regularity and precise sequence, correspond to the regular interaction of the celestial and terrestrial forces of nature. The matter becomes still more complicated by a reference to the higher and lower spiritual power. "Music lays stress on harmony, impresses the mind and follows heaven. Ceremonies make a sharp distinction between the various functions, they reside in the spirit and follow earth " (t).

The *Tso-chuan* refers ceremonies to both heaven and earth, calling them the principles of heaven and earth, their warp and woof (u), which is, at any rate, not a very clear conception.

The sage, or the great man, is not subordinate to heaven and earth, but their equal. Therefore it cannot be a matter for surprise that by music and ceremonies he may affect them and induce them to corresponding actions (x).

V. ANALOGIES OF HEAVEN AND EARTH WITH MAN, ANIMALS AND NUMBERS.

The relations supposed to exist between heaven and earth and man are still much more extensive. The *Li-hai-chi* (y), a rather late source, it is true, maintains that man contains heaven and earth in himself in their entirety, as far as the fluid and the form is concerned, and thus he distinguishes himself from animals. The *head* of

---

(t) *Eod.* 樂 者 敦 和 率 神 而 從 天 禮 者 別 宜 居 鬼 而 從 地.

(u) *Tso-chuan, Duke Chao,* 25th year : 禮 上 下 之 紀 天 地 之 經 緯 也.

(x) *Liki* II., 115.

(y) Written by *Wang K'uei* 王 逵 between 1068 and 1078 A.D.

man corresponds to heaven, being round like heaven and uppermost, the *foot* to earth, being square like earth and below. The *four limbs* take the place of the four seasons, and the *five inner parts* of the five elements (*z*).

The *Yiking* already likens heaven to the *head* and earth to the *belly* (*a*). The head, says the commentary, belongs to Yang, is noble and above like heaven, the belly belongs to Yin and is concealed. But with animals parallels are drawn too : Heaven is compared to the *horse*, earth to the *ox* (*b*). *Tertium comparationis* for the horse is said to be its strength and constant motion, for the ox its docility and the carrying of heavy loads. Another commentator thinks that the horse resembles heaven, because of its having round hoofs, and the ox earth for having divided hoofs. This is mere trifling. Such associations of ideas are quite foreign to us.

The Chinese, also, imagine to have discovered certain relations between heaven and earth and numbers. The odd numbers, 1, 3, 5, 7, 9, belong to heaven, the even numbers, 2, 4, 6, 8, 10, to earth (*c*). The odd ones are Yang, the even Yin numbers, and heaven representing the Yang and earth the Yin principle, one has simply distributed the numbers on heaven and earth in the same manner. The notion of the Yang and Yin numbers is said to be derived from the "Tablet of the Yellow River" (*d*).

(*z*) *T'u-shu chi-ch'êng* 乾 象 典 chap. 7 天 地 總 部 雜 錄 p. 8 v. 蠡 海 集. 天 形 圓 而 在 上 人 之 首 能 應 之 地 形 方 而 在 下 人 之 足 能 應 之 四 時 運 於 表 四 肢 應 之 於 外 五 行 處 於 裏 五 藏 應 之 於 內.

(*a*) *Yiking*, App. V., p. 429. 說 卦 傳. 乾 爲 首 坤 爲 腹.

(*b*) *Loc. cit.*, 乾 爲 馬 坤 爲 牛.

(*c*) *Yiking*, App. III., p. 365. 繫 辭 上 傳. 天 一 地 二 天 三 地 四 天 五 地 六 天 七 地 八 天 九 地 十.

(*d*) *Legge, Yiking*, Introd. p. 15 seq.

The development can simply have been this, that as a symbol for Yang an unbroken line, for Yin a broken line, was used, viz., — and ----; consequently Yang had one and Yin had two lines, or 1 stands for Yang and 2 for Yin. If the numbering is continued, 3 falls to Yang, 4 to Yin, and so forth. Thus five numbers are apportioned to heaven and to earth five also, but an addition of the five odd numbers gives 25, of the even ones 30, and the numbers of heaven and earth are 55, the sum of 25 and 30 (*e*).

Whereas after this scheme the number of heaven is 5 or 25, in another passage of the *Liki* 12 is given as the number of heaven (*f*). This may possibly be a reference to the " Twelve Branches " or cyclical signs by which the points of the compass are designated, and the horizon or circle of heaven is divided into 12 equal parts.

But there are still other combinations of numbers. To heaven the number 3, to earth 2, is assigned (*g*). As a reason, the commentary adduces the fact that, the diameter being 1, the circumference (heaven) is 3, and one side of a square (earth) being 1, its circumference is 4, and the four sides form 2 pairs. Then it would be more logical, however, to give to the quadrangle of earth the number 4. *Kuan-tse* claims that heaven is governed by the number 9, and earth by 8 (*h*), but a reason is not given (*i*).

(*e*) *Loc. cit.*

(*f*) *Liki* I., 430. 郊 特 牲 祭 之 曰 王 被 袞 以 象 天 載 冕 璪 十 有 二 旒 則 天 數 也.

(*g*) *Yiking*, App. V., p. 422. 參 天 兩 地 而 倚 數.

(*h*) *Kuan-tse* XIV., 10 r. 五 行 篇 天 道 以 九 制 地 理 以 八 制.

(*i*) The commentary says that 9 is the number of the " old Yang " 老 陽 and 8 the number of " young Yin " 少 陰, which does not bring us much farther.

VI. Worship of Heaven and Earth.

Since time immemorial the Chinese have offered divine worship to Heaven and Earth in the form of sacrifices. These were the highest sacrifices which could only be performed by the emperor (k). The sacrifice to Heaven took place at the winter solstice in the suburbs, that for Earth at the summer solstice in the city itself (l). As a sacrificial offering to Heaven wood was burned on the great altar of Heaven; for Earth the victim was buried in a huge pit (m). Still in recent times the ox offered to Earth is buried, but instead of the wood they have substituted an ox for Heaven as well, which is burned in a porcelain furnace. The reason is obvious. Heaven enjoys the smell of the odours rising from the sacrifice, whereas earth incorporates the food offered her.

Wang Ch'ung relates that to Heaven and Earth millet, rice cakes, and soup were sacrificed on round hills (n). This, however, cannot have been the great State sacrifice, but some unsanctioned kind of veneration perhaps by private individuals.

VII. Heavenly Bodies : Sun, Moon, Stars.

The sun, the moon, and the stars are the principal parts of heaven and attached to it (o), but by most scholars they are not considered to be homogeneous. We saw that

---

(k) *Liki* I., 116. 曲 禮. 天 子 祭 天 地.

(l) *Liki* I., 385. 禮 運. 祭 帝 於 郊 所 以 定 天 位 也. 祀 社 於 國 所 以 列 地 利 也.

(m) *Liki* II., 202. 祭 法. 燔 柴 於 泰 壇 祭 天 也. 瘞 埋 於 泰 折 祭 地 也 用 騂 犢.

(n) *Lun Hêng* I., 510.

(o) *Yiking*, App. I., p. 237, 離 卦. 日 月 麗 乎 天. *Yü-lung-tse* 御 龍 子 objects that the moon passing before the sun at an eclipse

in *Lieh-tse* the sun, the moon and the stars were all described as the lights of heaven (*p*), which would involve their homogeneity, but this is not the common opinion. The dualism of Yin and Yang has been transferred to the sun and the moon, so that both must be made of different material. As *Huai-nan-tse* has it, the sun is the fiery essence and the moon the watery fluid, and the stars are produced by the sexual intercourse of the sun and the Moon (*q*). *Wang Ch'ung*, too, holds that the stars are of the same stuff as the sun and the moon (*r*). According to the *Erh-ya-su* of *Kus-p'o* (third to fourth century A.D.). Yin and Yang are names of the sun and the moon. Still at present *T'ai-yang* is the most common term for the sun. The expression *T'ai-yin* for the moon occurs too, but is not so much used (*s*). *Kuan-tse* makes the sun rule over the Yang, and the moon over the Yin (*t*).

Between the sun and the moon there is a certain contrast, the sun being the hot diurnal luminary with a brilliant light, the moon the cool companion of night shedding its mild rays. It is, therefore, but natural to think of the sun as the star of light or the Yang element and of the moon as the star of darkness or Yin, and to transfer the contrast of Yin and Yang existing already between heaven and earth to the sun and the moon likewise. The idea to look upon the little stars as the children of the sun and the moon suggests itself very easily. Of course, the sun endowed with the male Yang must be the

---

would fall off from heaven, which may be the reason why *Hsü Chêng* placed the sun and the moon 7,000 Li below the sky (*T'u-shu chi-ch'êng*, 乾 象 典, chap. 31, 日 月 部 雜 錄 7 r.)   Cf. above, p. 61.

(*p*) See above, p. 44.
(*q*) Cf. p. 38.
(*r*) *Lun Hêng* II., 174.

(*s*) 太 陽 and 太 陰.

(*t*) *Kuan-tse* XIV., 10 r. 四 時 篇. 日 掌 陽 月 掌 陰.

father, and the moon imbued with the female Yin the mother.

The relation between the emperor and the empress has been likened to that of the sun and moon and Yin and Yang. " The ruler of men regards heaven as his father, earth as his mother, the sun as his brother, and the moon as his sister " (*u*). The sun and the moon as children of heaven must of course be the nearest kindred of the " son of heaven."

In *Greek-Roman* mythology *Sol* and *Helios* always appears as a man, while *Luna, Selene* is a woman, a conception which remained later. In *Ptolemian* astrology the sun corresponds to man, the moon to woman. The *Christian Platonists* speak of the Sun king and the Moon queen (*x*). We meet with similar notions among the *American Indians*. The *Taos, Isleta* and *Zuñi* call the sun father and the moon mother. Both travel daily over the great water of heaven. In the evening they pass through a lake in the lower world, travel the whole night eastward and on the next morning emerge from the lake (*y*). The *Peruvians* likewise believe that at night the sun swims beneath the earth and in the morning rises refreshed from its bath (*z*).

The *Bakairi*, or *Caraib* tribe, have much more naïve, but very poetical conceptions of the sun and moon. The sun is a ball of the feathers of the red *macaw* and the *toucan* and the moon a ball of the feathers of the *cassicus*. At night the sun is covered with a big pot. During the

---

(*u*) *Liki* II., 434 昏 義. 天 子 之 與 后 猶 日 之 與 月 陰 之 與 陽 *Ch'un-ch'iu kan-ching fu* 春 秋 感 精 符. 人 主 父 天 母 地 兄 日 姊 月.

(*x*) *Bouché-Leclercq*, pp. 89, 449; Porphyr. Isagog. 181-182.

(*y*) *Harrington*, p. 46. See also above, p. 31.

(*z*) *Beuchat*, p. 631.

rainy season it is carried by a snail, in the dry season by a swift, flying humming bird (*a*). In the popular belief of the *Aztecs* the sun and the moon are balls with which the gods play. The *Australians* fancy that these balls are thrown by the people in the east and caught by those in the west (*b*).

In the production of the seasons which, as we saw, primarily is the work of heaven and earth, the sun and moon play a certain rôle. " By the motions of the sun and the moon winter and summer are produced," says the *Shuking* (*c*). According to the commentary this means that from the course of the sun and moon and their position in the sky with reference to the north and south pole, the celestial equator and the ecliptic the season can be known. The *Liki* (Yüeh-ling) gives for each month the position of the sun in one of the twenty-eight solar mansions. Accordingly the sun in the third month of spring, approximately corresponding to our February, stays in the sign *Stomach* 胃 (Musca borealis) W., in the third month of summer in the sign *Willow* 柳 (Hydra) S., in the third month of autumn in the sign *House* 房 (Scorpio) E., and in the third month of winter in the sign *Virgin* 女 (Aquarius) N. The *Po-hu-t'ung* notes that in summer the sun stands in the sign *Well* 井 (Gemini) S.S.W., rising in E.N.E., and setting in W.N.W. In winter it stands in the sign *Ox* 牛 (Aries-Sagittarius), rising in E.S.E. and setting in W.S.W. (*d*).

For the deviation of the proper motions of the sun, the moon, and the planets which move eastward, while heaven

---

(*a*) *Hastings* IV., 168, art. by *R. L. Lowrie.*

ᐟ(*b*) *P. Ehrenreich*, Mythen und Legenden der Südamerikanischen Urvölker, 1905, p. 34, Anm. 2.

(*c*) *Legge, Shuking,* p. 342. 周書洪範. 日月之行則有冬有夏.

(*d*) *T'u-shu chi-ch'êng* 乾象典 chap. 29; 日月部彙考 I., 3 v, 4 r. 白虎通, 日月.

turns to the west, the same authority has an explanation characteristically Chinese. These stars in regard to heaven must be looked upon as Yin and therefore must move in opposite direction to Yang = Heaven. The other inquiry why the motion of the sun is so much slower than that of the moon, which according to Chinese views every day advances thirteen degrees to the east, while the sun makes an advance of only one degree, is answered with the naïve statement that the sun is the peacefully living prince and the moon the bustling and busy minister (*e*).

1. *The Sun.*

The sun is the principal centre of the Yang fluid of heaven. *Kuan Tse-yang* (*f*) of the former *Han* dynasty says that the sun is the celestial Yang, fire being the terrestrial Yang. In the same manner *Wang Ch'ung* defines the sun as the heavenly fluid or fire (*g*), but he does not grant it a round form, because it is fire and fire is not round on earth either. All the stars, he maintains, are not round, as can be seen from the meteors, which are nothing else but fallen stars (*h*).

We have already noticed the curious conception of a Yin and Yang independent of the sun, by which light and darkness are produced (*i*). According to this hypothesis the sun would disappear in the Yin at night and during the day combine its light with the Yang. An old tradition makes the sun rise in the East in the " Valley of Light " 暘 谷, shine in the South in the " City of Brightness "

(*e*) *Loc. cit.*

(*f*) 關 子 陽. 日 爲 天 陽 火 爲 地 陽, quoted in 桓 譚 新 論, T'u-shu chi-ch'êng 乾 象 典 chap. 1, 天 地 總 部 彙 考 I., 13 r.

(*g*) *Lun Hêng* I., 249, 357; II., 174.

(*h*) *Lun Hêng* I., 271.

(*i*) *Vide*, p. 14.

明都, go down in the West in the " Valley of Dusk " 昧谷 and vanish in the North in the " City of Darkness " 幽都 (*k*).

The Chinese having observed that at different times of the day the sun seems to be of different size attempted to draw conclusions as to its distance from this fact. *Lieh-tse* reports a pretended dispute of two boys, one of which claimed that the rising sun was nearer to us than at noon, arguing that at sunrise it appeared bigger than at noon. The other boy rejoined that the sun while rising is much cooler and therefore farther away than at noon, when we feel its heat most. Confucius is said to have been unable to settle the question and therefore was laughed at by the boys (*l*), one of the favourite insidious attacks of the Taoists against Confucianism.

Kuan Tse-yang took sides with the first boy, pointing out that clusters of stars which at their rise in the east seem to be over ten feet apart, at midnight, high up in the sky, are only one to two feet distant from each other, which proves that the sky above us, as well as the sun gliding over it, are more distant than at the horizon. The objection that the sun at noon is hotter than in the morning, ergo nearer, he tries to invalidate by the suggestion that the sun, as the heavenly Yang pours out toward the earth, has a fire in the direction of its flame always hotter than from the side. Moreover, in the morning the sun just issues from the great Yin, and therefore must be cooler than later. *Chang Hêng* regards the observed

---

(*k*) *Ch'ü-Yuan, T'ien-wên, Ch'u-tse* III., 1 v.; lets the sun start from the " Hot Valley " and halt on the " Shore of Dimness ": 出自湯谷次於蒙汜自明及晦所行幾里. The *Erh-ya* has 大蒙 for 蒙汜 and *Huai-nan-tse* writes 蒙谷. He gives a full itinerary of the sun's course with many more fanciful stages. Cf. *Mayers's* Reader under 日 No. 235.

(*l*) *Lieh-tse* V., 9 r.

difference of size as an optical illusion. A light in the dark, or seen from the dark appears bright and of full size, whereas in broad daylight it looks less brilliant and smaller. So we behold the sun in the morning twilight in its full size, at noon, however, part of its radiance is robbed by the light of the earth, *i.e.*, daylight, and it looks smaller. *Shu Hsi* (Chin dynasty) (*m*) holds likewise that we have here a delusion of our senses and a confusion of our eyes. Of sense delusions he gives several examples, which are remarkable considering the time in which Shu Hsi lived. He draws our attention to the fact that in a huge hall a sacrificial vessel holding an entire ox looks like a pot, and the tallest man small. When clouds are floating over the moon, the moon seems to travel and the clouds to stand still, and when sailing on a ship we often have the sensation that the water flows on and our ship does not move (*n*).

Ch'iu Kuang-t'ing (*o*) (tenth century) is at great pains to clear Confucius of the reproach of ignorance. A sage like him, he thinks, could explain the phenomenon, but considered it below his dignity to mix in a quarrel of street boys. It was his principle not to concern himself with questions indifferent to morality, just as he declined to give his views on demons and ghosts. In Ch'iu Kuang-t'ing's opinion the sun is always at the same distance from earth. Things, when viewed horizontally, always appear to us greater than when they are vertically above us. In the morning the sun does not yet emit as much heat as at noon (*p*). *Ch'ang Huang* (*q*) (Ming time) holds the same view, that

---

(*m*) 晉著作郎陽平束皙字廣微.

(*n*) *T'u-shu chi-ch'êng* 乾象典 chap. 1, 天地總部彙考, 13 r. seq.

(*o*) 丘光庭.

(*p*) *T'u-shu chi-ch'êng, loc. cit.* chap. 33, 日部總論, 6 r.

(*q*) 章潢, 圖書編. This work was written in A.D. 1585.

the difference in size, colour, and heat in the morning, at noon, and in the evening, is exclusively a consequence of the different emission of the solar fluid. The sun resembles a coal which briefly, after being ignited, seems red, is still dark inside, and does not shine much. Only by burning through it becomes hotter and more brilliant, but assumes a paler colour. Thus the sun in the morning has just been composed of the Yang fluid, therefore it appears big, red, and faintly shining, for its inner substance is still dark like that of the coal prior to its pouring forth its inner fire. At noon, however, it emits its heat entirely, whence its shape grows smaller, its effulgence brighter, but paler (r).

Just as the uninterrupted and regular motion of heaven is emphasised, the regularity of the course of the sun and moon is also insisted upon by Chinese writers. Yet tradition gives some few instances of a supposed breach of this natural law. *Huai-nan-tse* tells us that " when the Duke of *Lu-yang* was at war against *Han* (in the fifth century B.C.), during the battle the sun went down. The Duke, swinging his spear, beckoned to the sun, whereupon the sun, for his sake, came back and passed through three solar mansions " (s). It is well known that in the war of the *Jews* against the *Amorites* something very similar happened, for we read in *Joshua* (t) : " *Then Joshua spake in the presence of Israel: Sun, stand thou still above Gibeon, and thou moon, in the valley of Ajalon! And the sun stood still and the moon stayed, until the people had avenged themselves upon their enemies. Is this not written in the Book of the Upright? And the sun stood still in the midst of heaven, and hasted not to go down for the space of about a whole day* " (u).

(r) *T'u-shu chi-ch'êng, loc. cit.,* 6 v.
(s) *Huai-nan-tse* VI., 1 v.
(t) *Joshua* X., 12, 13.
(u) *Schiaparelli,* Astron. of Old Testament, p. 40.

The similarity between the two stories is so striking that *Gaubil* (*x*) assumes that *Huai-nan-tse* was acquainted with the story of Joshua. Most likely it is nothing but a strange coincidence such as will happen sometimes between nations living wide apart. The idea to arrest the course of the sun at a very momentous event, or even to cause it to turn backwards, may originate independently in the heads of many. If such a sympathetic action of the sun were possible, a big decisive battle would be a very appropriate moment for it.

Duke *Lu-yang* induces the sun to revert, *Joshua* only prevails upon it to stand still in the midst of heaven. In the historical section of *Isaiah*, however, the Jewish prophet likewise makes the sun come back, and in the Second Book of Kings, invoking Jahwe, he causes the shadow of the sun to recede 10 ma''aloths (steps of the palace) (*y*).

In Chinese sources still other similar cases are mentioned. The King of *Ch'in* promised Prince *Tan of Yin* that he would allow him to return home provided that the sun returned to the meridian, and the sun actually came back to the meridian. This is said to have taken place in 230 B.C. (*z*). In the year 163 B.C. a similar case happened under the regime of *Han Wên-ti*. *Hsin-yuan P'ing* waited for the event, and when the sun returned to the meridian the emperor selected this memorable year, the seventeenth of his reign, and with it commenced his reign again, calling it the "Later Beginning" 後 元 (*a*).

We learned that the emperor is to regard the sun as his brother. But another conception is current too, viz., that the sun is the father, as it were, or the heavenly sperm from which the emperor is born in a supernatural way.

(*x*) *Gaubil*, Astron. chin., p. 245.
(*y*) *Schiaparelli*, p. 97.
(*z*) *Lun Hêng* II., 176.
(*a*) *Shi-chi*, 28, 7 v.; *E. Chavannes*, Mémoires Historiques de Se-ma Ts'ien, Vol. III., p. 459.

Such a supernatural birth is borne witness to for several rulers in the official histories. The mother of the *Wei* emperor *Hsüan Wu-ti*, 500-516 A.D., dreamed that she was pursued by the sun and concealed herself under the bed. Then the sun transformed himself into a dragon, which twined around her several times. The empress became enceinte and in the year 484 A.D., in the fourth intercalary month, gave birth to the later Hsüan Wu-ti (*b*). Already in her youth she had had a similar dream that the sun pursued her, casting ardent looks through the window, and did not desist until she escaped (*c*). The mother of the *Liang* emperor *Wu-ti*, 502-550 A.D., embraced the sun in her dream (*d*). The empress *Hu* of the *Northern Ch'i* dynasty dreamed that she was sitting in a jade basin on the ocean and that the sun pierced her gown. On the fifth day of the fifth month, 556 A.D., she bore the emperor *Hou-chu* (*e*). The sun fell into the bosom of the empress *Hsüan-chien* in her dream, which was the cause of the birth of *T'ai Tsu* (*f*), 907-927 A.D. The *Hsü Po-wu-*

(*b*) *Wei-shu*, chap. 8, p. 1 r. 世宗本紀．世宗宣武皇帝母曰高夫人初夢爲日所逐避於牀下日化爲龍繞己數匝寤而驚悸旣而有娠太和七年閏四月生帝於平城宮．

(*c*) *Wei-shu*, chap. 13, p. 6 v. 皇后傳．孝文昭皇后高氏幼曾夢在堂內立而日光自窗中照之灼灼而熱后東西避之光猶斜照不已如是數夕．

(*d*) *Nan-shih*, chap. 6, p. 1 v. 梁武帝紀．皇妣張氏常夢抱日巳而有娠遂產帝．

(*e*) *Pei Ch'i shu*, chap. 8, p. 1 r. 後主本紀．母胡皇后夢於海上坐玉盆日入裙下遂有娠天保七年五月五日生帝於幷州邸．

(*f*) *Liao-shih*, chap. 1, p. 1 r. 太祖本紀．太祖母宣簡皇后蕭氏夢日墮懷中有娠乃生帝．

ch'ih relates that *Lao-tse* was born in a similar manner, his mother seeing the solar essence falling down like a shooting star and entering her mouth (*g*). In all these reports, which of course have the tendency to prove the divinity of the emperor, it is noteworthy that a mere dream suffices to cause pregnancy.

Mythologically the sun has not had the same influence on the imaginative power of the Chinese as the moon. Solar myths are few. *Huai-nan-tse* and *Wang Ch'ung* inform us that the ancient literati believed in the existence of a *three-legged raven* living in the sun. Wang Ch'ung sets himself to demonstrate the impossibility of any animal living in a fiery mass (*h*).

2. *The Moon.*

The moon consists of the Yin fluid or water. *Wang Ch'ung* expresses himself to this effect repeatedly (*i*), and the *Shuo-wên* defines the moon as the essence of the *T'ai-yin* (*k*). The *Erh-ya-su* connotes the fiery essence of the sun as external radiance and the watery essence of the moon as the internal light (*l*). To us the idea that the moon consists of water appears strange, yet the comparison of the faint moonlight with glittering water is not at all very far-fetched. The *Greek physicists* likewise averred the moist nature of the moon, which could be proved by the dampness of the nights—the dew is supposed to fall down from the moon—and by the influence of the moon on the tides. Generally speaking, to the Greeks not less

---

(*g*) 續博物志 老君其母曾見日精下落如流星飛入口中有娠.

(*h*) *Mayers*, Reader No. 235—*Lun Hêng* I., 268.

(*i*) *Lun Hêng*, I., 268; II., 341, 350.

(*k*) *Shuo-wên* : 月闕也太陰之精.

(*l*) *Erh-ya-su*, 釋天. 火則外光水則含景.

than to the Chinese the virile energy seemed analogous
to heat and the feminine functions related to the moist
principle (*m*). One may call to mind that the sun is the
representative of the masculine, fiery Yang fluid, whereas
the moon is the repository of the feminine, moist Yin
essence.

Now, provided that the moon is not fiery like the sun
and has water as its element, whence does it obtain its
light? If we are to believe the commentary, then the
author of the *Chou-pi* was aware already that the moonlight
is borrowed from the sun. "The sun," says the Chou-pi,
"gives to the moon her appearance. So the moonlight
comes forth, and the bright moon is complete" (*n*). Perhaps
a passage in *Wên-tse* refers to the same phenomenon :
"When the moon is in opposition to the sun, she robs her
light. The Yin cannot take the place of the Yang" (*o*).
Ching Fang (1st cent. B.C.) is quite explicit saying, "The
moon and the stars are Yin. They have shape, but no
light. This they receive only when the sun illuminates
them. The former masters thought that the sun is like
a ball and the moon like a mirror, or they took the moon
for a ball too. The spots illuminated by the sun appear
bright, those not illuminated dark" (*p*). The commentary
to the above-quoted passage of the *Chou-pi* runs thus (*q*) :
"The moonlight comes from the irradiation of the sun,

(*m*) *Bouché-Leclercq*, p. 92.

(*n*) *Chou-pi* II., 1 r. 故日兆月月光乃出故成明月.

(*o*) *Wên-tse* VI., 4 r. 上德篇. 月望日奪光陰不能
以承陽.

(*p*) *Erh-ya-su.* 京房云. 月與星辰陰者也有形無光
日照之乃有光先師以爲日似彈丸月似鏡體或
以爲月亦似彈丸日照處則明不照處則暗.

(*q*) *Chou-pi, loc. cit.* 故月光生於日所照魄生於日
所蔽當日則光盈就日則明盡.

and the waning of the moon, when the sun obscures it.
When the moon is opposite to the sun, her brilliancy
increases, when she comes near the sun, her light vanishes."

In its astronomical section the *Sui-shu* says about the
moon : " When the sunlight illumines her, we see her
bright, that part, however, which the sunshine does not
strike is called the dark disk. On the fifteenth day of
every month the sun and the moon are in opposition, and
men staying in the middle between the two then perceive
the moon completely bright, wherefore she appears round.
On a day of the two quarters the sun illumines but one
side of the moon. Men then only behold this side, and
one side of the moon is bright, the other dark. On the
last and first day of every month the sunshine falls on the
outer side of the moon. People are situated at the inner
side, and therefore cannot see the moon at all " (r).

The light of the moon and her phases have from olden
days enlisted the interest of humanity. The ancient
civilised nations did not yet know the reason. At the time
of *Berosos* the *Chaldeans* taught that the moon was a ball
with one shining and one dark side. It is a curious fact
that the *Hindus* at the time of the *Vedas* also thought of
the sun as having one bright side by which the day was
produced and one dark side causing night (s). This old
conception was subsequently changed by Buddhism. From
the *Li-shi a-pi-tan lun*, translated 558 A.D. by *Parā-
martha* (t), we take the following outline of a new theory :

(r) *Sui-shu* XX., 6 r. 天文志.月者陰之精也.其形圓
其質清日光照之則見其明日光所不照則謂之
魄故月望之日日月相望人居其間盡覩其明故
形圓也二弦之日日照其側人觀其傍故半明半
魄也朔之日日照其表人在其裏故不見也.

(s) *Bouché-Leclercq*, p. 43.

(t) *Bunyiu Nanjio*, Catalogue of the Buddhist Tripiṭaka, No. 1297;

" What does the *dark half* mean and what the *bright half*? The sun is the cause of the dark half, and the sun is the cause of the bright half. The sun constantly pursues the moon and every day comes 48,080 yocana nearer. While the sun is retiring from the moon, the daily progress is the same. The sun advancing upon the moon, the moon disk becomes overshadowed, viz., $3\frac{1}{3}$ yocana every day more. In this manner the overshadowing of the moon increases fifteen days, until at the commencement of the last day the dark half of the moon is complete. As soon as the sun begins to recede from the moon more and more from day to day, the distance covered is also of 48,080 yocana, and the moon becomes every day cleared $3\frac{1}{3}$ yocana. In this manner after fifteen days the moon is perfectly bright and quite round, so that people then say that the bright half is full."

" When the sun and the moon are at the greatest distance from one another, at that time the moon is full, and they then say that the bright half is full. When the sun and the moon are united in one place, one calls that their conjunction, and people say that the dark half is full. The sun following in the train of the moon, the sunshine falls on the moonlight. This light is much coarser, therefore when hit by the sunshine it produces shade, and this shade of the moon covers the moon itself. Thus the backside of the moon does not appear round. For this reason the obscuration of the moon gradually increases and after fifteen days it is complete. When the sun passes behind the moon one speaks of the dark half, when it passes before the moon, the moon becomes clearer from day to day in a similar way, and after fifteen days it is

A. Forke, Katalog des Pekinger Tripiṭaka der Koeniglichen Bibliothek zu Berlin, No. 782.

perfectly round. While the sun passes before the moon, one speaks of the bright half " (*u*).

It is worthy of notice that according to this theory the moon shines with its proper light. The sun and the moon being wide apart the proper light of the moon shines without any impediment, and we have full moon. When the sun and the moon meet, the sun deprives the moon of its light covering it, which actually takes place only at an eclipse of the moon. When the moon is waxing or waning, the shade is said to be the result of the sunshine which in some inexplicable way produces a shadow on the fainter moonlight. This view is still far away from the right one already understood by *Ching Fang*.

Having once made the moon the representative of the Yin element or water, it is not surprising that the Chinese should assign to it a certain influence on the water on earth and the animals living therein. We do not know whether they were guided by these considerations or by direct observations; at all events in the *Han* time already they were fully cognizant of the influence of the moon on the ebb and high tides. " The rising of the waves follows the growing and waning, the bigness and smallness, the fullness and extinction of the moon " (*x*) says *Wang Ch'ung* in a discussion on the famous bore or spring-tide of Hangchou. Among the *Romans Caesar* was the first who noticed that at full moon the tide was higher than usual, and *Pliny* ascribed it directly to the influences of the sun and the moon.

As all nations do, the Chinese also have endowed the moon with *sympathetic forces*, which become manifest in things proceeding like the moon from the Yin fluid.

(*u*) *T'u-shu chi-ch'êng*, 乾 象 典 chap. 43, 月 部 雜 錄 4 r. 立 世 阿 毘 曇 論 sub 法 苑 珠 林.

(*x*) *Lun Hêng* II., 251.

According to *Huai-nan-tse*, at the waning of the moon the brains of fish grow smaller, and at new moon shells and oysters shrink together (*y*). Crabs, pearls, and turtles likewise grow and decrease in conjunction with the moon (*z*). *Lü Pu-wei* informs us that "the moon is the source of all Yin. At full moon all shells and oysters are full, and all Yin is exuberant, at new moon shells and oysters are empty, and all Yin fades away" (*a*). Pearls are considered to be direct products of the moonlight. "The moon is the essence of the T'ai-yin," says one writer; "sea-shells consume its brilliancy and by so doing produce pearls" (*b*). *Wang Ch'ung* extends the influence of the moon even to snails and corn-weevils, which are believed to decrease at eclipses of the moon (*c*).

Very similar ideas were prevalent during the Middle Ages in Europe until the beginning of modern times. *Tycho de Brahe* and *Melanchthon* were firmly convinced that with the waxing and waning moon the brains of animals, the marrow of bones and trees, and the flesh of crabs and snails grew and shrank together (*d*).

The *Hsiung-nu* must have been of opinion that the phases of the moon affected human fate also, for the *Han-shu* reports about them that they would only fight with the waxing moon, the waning moon (*e*) probably being a bad augury for the outcome of the battle.

(*y*) *Huai-nan-tse* III., 2 r. 天文訓. 月虛而魚腦減月死而蠃蛖膲.

(*z*) *Eod.* IV.; 7 v. 墜形訓. 蛤蟹珠龜與月盛衰.

(*a*) *Lü-shih ch'un-ch'iu* IX., 12 v. 精通篇. 月也者羣陰之本也月望則蚌蛤實羣陰盈月晦則蚌蛤虛羣陰虧.

(*b*) 春秋感精符. 太陰之精海蚌食其光生珠.

(*c*) *Lun-Héng* II., 341.

(*d*) *Troels-Lund*, p. 209 seq.

(*e*) *Ch'ien Han-shu*, chap. 94a, p. 4 r. 匈奴傳上.

A variety of myths are connected with the moon in China, all invented doubtless with the object of accounting for the dark spots visible in the moon. In the moon there lives *Ch'ang-o*, the wife of *Hou I*, transformed into a three-legged toad, a hare, a Taoist adept, an old man, and there grows a cassia-tree (*f*). Of these stories that of the toad and the hare seem to be the oldest. The hare in the moon was already known before the 4th century B.C., for in the " Questions " *Ch'ü Yuan* inquires : " The light of the night what excellent quality has it, that it dies and is recalled to life again? And what advantage has it from the hare which we behold in its womb?" (*g*) These two sagas are attacked by *Wang Ch'ung* from his rationalistic view-point on the ground that the moon is water in which toads and hares could not live (*h*). *Chang Hêng* (1st—2nd cent. A.D.) narrates the story of *Ch'ang-o* (*i*). The myth of the toad must have been current in the former *Han* epoch already, that of the hare in the *Chou* period. There-fore we cannot concur with *Mayers*, who quoting a very unreliable authority *De Gubernatis*, advocates the Indian origin of these stories. The hare in the moon is also found with the old Mexicans (*k*), who never had any traceable relations with China.

The adept *Wu Kang* (*l*), who for some misdemeanour was condemned to cut down the cassia-tree in the moon, which after each stroke closed again, seems to be first mentioned by the *Yu-yang tsa-tsu* (8th cent. A.D.) (*m*).

(*f*) Cf. *Mayers*, Reader No. 957, who relates all these stories.

(*g*) *Ch'ü Yuan*, *T'ien-wên*, *Ch'u-tse* III., 1 v. 夜 光 何 德 死 則 又 育 厥 利 維 何 而 顧 菟 在 腹.

(*h*) *Lun Hêng* I., 268.

(*i*) *T'u-shu chi-ch'êng*, 乾 象 典 chap. 43, 月 部 雜 錄 15 r.

(*k*) *Tylor* I., 355.　　　　　　　　(*l*) 吳 剛.

(*m*) 酉 陽 雜 俎 in *T'u-shu chi-ch'êng*, 乾 象 典, chap. 43, 月 部 外 編, 4 r. and *Mayers*, No. 864.

In the *Hsü Yu-kuai-lu* (*n*), also of the 8th century, we read the story of the old man in the moon, who with red threads binds together the legs of future husbands and wives.

The myth of the cassia-tree is perhaps borrowed from India. In the *Ch'i-shih ching* (*o*), translated by *Jñānagupta*, 561—578 A.D., we have the following reference to it: " And whence come all the shadows visible in the moon palace? In our great continent there is the *Jambu* tree, from which the name Jambu-dvīpa is derived. This tree is very high, and its shadow appears on the disk of the moon." In another passage of the *Yü-ch'ieh lun* (*p*) it is said, " The shadows of the fishes and turtles from the ocean appear on the disk of the moon. Therefore, black spots are visible on this."

The author of the *Yu-yang tsa-tsu* was familiar with these Indian conceptions, for where he speaks about the adept and the cassia-tree, said to be 5,000 feet high, he expressly adds : " The Buddhist books mention that south of Mount *Sumeru* there stands a Jambu tree. When the moon passes this tree, its shadow falls on the moon. Some say that the toad and the cassia-tree in the moon are shadows of the earth, and the empty spaces the reflex of the water (of the ocean). This view comes near to the truth " (*q*). *Ch'iu Kuang-t'ing* disclaims the possibility of a cassia-tree growing on the moon, because the moon has

---

(*n*) 續 幽 怪 錄 in *T'u-shu chi-ch'êng*, *loc. cit.* and *Mayers*, No. 838.

(*o*) 起 世 經, *Bunyiu Nanjio*, No. 550, and *Peking Tripiṭaka*, No. 57, quoted in 月 部 外 編, 1 v. seq. sub 法 苑 珠 林.

(*p*) 瑜 伽 論 *loc. cit.* Perhaps the *Yogaśāstra*, *Bunjiu Nanjio*, No. 1170, is meant.

(*q*) 釋 氏 書 言 須 彌 山 南 面 有 閻 扶 樹 影 入 月 中 或 言 月 中 膽 桂 地 影 也. 處 水 影 也 此 語 差 近.

no earth, and thinks himself that the shadow of the earth on the moon takes the shape of a tree (r).

Perhaps the idea to conceive of the spots in the moon as shadows or reflections of things on earth may also have been suggested by the study of Buddhist works. *Wang An-shih* (s) expresses it quite clearly, saying that the things which seem to be in the moon are the shadows of mountains and rivers (t), of the earth of course. *Su Tung-p'o*, who wishes to do away with stories about the toad, the hare, and the cassia-tree, indited the following verses on the moon : "It is just like a huge, round mirror in which our mountains and rivers delineate themselves. The unfounded assertions about the cassia-tree, the hare and the toad ought to be discarded" (u). The device to have the earth mirrored in the moon, thought of as an enormous drop or a surface of water, is not so bad. The *Mao-shih ming-wu chieh*, which gives an account of all these various opinions, however, voices the following doubt : When any object is reflected in one half of a mirror, it nevertheless appears complete, whereas the reflexes in the half moon disk are only half (x).

3. *Eclipses of the Sun and the Moon.*

Eclipses of the sun and the moon have been observed in China from the remotest times. In the *Han* epoch

---

(r) 唐 丘 光 庭 兼 明 書. 辨 月 桂. 月 中 無 地 安 得 有 桂 蓋 以 地 影 入 于 月 中 似 樹 形 耳.

(s) 王 安 石 A.D. 1021—1086.

(t) 月 中 彷 彿 有 物 乃 山 河 影 也.

(u) 東 坡 先 生 亦 有 正 如 大 圓 鏡 寫 此 山 河 影 妄 言 桂 兎 蟆 俗 說 皆 可 屏 之 句.

(x) 毛 詩 名 物 解 in *T'u-shu chi-ch'êng* 乾 象 典 chap. 43, 月 部 雜 錄 p. 6 r. The author is *T'sai Pien* 蔡 卞, A.D. 1054—1112.

the cause of the eclipses of the sun was known. The literati knew, at least part of them, that the eclipses of the sun are caused by the moon. Since such eclipses would always happen on the last and the first day of a month, when the sun and the moon were in conjunction, they inferred that the moon eclipsed the sun. "Some says," *Wang Ch'ung* tells us, "that, when the sun is eclipsed, the moon covers him" (*y*). Wang Ch'ung himself militates against this correct view with insufficient reasons, particularly he takes exception to the fact that the eclipse is mostly incomplete. He mentions still another theory, according to which an eclipse of the sun takes place, when the Yang is weak and the Yin strong, and he by a counter-argument shows that at new moon the Yin fluid of the moon then completely vanishing cannot be strong. Wang Ch'ung's own view is that at an eclipse the sun shrinks spontaneously. As a rule, according to Wang Ch'ung every 41—42 months there is an eclipse of the sun and every 180 days of the moon. In another passage he gives the interval between two eclipses of the moon as 56 months (*z*).

The popular Chinese explanation of eclipses is that they originate from the "celestial dog" (*a*) devouring the sun or the moon. One might think of a loan from India, where the head of the demon *Râhu* devours the sun and the moon, thus causing the eclipses, if similar conceits of a monster devouring the moon did not exist among the American Indians as well, and if the custom to come to the assistance of the moon in her trouble by shouting and making every kind of noise, as the Chinese do to this day, were not practised all over the world. *Tylor*, who has collected the material concerning this interesting chapter of

---

(*y*) *Lun Hêng* I., 270.
(*z*) *Eod.* II., 14.
(*a*) 天 狗.

primitive astronomy (*b*), says, " The *Chiquitos* of the southern continent thought the moon was hunted across the sky by *huge dogs*, which caught and tore her till her light was reddened and quenched by the blood flowing from her wounds, and then Indians, raising a frightful howl and lamentation, would shoot arrows into the sky to drive the monsters off."

The *Caribs* believe that the demon *Maboya* devours the sun and the moon, and they dance and howl at an eclipse. In the *Tupi* language the term " Jaguar has eaten Sun " refers to an eclipse of the sun. The *North American Indians* speak of a big dog devouring the sun. Although the *Aztecs* had an idea of the true cause of eclipses, yet they kept the expression of the sun and moon being devoured, just as the Chinese still at present speak of the " eating of the sun " or the " eating of the moon " (*c*).

In *Sumatra* prevails the idea that at an eclipse the sun and the moon devour one another, and people make the noise to prevent this.

The *Romans* felt bound to help the moon in her distress. " *Laboranti succurrere lunae* " was the expression. To that end they flung up firebrands into the air, blew trumpets, and clanged brazen pots. In *France* the phrase " *Dieu garde la lune des loups* " has survived as a reminiscence of an old popular belief. Up to the 17th century people in *Ireland* and *Wales* were in the habit of running about wildly at an eclipse, beating kettles and pans with a view to assisting the suffering luminary. That in ancient times already the Chinese offered the same assistance seems to result from a notice in *Hsün-tse* (4th cent. B.C.) to the effect that, " When the sun and moon

---

(*b*) *Tylor* I., 328 seq.

(*c*) 日 食 and 月 食.

are being eaten, one helps them " (*d*). Presumably at that time already the two orbs were eaten by the heavenly dog.

4. *Stars.*

As to the origin and substance of the stars opinions are divided. We saw that *Huai-nan-tse* considered them to be the children of the sun and the moon, to which *Wang Ch'ung* assents (*e*). In opposition to this the *Erh-ya-su* (*f*) holds that the stars effloresced from the Yang fluid. This fluid first becomes the sun, from which the stars separate. Such is the meaning of the character 星 for star, viz., " born from the sun " (*g*). On the other hand *Ching Fang*, as we saw, regards the stars as Yin, because they have no light of their own and are illuminated by the sun (*h*).

To the *Mintera* of the *Malay Peninsula* the stars are children of the moon. The sun also had his children, but he has devoured them, which of course must be explained cosmically (*i*).

Wang Ch'ung believes that the stars are not round, as little as the meteors or falling stars are, but that they are much bigger than they appear to us, perhaps 100 Li. *Hsü Chêng* distinguishes three classes of stars, of 100 Li, 50 Li, and 30 Li in diameter (*k*). Of the " Seven Stars " he states that they are 9,000 Li distant one from another,

---

(*d*) *Hsün-tse* XI., 17 v. 天 論 篇. 日 月 食 而 救 之.

(*e*) Cf. p. 80.

(*f*) *Erh-ya-su*, 釋 天. 陽 精 爲 日 日 分 爲 星 故 其 字 日 下 生 也.

(*g*) This etymology is hardly correct, for 生 is the phonetic element and 日 abridged for 晶 meaning stars already. Cf. *L. Wieger*, Leçons Etymologiques, p. 247.

(*h*) *Vid.*, p. 90.

(*i*) *Tylor* I., 356.

(*k*) Cf. p. 61.

an estimate most likely based on the putative circumference of heaven = 730,000 Li. All stars, in his opinion, consist of the finest water essence of the original fluid (*l*).

The pregnancy of an empress mother may eventually be brought about by a *shooting star* quite as well as by the sun. The mother of the mythical emperor *Chuan Hsü* saw the *Yao kuang* star pass through the moon, and afterwards gave birth to the emperor (*m*). The mother of the emperor *Yü*, prior to her pregnancy, had beheld a falling star enter into the Pleiades and subsequently dreamt that she swallowed a magic pearl (*n*).

B. MODERN TIMES.

Chinese philosophy and the sciences combined with it had a renaissance in the *Sung* dynasty beginning in the 10th century. From this date on we may count the modern times of Chinese sciences. As by the Sung philosophers Confucianism was rejuvenated, so in their speculations on the philosophy of nature they likewise resumed the old ideas about the shape, the origin and the formation of the universe and further developed them. In so doing they try, as far as possible, to remain in accordance with the old classics. The basic notions remain the same and are only expanded.

(*l*) *T'u-shu chi-ch'êng*, 乾象典, chap. 55, 星辰部彙考 12, 6 v.

(*m*) *Bamboo Annals*, chap. 1. 竹書紀年. 帝顓頊高陽 氏. 母曰女樞見瑤光之星貫月如虹感己於幽房 之宮生顓頊於若水.

(*n*) *Eod.*, chap. 3. 帝禹夏后氏, 母曰修己出行見 流星貫昴夢接意感旣而吞神珠修己背剖而生 禹於石紐.

I. System of the Universe.

Of the various systems of antiquity the *Hun-t‘ien* theory of the spheroid shape of heaven has obtained the exclusive sway. *Chu Hsi* frequently alludes to this fact. Against the *Kai-t‘ien* system he urges that agreeably to it the vault of heaven would be similar to an umbrella and it could not be explained how in its rotation it could keep in touch with earth (*o*). The same objection against the Kai-t‘ien theory had been raised by *Wang Ch‘ung*. Chu Hsi correctly observes that, if one half of heaven is above earth, the other half must be underneath (*p*). How he conceives the universe is apparent from the following statement : " The shape of heaven and earth is as if somebody joins two bowls with water inside. As long as he constantly turns them around with his hands, the water remains inside and is not spilled, but no sooner does he stay his hands for a moment than it runs out " (*q*). It is needless to say that the two bowls represent the two hemispheres which are in constant rotation, and the water the ocean surrounding the earth, which, in spite of the revolution of the vault of heaven, remains quiet.

Since heaven encompasses earth from all sides, it is natural that she should be supported by heaven below, but not only does heaven support the earth, but the earth also supports heaven, so that they mutually support each other. That is the idea of *Shao K‘ang-chieh* (*r*) which Chu Hsi adduces approvingly, declaring that heaven reposes on

---

(*o*) *Chu Hsi's* Complete Works, chap. 50, p. 16 r. 朱 子 全 書. 天 度.

(*p*) *Chu Hsi* 50, 12 v. 天 度.

(*q*) *Chu Hsi* 49, 14 r. 天 地. 又 曰 天 地 之 形 如 人 以 兩 盌 相 合 貯 水 於 內 以 手 常 常 掉 開 則 水 在 內 不 出 稍 住 手 則 水 漏 矣.

(*r*) 邵 雍 or 邵 康 節, the philosopher *Shao-tse*, A.D. 1011—1077.

earth, and earth on the air of heaven (*s*). This would seem
contradictory, for if heaven enfolds the earth it cannot well
repose on it. Chu Hsi seems to have in view the atmosphere amassed on earth, which to the Chinese is a portion
of heaven. " Heaven," says Chu Hsi, " as air reposes on
the mass of earth, and earth as a mass lies on the air of
heaven. The air of heaven encircles the earth, which is
but an object within heaven. Heaven as air gyrates
outside. Therefore earth solidly reposes upon it like a
swimming bridge in the centre of heaven and does not
move. If the motion of heaven stopped only one moment,
earth would tumble down " (*t*). Consequently the whirling
power of heaven keeps earth in equilibrium, just as the
turning bowls do the water.

Of water, or the ocean, Chu Hsi does not speak at all,
but in another passage where he assails the assertion of the
Huang-ti shu that outside of heaven there is water by
which both heaven and earth are carried (*u*), he states that
there is no water outside of heaven, but under the earth,
which alone swims upon it (*x*). But how does that tally
with the above statement that earth reposes on the air of
heaven? Probably Chu Hsi thinks of earth as swimming
upon the ocean and of the ocean as surrounded by heaven
below. *Wang K'o-ta* (*y*) (Ming dynasty) also holds that

(*s*) *Chu Hsi* 49, 22 r. 天 地. 似 康 節 說 得 那 天 依 地 地
附 天 天 地 自 相 依 附 天 依 形 地 附 氣 底 幾 句.

(*t*) *Loc. cit.* 天 以 氣 而 依 地 之 形 地 以 形 而 附 天 之
氣 天 包 乎 地 地 特 天 中 之 一 物 爾 天 以 氣 而 運 乎
外 故 地 榷 在 中 間 隤 然 不 動 使 天 之 運 有 一 息 停
則 地 須 陷 下.

(*u*) See above, p. 18.

(*x*) *Hsing-li ta-ch'üan* 26, 14 v. 天 地. 朱 子 曰 天 外 無 水 地
下 是 水 載.

(*y*) 王 可 大 象 緯 新 篇.

within heaven earth swims upon the water. *Chang Huang* (z) (Ming time) is right in making the following criticism : " The statement of the *Sui-shu* that the sun enters into the water is erroneous. The water issues from the earth and does not part from her. On all sides around the earth there is heaven, whence could the water come? If they say that heaven floats upon the water and earth is carried by it, this is still more preposterous " (a). Chang Huang seems to be aware that the oceans are parts of the earth and do not encircle or carry her.

Heaven, in pursuance of Chu Hsi's view, consists of air in constant rotation, which is designed to account for the gyration of the vault of heaven. By this fast motion air becomes so concentrated that it appears hard. This is the " *hard wind* " of the Taoists. In this way Chu Hsi at the same time obtains the quality of hardness ascribed to heaven in the Yiking. The strata of air forming heaven, however, are not uniform (b). The uppermost contain the purest air, rotate quickest, and are the hardest, so hard that Chu Hsi presumes that the outermost layer even forms a hard shell enfolding all the others. The nearer one approaches earth the more turbid becomes the air and the slower it rotates. Chu Hsi distinguishes nine such layers of air and identifies them with the Nine Heavens men-

---

(z) 章 潢.

(a) 圖 書 編. 天 地 總 論. 隋 書 謂 日 入 水 中 妄 也. 水 由 地 中 行 不 離 乎 地 地 之 四 表 皆 天 安 得 有 水 謂 水 浮 天 載 地 尤 妄 也.

(b) *Chu Hsi* 49, 19 v. 天 地. 問 天 有 形 質 否 曰 只 是 箇 旋 風 下 軟 上 堅 道 家 謂 之 剛 風 人 常 說 天 有 九 重 分 九 處 爲 號 非 也 只 是 旋 有 九 耳 但 下 面 氣 較 濁 而 暗 上 面 至 高 處 則 至 清 至 明 耳.

tioned in the *Li-sao* and in other old sources (*c*). We cannot dispute the ingenuity of these arguments.

The author of the *Hai-han wan-hsiang lu* describes a model very well illustrating the universe in accordance with Chu Hsi's theory : " When I was small, I played with a pig's bladder, filling it half full of water and putting in it a big, hard clay ball. Then I blew it full of air, and I saw the water in the bladder below, the clay ball swimming in the water, and the air moving like clouds. It was a model of heaven and earth. Round the ' Great Void ' there must be the ' hard air ' " (*d*). This last expression, of course, refers to Chu Hsi's theory. The "hard air " here is the bladder, the water represents the ocean, and the clay ball is the earth.

Shih Po-hsüan (*e*) speaks doubtfully about Chu Hsi's supposition that the earth is surrounded by the whirling air of heaven and floating on water. Thus tossed about by air and water it might easily come to destruction. To avert that he suggests that the axis of the earth which passes through the south pole must stick fast in heaven. If such an axis were more than a mere abstraction and had real existence, this would indeed be a contrivance to make

---

(*c*) *Chu Hsi* 49, 25 v. 天地. 離騷有九天之說注家妄解云有九天據某觀之只是九重蓋天運行有許多重數裏面重數較軟至外面則漸硬想到第九重只成硬殼相似那裏轉得又愈緊矣.

(*d*) *T'u-shu chi-ch'êng* 乾象典 chap. 7, 天地總部雜錄 p. 12 r. 海涵萬象錄. 予幼時戲將豬水胞盛半胞水置一大乾泥丸於內用氣吹滿胞畢見水在胞底泥丸在中其氣運動如雲是即天地之形狀也此太虛之外必有固氣者. The author is *Huang Jun-yü* 黃潤玉 of the Ming dynasty.

(*e*) 史伯璿.

the earth steady. In the *Ching-kuan so-yen* (*f*) *Shih Po-hsüan* is excoriated for the absurdity of his view.

Conformably to the calculations of the *Chou-pi* the distance between heaven and earth measures 80,000 Li (*g*). The *Mo-wang* assumes it to be 84,000 Li, which it divides as follows : The upper 36,000 Li of heaven are 36 regions filled with the Yang fluid, the lower 36,000 Li. reaching down to earth are 36 regions filled with the Yin fluid. Between these Yang and Yin regions there is an intermediate zone of 12,000 Li where Yang and Yin are blended (*h*).

II. CREATION.

Modern cosmological theories closely follow those of the ancients. The fundamental thoughts are the same, only in details we find differences, and the theories have been further developed. The investigations of *Chu Hsi*, which may be considered the most thorough, bear a close relation to those of *Lieh-tse* and *Chang Hêng* (*i*). His own words are :

" Heaven and earth were first the Yin and Yang fluid. This one fluid was in motion, and by the grinding of the particles against each other a violent friction ensued, which resulted in the secretion of a great quantity of sediments. There being no space in the centre to escape they coagulated and formed an earth in the centre. The

---

(*f*) 非 觀 瑣 言, later *Sung* or *Ming* period.

(*g*) Cf. p. 57.

(*h*) 脉 望. 天 地 相 去 八 萬 四 千 里 自 天 以 下 三 萬 六 千 里 應 三 十 六 陽 候 自 地 以 上 三 萬 六 千 里 應 三 十 六 陰 候 所 謂 天 上 三 十 六 地 下 三 十 六 中 間 一 萬 二 千 里 乃 陰 陽 都 會 之 處 天 地 之 中 也. The *Mo-wang* is written by *Chao T'ai-ting* 趙 台 鼎, *Ming* epoch.

(*i*) Cf. pp. 34 and 38.

purest particles of fluid became the sky, the sun, the moon
and the stars, which are permanently revolving and turning round outside. The earth was in the centre motionless,
but not below. Heaven moved unceasingly, turning round
day and night. Thus earth was in its centre like a
swimming bridge. Should heaven stop only one instant,
earth must fall down. But the gyration of heaven was so
fast, that a great amount of sediment was amassed in the
middle. This sediment of the fluid is the earth. Therefore they say that the purer and lighter parts become
heaven, the grosser and more turbid, earth " (k).

The conception of earth as a kind of silt or sediment
pressed out by the violent friction of the rotating Yin and
Yang particles is new, as is the idea that the equipoise
of earth is preserved by the force of the circling sky,.
already pointed out. In accordance with the *Hun-t'ien*
system earth must occupy a central position and cannot
be below the sky, a mere delusion of sight.

Chu Hsi assumes that, before chaos was divided, there
were only *water* and *fire*, i.e., Yin and Yang. From the
silt of the muddy water thrown out by rotation the earth
was formed. These earthly particles are compared with
sand thrown up by the tide. Chu Hsi points to the
wave-like shape of mountains, from which he infers that
in primeval times they must have been under water and

(k) *Chu Hsi* 49, 19 r. 天地. 天地初間只是陰陽之氣
這一箇氣運行磨來磨去磨得急了便楼許多渣
滓裏面無處出便結成箇地在中央氣之清者便
爲天爲日月爲星辰只在外常周環運轉地便只
在中央不動不是在下天運不息晝夜輥轉故地
榷在中間使天有一息之停則地須陷下惟天運
轉之急故凝結許多渣滓在中間地者氣之渣滓
也所以道輕清者爲天重濁者爲地.

soft. We have in him an advocate of Neptunism. From
the essence of fire, wind, thunder and lightning, the sun
and the stars were evolved (*l*). Before Yin and Yang
separated, there reigned complete darkness, and only at
their separation a bright light shone forth (*m*).

The cosmogony of Chu Hsi's predecessor *Shao-tse*, in
his *Huang-chi ching-shi* (*n*) is much more sophisticated.
He depends on a passage in a commentary of the Yiking
saying that the principle of heaven is *Yin* and *Yang*, and
that of the earth the *Soft* and the *Hard* (*o*). Conformably
to the ordinary view Yang is the principle of heaven, and
Yin the principle of earth. Creation being completed, both
elements occur throughout the universe, in heaven as well
as on earth, so that they cannot be claimed for heaven
alone. Softness and hardness are qualities of substances,
but not elements that might be contrasted with Yin and
Yang. However that may be, the authority of a Yiking
commentary attributed to Confucius does not allow of
any criticism by a Chinese philosopher, he has to abide
by it, and Shao-tse does so, evolving the cosmos from
the afore-mentioned four principles.

From Chaos springs the Absolute or the primary

(*l*) *Loc. cit.* 49, 19 v. 天地. 天地始初混沌未分時想
只有水火二者水之滓腳便成地今登高而望羣
山皆爲波浪之狀便是水泛如此只不知因是麼
時凝了初間極軟後來方凝得硬問想得如潮水
湧起沙相似曰然水之極濁便成地火之極清便
成風霆雷電日星之屬.

(*m*) *Eod.* 49, 20 r. 天地. 方渾淪未判陰陽之氣混合
幽暗及其旣分中間放得開闊光朗而兩儀始立.

(*n*) 邵子. 皇極經世. 觀物內篇.

(*o*) *Yiking*, App. V., 423. 大傳. 立天之道曰陰與陽立
地之道曰柔與剛.

principle *T'ai-chi*, which splits into the two modes, heaven and earth. Heaven originates from motion, earth from rest. At the inception of motion Yang is produced, at its close, Yin. At the beginning of rest the Soft is created, at its end, the Hard. Motion and rest, Yin and Yang, Softness and Hardness continually alternate and follow each other. To this *Shao Po-wên* (A.D. 1057—1134), the son of *Shao-tse*, adds the following remarks :—" In view of its substance heaven is considered in motion, and earth at rest, but as regards its manifestation heaven is both moved and unmoved, possessing Yin as well as Yang. Earth, on the other side, possesses softness and hardness, the Soft is said to be at rest and the Hard in motion " (*p*). This reasoning is not very convincing. The philosopher takes great care to docket his notions correctly, but does not pay any heed to nature as it really is.

The four principles are again subdivided by the younger *Shao* into eight. According as motion and rest are more or less complete and softness and hardness exist in larger or smaller quantities we obtain : *T'ai-yang* = abundant Yang, *Shao-yang* = scanty Yang, *T'ai-yin* = abundant Yin, *Shao-yin* = scanty Yin, *T'ai-kang* = great Hardness, *Shao-kang* = small Hardness, *T'ai-jou* = great Softness, *Shao-jou* = small *Softness* (*q*). From these eight principles or elements the different parts of heaven and earth were produced:

(*p*) *Hsing-li ta-ch'üan* IX., 2 r. 天生於動者也地生於靜者也 .... 動之始則陽生焉動之極則陰生焉 .... 靜之始則柔生焉靜之極則剛生焉 ....〔言其體則天動而地靜言其用則天有陰陽陰靜而陽動也地有柔剛柔靜而剛動也.〕

(*q*) *Eod.* IX., 5 r. 〔混成一體謂之太極太極既判初有儀形謂之兩儀兩儀又判而爲陰陽剛柔謂之四象四象又判而爲太陽少陽太陰少陰太剛

(1) T'ai-yang = the *Sun*, Yang of the highest potency. On earth *fire* corresponds to it.

(2) T'ai-yin = the *Moon*, Yin in the highest degree. On earth *water* corresponds to it.

(3) Shao-yang = the *Stars*, formed of the residue of the solar fire, therefore a scanty Yang. On earth *stones* correspond to it.

(4) Shao-yin = the *Space of Heaven*, the blue empyrean, which corresponds to the *soil* on earth.

(5) T'ai-jou = *Water*, the softest substance on earth. In heaven the *moon* corresponds to it.

(6) T'ai-kang = *Fire*, the hardest substance (*sic*!) on earth. In heaven the *sun* corresponds to it.

(7) Shao-jou = *Earth*, soft, though in a lesser degree than water. In heaven the *space of heaven* corresponds to it.

(8) Shao-kang = *Stones*, hard though in a lesser degree than fire. In heaven the *stars* correspond to it.

The sun, the moon, the stars, and the spaces of heaven are the four celestial forms to which the four terrestrial formations—fire, water, stones and earth—exactly correspond. The sun consists of fire, the moon of water, the stars of stone, as the meteors prove, and the blue dome of heaven must be something analogous to the soil of the earth. The objection that the Five Elements—metal, wood, water, fire and earth—are other than his four parts of earth, *Shao Po-wên* rebuts with the remark that his parts are the original ones from which some of the elements developed later, viz., metal came from stones and wood grew from earth.

With his eight principles *Shao Po-wên* works rather mechanically, and by so doing arrives at some very odd results. According to his deductions, the sun produces heat, the moon cold (!), the stars daylight (!), the spaces of heaven night (!). Water becomes rain, fire wind (!), earth dew (!), and stones thunder (!) (*r*). The reasons given are either mere repetitions of the statement or quite futile, and so it goes on.

III. DESTRUCTION OF THE WORLD AND WORLD PERIODS.

The Sung philosophers believed in a destruction of the world, but followed by a reconstruction. Creation and destruction are repeated in regular periods. Questioned as to whether the world could be annihilated *Chu Hsi* replied in the negative, but, he added, when the depravity of men had reached the utmost limit, then everything would collapse, men would be exterminated and chaos prevail again. Yet from out of this chaos a new world would spring forth (*s*). According to *Shao-tse*, whom Chu Hsi quotes, such a world period from the time of creation to that of destruction would last 129,600 years (*t*).

Chu Hsi even endeavours to base his opinion regarding the revolutions caused by the destruction of the world on experience, calling attention to the petrifactions discovered

少 剛 太 柔 少 柔 而 成 八 卦 太 陽 少 陽 太 陰 少 陰 成 象 於 天 而 爲 日 月 星 辰 太 剛 少 剛 太 柔 少 柔 成 形 於 地 而 爲 水 火 土 石 八 者 具 備 然 後 天 地 之 體 備 矣.〕

(*r*) *Loc. cit.* IX., 6 v. seq. 〔觀 物 內 篇. 日 爲 暑. 月 爲 寒. 星 爲 晝. 辰 爲 夜. 水 爲 雨. 火 爲 風. 土 爲 露. 石 爲 雷.〕

(*s*) *Chu Hsi* 49, 20 r. 天 地 又 問 天 地 會 壞 否 曰 不 會 壞 只 是 人 無 道 極 了 便 一 齊 打 合 沌 混 一 番 人 物 都 盡 又 重 新 起.

(*t*) *Eod.* 49, 20 v. 邵 康 節 以 十 二 萬 九 千 六 百 年 爲 一 元 則 是 十 二 萬 九 千 六 百 年 之 前 又 是 一 箇 大 闔 闢 更 以 上 亦 復 如 此 直 是 動 靜 無 端 陰 陽 無 始.

on high mountains. " One frequently sees on high mountains conches and oyster-shells, sometimes embedded in stones. These stones in pristine times were earth, and the shells and oysters lived in water. Subsequently all was inverted, things from the bottom came to the top, and the soft became hard. A careful consideration of this fact leads to far-reaching conclusions " (*u*).

IV. INFINITY.

Shao Po-wên disclaims the boundlessness of space, whereas *Chu Hsi* affirms it. " Heaven and earth," says the former, " are things also and the largest of all. If they are regarded as things, they must be limited likewise " (*x*). Chu Hsi makes a distinction between heaven and earth as bodies and the surrounding air. As bodies they are limited, *i.e.*, the vault of heaven occupies a certain space, but the air outside is unlimited (*y*). We would say at present that the empty space outside of the visible heavenly bodies is infinite.

With reference to time Shao-tse as well assumes infinity. Chu Hsi avers many a time that motion and rest, Yin and Yang, are without beginning or end. Every world-period is preceded and followed by another. *Huan-lung-tse* enunciates this with great precision. To the inquiry about the origin of the world he once replied that it had none

(*u*) *Eod.* 嘗見高山有螺蚌殼或生石中此石卽舊日之土螺蚌卽水中之物下者却變而爲高柔者却變而爲剛此事思之至深有可驗者.

(*x*) *Hsing-li ta-ch'üan* IX., 1 r. 皇極經世,觀物內篇.〔天地亦物也天地有物之大者耳旣謂之物則亦有所盡也.〕

(*y*) *Chu Hsi* 49, 21 v. 天地.天地無外所以其形有涯而其氣無涯也.

and another time that it had one (*z*), adding by way of explanation, " Speaking of but one world-period it has a commencement, having in view all the world-periods, however, it has none."

V. HEAVEN AND EARTH.

A. *Natural Science.*

On heaven and earth in particular the modern age has not had many original ideas. *Chu Hsi* concurs with Lieh-tse in asserting that heaven is an accumulation of air and that the stars are lights in this air (*a*). He also knows that blue is not the real colour of heaven. If heaven were bright, he thinks that the sun and the moon would be invisible. The deepest black of midnight is the true colour of the universe (*b*). Chu Hsi, without being conversant with the nature of light or the perception of colours, has hit the truth.

According to *Chu Hsi* the air of heaven pervades everything, even stones and metals. When it enters the earth, the earth receives it and therewith produces the ten thousand beings (*c*). The first generation of living beings through Yin and Yang is spontaneous (*generatio*

(z) 蔡龍子. 或問天地有始乎曰無始也天地無始乎曰有始也. 未達曰自一元而言有始也自元元而言無始也.

(a) See above, p. 44, and *Chu Hsi* 49, 27 v. 天地. 列子曰天積氣日月星宿亦積氣中之有光耀者此言得之.

(b) *Chu Hsi* 49, 22 r. 天地. 天明則日月不明天無明夜半黑淬淬地天之正色.

(c) *Eod.* 49, 27 r. 天地. 陽氣昇降乎其中無所障礙雖金石也透過去地便承受得這氣發育萬物.

aequivoca), but as soon as male and female creatures are produced, their further propagation is sexual through these. Spontaneous generation still takes place at present in many instances, *e.g.*, with lice (*d*). The first man likewise was produced spontaneously by Yin and Yang and the Five Elements. Chu Hsi expressly characterises the technical term for *generatio aequivoca* 化 生, the equivalent of Sanscrit *anupapādaka*, as of Buddhist origin (*e*). We know that it is applied to *Dhyani Buddhas*, who are supposed to be born without a father through a process of nature.

By the co-operation of the celestial and terrestrial fluids *the seasons* are produced. Regarding this view of the ancients *Chang-tse* (*f*), in his *Chêng-mêng*, makes the following remark : " The earth ascends and descends, and the sun has a shorter or a longer course. Although earth is a massive body and not dispersing, yet the two fluids in the middle rise and fall and incessantly follow each other. When the Yang daily ascends and earth descends, the lower space becomes empty. When the Yang daily descends and earth advances, the upper space is filled. This causes the periods of cold and heat every year " (*g*).

(*d*) *Eod.* 49, 26 r. 天 地. 生 物 之 初 陰 陽 之 精 自 凝 結 成 兩 箇 盂 是 氣 化 而 生 如 虱 子 自 然 爆 出 來 既 有 此 兩 箇 一 牝 一 牡 後 來 却 從 種 子 漸 漸 生 去 便 是 以 形 化 萬 物 皆 然.

(*e*) *Eod.* 49, 20 r. 天 地. 又 問 生 第 一 箇 人 時 如 何 曰 以 氣 化 二 五 之 精 合 而 成 形 釋 家 謂 之 化 生 如 今 物 之 化 者 甚 多 如 虱 然.

(*f*) 張 載, A.D. 1020—1076, or 張 子.

(*g*) *Hsing-li ta-ch'üan* V., 11 v. 張 子, 正 蒙. 參 兩 篇. 地 有 昇 降 日 有 修 短 地 雖 凝 聚 不 散 之 物 然 二 氣 昇 降

The meaning of this passage is very dubious. It seems to be a paraphrase of some utterances of *Huai-nan-tse* and the *Liki* to the effect that, when the warm fluid of heaven descends and the cold fluid of earth ascends, warm or mild weather is the outcome, whereas, when the fluid of heaven is emitted upwards and the fluid of earth downwards into space, wintry cold ensues (*h*). Then Chang-tse cannot have understood by earth, earth itself, but the fluid of earth sometimes ascending, sometimes descending. From the wording, however, this is not directly apparent. The successors of Chang-tse, for instance, *Wang K'o-ta* (*i*) (Ming time) have taken his words literally, assuming a rising and falling of earth which does not only affect the weather but also the course of the sun. With this idea still another strange theory has been amalgamated, that of the "four wanderings" 四 遊 of earth. In pursuance of this, earth would not barely move up and down, but in the four directions likewise. *Chu Hsi* already alludes to this theory. At the commencement of summer earth moves to the South toward the sun, at the beginning of winter to the North away from the sun, in spring eastward, and in autumn westward, and in each direction about 30,000 Li. Wang K'o-ta combats this view, stating that according to the calculations of Duke *Chou* the distance from Yang-chêng, the centre of the earth, to the southernmost point of the sun measured but 15,000 Li and that the sun under the southernmost point did not produce any shade. At a distance of 30,000 Li the shade conditions would be still more extreme. The sun would stand in the north and her shade fall to the south. Constellations like

---

其 間 相 從 而 不 已 也 陽 日 上 地 日 降 而 下 者 虛 也
陽 日 降 地 日 進 而 上 者 盈 也 此 一 歲 寒 暑 之 候 也.

(*h*) Cf. p. 63.

(*i*) 王 可 大.

the Seven Stars would change their positions on the sky considerably, shifting them up or down, to the East or to the West. Actually the differences in successive seasons measure scarcely one degree, consequently the entire theory of the wandering of earth could not be correct.

Wang K'o-ta accounts for the differences of temperature and of the length of the days merely by the course of the sun. The zodiacal signs " Well " and " Devil " (Gemini and Cancer) are near the pole, "Bushel " and " Ox " (Sagittarius and Aries) are far from it. These are the northern and the southern limits which the sun reaches on the ecliptic. When it stands in the signs " Well " and " Devil," heaven has its greatest height, and the sun is near to us. Consequently the orbit of the sun is long and so is the duration of the day. When the sun stays in the signs " Bushel " and " Ox," heaven is very low. The sun then is far distant from us, its course short and the length of the day likewise. The sun being in the proximity of the pole we have heat, it being at a long distance we have cold. In the first case the fluid of earth can expand and intermingle with that of heaven, which results in a general growth of vegetation, while in the second it remains blocked and obstructed (*k*). Wang K'o-ta probably thinks of the different altitudes of heaven

---

(*k*) 王 可 大, 象 緯 新 篇. 經 星 井 鬼 近 極 斗 牛 遠 極
此 南 北 兩 端 日 黃 道 必 經 之 處 日 躔 井 鬼 之 次 當
天 極 高 之 體 且 於 人 近 見 日 之 度 常 多 故 晝 晷 長
日 躔 斗 牛 之 次 當 天 最 低 之 體 且 於 人 遠 見 日 之
度 常 少 故 晝 晷 短 ‥‥ 二 氣 之 通 塞 皆 日 之 進 退
主 之 日 大 火 也 故 近 極 而 暑 遠 極 而 寒 寒 則 地 氣
閉 塞 而 不 達 暑 則 地 氣 暢 達 而 發 育 此 一 歲 寒 暑
之 所 由 也.

as being caused by the rising and sinking of the axis of heaven during the various seasons.

Chang Huang also sees the cause of the change of the seasons in the course of the sun, but describes it in a different way : " At the time of the winter solstice the sun during the day approaches the south pole and moves in the southern part of heaven. The Yang fluid then is at a long distance from men, therefore it is cold. At night the sun hides in the empty space below the earth, and the Yang fluid is just under our feet, whence the springs appear warm. At the time of the summer solstice the sun during the day comes near to the north pole and passes just over the heads of men. The Yang fluid darts down in a straight line, and it becomes hot. At night the sun absconds outside the region of earth in the empty void of the north. The Yang is not underneath the earth, therefore the springs are cold. That plants come forth in spring and grow in summer is because then the solar heat rises from under the earth, and that in autumn they are harvested and in winter stored away is because then the solar heat recedes more and more from under the earth." Chang Huang closes these strange lucubrations with the assurance that all this is as clear as daylight, but that the beclouded do not perceive it. This shows us that his views did not win the undivided applause of his contemporaries (*l*).

(*l*) 章潢, 圖書編. 天地總論. 冬至之日晝則近南極而行在天之南方而陽氣去人甚遠故寒夜則潛於地底之虛空而陽氣正在人之足下所以井泉溫夏至之日晝則近北極而行正在人之頂上而陽氣直射於下故熱夜潛於地外在北方之虛空處而陽不在地底所以井泉冷萬物春而生夏而長由地底太陽之氣自下蒸上也秋而收冬而

B. *Philosophy.*

The study of heaven and earth in ancient times imperceptibly passed from the field of science into that of mythology and religion. Heaven and earth were anthropomorphised and looked upon as a married couple with human qualities. The moderns more and more abandon this conception. There is less a tendency to deify than to speculate on the nature of heaven and earth. Here we are confronted with two viewpoints; some thinkers hold that heaven alone is a spirit and earth a body, others regard them both as spiritual beings.

(a) *Heaven a Spirit, Earth a Body.*

Chang-tse boldly contends that " Earth is a thing and heaven is a spirit." But no thing, he thinks, can dispense with spirit, therefore earth needs a spirit, and this spirit is heaven (*m*). Moreover, he trusts to be in a condition to deduce the spirituality of heaven from its purity stating : " The great void is pure, purity meets with no obstruction, and this being without obstruction is spirituality. What is pure in the fluid can freely move about, what is turbid becomes congested. Purity of the highest degree becomes spirit " (*n*).

Ho T'ang (*o*) (Ming period) uses similar arguments

藏 由 太 陽 之 氣 去 地 底 以 漸 而 遠 也 此 理 昭 然 而 昧 者 自 不 知 耳.

(*m*) *Hsing-li ta-ch'üan* V., 11 v. *Chang-tse Chěng-měng* 參 兩 篇.

地 物 也 天 神 也 物 無 蹤 神 之 理 顧 有 地 斯 有 天 若 其 配 然 爾.

(*n*) *Loc. cit.* V., 5 v. seq. 太 和 篇. 太 虛 爲 清 清 則 無 礙 無 礙 故 神 .... 凡 氣 清 則 通 昏 則 壅 清 極 則 神.

(*o*) 何 塘.

inferring the spirituality from the aerial state of the
heavenly fluid. Heaven is Yang and air, earth is Yin
and a body. Air still possesses a shape, therefore Ho T'ang
believes that it is better to substitute the word " spirit."
Spirit is the wonderful manifestation of living air (*p*).
This idea reminds us of the old notion of the soul as a
breath or an *aura*.

The inexplicable effects of Yin and Yang according to
Ho T'ang, are spiritual. In earth there are none, therefore she is not a spirit. The wonderful forces active in
earth were imparted by heaven. The reasoning is very
weak, and Wang Ting-hsiang's attacks are justified.

(b) *The Spirit of Heaven and Earth.*

To prove that heaven and earth are animated *Chu Hsi*
quotes a Yiking commentary saying : " Do we not see in
the diagram Fu that heaven and earth have a spirit ? " (*q*).
In the absence of a regulating spirit Chu Hsi thinks it
possible that an ox might produce a horse or that plum
blossoms might grow on a peach tree (*r*). The spirit is the
regulating principle manifested by heaven and earth in
producing things. Questioned about the difference between
the general principle of heaven and earth and their spirit,
Chu Hsi replied that the spirit is a regulator, but identical
with the general principle of the world. Besides the spirit
there does not exist a general principle, nor a spirit in

(p) 王廷相, 陰陽管見辯。天陽爲氣地陰爲
形 .... 凡屬氣者皆陽凡屬形者皆陰此數語甚
眞然謂之氣則猶有象不如以神字易之蓋神卽
氣之靈尤妙也.

(q) *Yiking*, App. I., p. 233. 復其見天地之心. Legge says
in his notes that the mind of heaven and earth is the love of life and of
all the goodness in nature.

(r) *Chu Hsi* 49, 23 v.

addition to this principle (*s*). Interrogated again as to whether the notion of spirit came near to that of God, he rejoined that the similarity between spirit and God was like that between man and heaven (*t*). This is an illustration of one unknown quantity by another not better known.

According to Chu Hsi the mundane spirit is not indifferent or without initiative like Tao, still he has not as many needless troubles and sorrows as man, so that the dictum of Ch'êng-tse "Heaven and earth create and transform things but indeliberately" holds good (*u*). The regular development of things in the course of the four seasons takes place without a special plan of the mundane spirit, and only in extraordinary cases, *e.g.*, when dried up wood begins to grow green again, it acts deliberately (*x*). Heaven and earth transfer their spirit to their creatures. When man obtains it, it becomes the human mind. The spirit of plants, animals, and men is nothing else than the mundane spirit (*y*).

(*s*) *Chu Hsi* 49, 23 r. 曰心固是主宰底意然所謂主宰者卽是理也不是心外別有箇理理外別有箇心.

(*t*) *Loc. cit.* 49, 23 r. 又問此心字與帝字相似否曰人字似天字心似帝字.

(*u*) *Eod.* 49, 22 v. 問天地之心亦靈否還只是漠然無爲曰天地之心不可道是不靈但不如人恁地思慮伊川曰天地無心而成化.

(*x*) *Eod.* 49, 24 r. 萬物生長是天地無心時枯稿欲生是天地有心時.

(*y*) *Eod.* 49, 24 r. 曰天地以此心普及萬物人得之遂爲人之心物得之遂爲物之心草木禽獸接著遂爲草木禽獸之心只是一箇天地之心.

Ho T'ang is of the opinion that the difference between the spirit of creation and the human spirit is only quantitative, but that in their essence they are identical, the spirit of creation being so much vaster than the human spirit, that its effects also must be much greater (*z*).

Wang T'ing-hsiang professes that though all things have received their fluid from heaven, yet they all have their particular spirit. There is a spirit of earth, a human spirit, and all other creatures have their own spirits as well (*a*).

The *Yü-hsiao ling-yin* insists on the different quality of the spirit of heaven and the spirit of earth. The essence of the spirit of heaven is the *zeal*, without which the constant movement of heaven could not take place. The essence of the spirit of earth is the *diligence* requisite for the constant rest of earth and for carrying all things upon her (*b*).

According to *Chu Hsi* the spirit of heaven is identical with the spirit of earth, and we may straightway speak of a uniform mundane spirit; according to *Wang T'ing-hsiang* and the *Yü-hsiao ling-yin*, however, the spirit of earth and the spirit of heaven are divergent.

(*z*) 續性理會通, *Wang T'ing-hsiang, Yin-yang kuan-chien pien*: 造化人物無異但有大小之分耳造化神氣大故所能爲者亦大人物神氣小故所能爲者亦小其機則無異也.

(*a*) *Eod.* 愚則以爲萬物各有禀受各正性命其氣雖出於天其神卽爲已有地有地之神人有人之神物有物之神.

(*b*) 玉笑零音 in *T'u-shu chi-ch'êng*, 乾象典 chap. 7, 天地總部雜錄 p. 12 v. The author is *T'ien I-hêng* 田藝衡, *Ming* time.

VI. Analogies between Heaven, Earth and Man.

The desire to find out certain analogies between the universe and man is noticeable even in modern times. The supposed similarities discovered by the ingenious younger *Shao* are worth mentioning : The *sun*, the *moon*, the *stars*, and the *spaces of heaven* are to be compared with the *ear*, the *eye*, the *mouth* and the *nose*. Shao-tse expends the old simile between heaven and a human head (*c*), simply contrasting parts of heaven with parts of the head. Aside from the sun and the moon, which may well be conceived as the eyes of heaven, the analogy can hardly be carried through. The further comparison of *water*, *fire*, *earth* and *stones*, with the human *blood*, *breath*, *flesh*, and *bones* is much better. The statement that *Yin* and *Yang*, the *Hard* and *Soft*, in the universe correspond to the human spirit dominating the ear, the eye, the mouth, the nose, blood, breath, flesh, and bones may pass too (*d*). Needless to say that by such analogies we gain very little; they are even rather dangerous, if, as often happens, similarities are transformed into identities. The myth of *P'an Ku* is the best proof (*e*).

VII. The Heavenly Bodies, the Sun, the Moon, and the Stars.

(a) *The Motion of Heaven and the Stars.*

Chang-tse informs us that the. *vault of heaven* turns from the left, *i.e.*, from East to West. The *fixed stars* have no proper motion and are attached to heaven, whose motion they share. Contrariwise the *sun*, the *moon*, and

---

(*c*) Cf. p. 77.
(*d*) *Hsing-li ta ch'üan* IX., 5 v. *seq.*; *Shao-tse, Huang-chi ching-shi,*
觀 物 內 篇.
(*e*) *Vid.*, above, p. 41.

the *planets* move in opposite direction to the revolution of heaven, *i.e.*, from the right or from West to East. They are not completely fixed on heaven and to some extent influenced by earth. *Earth* follows the motion of heaven and likewise turns from the left. The stars attached to her follow her motion, but are somewhat slower, whence results a movement in opposite direction, viz., from the right.

The motions of the sun, the moon, and the planets harmonise with their nature. The *moon* being Yin essence and opposed to Yang moves very fast in a direction opposite to that of heaven or Yang, namely from the right to the left. The *sun* is Yang essence, but its substance was originally Yin—a statement not further substantiated —therefore it moves from the right, but slowly, for it is not as strongly fastened to the sky as the fixed stars. *Venus* and *Mercury* attach themselves to the sun, sometimes advancing, sometimes receding in consequence of a kind of attraction. This does not mean gravitation, but a certain sympathy supposed to exist between these stars and the sun. *Saturn*, called the " earth star " is under the influence of earth, being of the same type; its course is very slow. *Mars* has Yin substance, but also contains some Yang like the sun; its fluid is much weaker, and its motion only half as fast as that of the sun. *Jupiter* traverses one space of heaven= 辰 *ch'ên*, equal to one· twelfth of the horizon in one year, and thus completes its circumvolution in twelve years. The planets have their proper motion, which does not come from without. A sort of propelling force is inherent in them (*f*).

Chu Hsi is never tired of repeating that the assertion of astronomers and commentators, claiming that heaven moves from the left side and the sun, the moon and the stars from the right, is not correct. The latter also follow

---

(*f*) *Hsing-li ta ch'üan* V., 10. 張 子 正 蒙, 參 兩 篇.

the motion of heaven, but are much slower. The sun makes daily a full revolution of the sky of $365\frac{1}{4}$ degrees; heaven itself turns in the same way, but one degree more, so that the sun remains one degree behind it. This causes the impression that the sun moves one degree to the left. The moon remains daily thirteen degrees behind heaven and seems to move as many degrees to the left. After 365 days = one year, the sun and heaven meet again at the same starting point, the moon and heaven already after every $\frac{365}{13}$ days = twenty-eight = one month. If astronomers speak of the retrograde motion of the stars, this is because from this point of view their motions are more easy to calculate (g).

(b) *Phases of the Moon.*

Chu Hsi emphasises the fact that the moon receives its light from the sun. Its phases are an increase and a decrease of this borrowed light, but not of the substance of the moon, which has the shape of a ball. The light of the sun always falls on one side of the moon. On the 15th of each month the sun in the West is directly opposite to the moon in the East, and the side of the moon visible to us receives the full sunlight (full moon). The sun and the moon cannot move through the outermost stratum of the sky, because there the air is too compressed and the current too strong, therefore they must pass through a layer

---

(g) *Chu Hsi* 50, 6 r. *seq.* 天度。天道與日月五星皆是左旋天道日一周天而常過一度日亦日一周天起度端終度端故比天道常不及一度月行不及十三度十九分度之七今人却云月行速日行遲此錯說也但曆家以右旋爲說取其易見日月之度耳.

See also: *Chu Hsi* 50, 7 v., 50, 8 r., 50, 15 v.

nearer to the centre. The earth is suspended in the centre
of heaven. On the 15th of the month the sun and the
moon are also in the middle of heaven and the earth stands
exactly between the two. But the earth being compara-
tively small the light of the sun reaches the moon from
all sides nevertheless, and only in the centre is the moon
somewhat obscured by the shadow of the earth. On the
1st day of every month the sun and the moon come
together and cover one another. The moon passes either
above or below the sun and does not receive any light (new
moon). In the meantime the sun and the moon withdraw
from each other and afterwards reapproach, consequently
the illuminated moon disk does not appear complete.
When the moon is increasing we have the first quarter,
when it is waning the last quarter (*h*).

As an advocate of the right view of the borrowed light
of the moon *Shên Hua* (1030-1093), the author of the well-
known collection *Mêng-ch'i pi-t'an* (*i*), is also mentioned.
But the theory that the moon and the stars shine with
their own light has likewise supporters, who, like the
Hindus, assign to the moon one bright and one dark side.

(*h*) *Chu Hsi* 50, 15. 天度。月只是受日光月質常圓
不曾闕如圓毬只有一面受日光望日日在酉月
在卯正相對受光爲盛天積氣上面勁只中間空
爲日月來往地在天中不甚大四邊空 .... 則光
從四旁上受於月其中昏暗便是地影望以後日
與月行便差背向一畔相去漸漸遠其受光面不
正至朔行又相遇日與月正緊相合日便蝕無光
月或從上過或從下過亦不受光 .... 及日月各
在東西日光到月者止及其半故爲上弦又減其
半則爲下弦.

(*i*) 沈括, 夢溪筆談.

As a minister always will show his respect to his prince, so the moon is believed always to turn its face to the sun, which means its bright side (*j*).

(c) *Eclipses of the Moon.*

We saw that as far back as in the Han period eclipses of the sun were traced back to the shadow of the moon. Later they looked for an explanation of the eclipses of the moon also, and recognised the shadow of the earth as the true cause. But this explanation did not meet with general approval any more than the correct explication of the eclipses of the sun. Many men of learning assumed that the eclipses of the moon came from the dark spots on the sun falling on the moon. The correct view is gainsaid with the argument that a shadow usually is much bigger than the object causing it. Consequently the moon ought to be covered almost permanently by the shadow of the earth and thus lose its light (*k*).

(d) *Precession of the Equinoxes.*

The precession of the equinoxes and solstices seems to have been first observed during the Han epoch, but the cause was unknown. *Chu Hsi* points out the fact, *Wang K'o-ta* attempts to give the reason. He supposes that the sky in its rotation has the tendency to extend its orbit outward, while the sun and the moon tend to contract their

---

(*j*) 非觀瑣言。是本沈括月本無光日耀之乃光之言矣復謂月與星皆是有光但月體半光半晦月常面日如臣主敬君.

(*k*) *Loc. cit.* 通論月食既疑先儒月爲日中暗處所射之說而主張衡暗虛之說以爲暗虛只是大地之影矣復疑影當倍形如此則月光常爲地影所蔽失光之時必多.

course inward. Accordingly the sky gradually shifts more and more to the West, the year, however, which is determined by the course of the sun and the moon to the East (*l*). It goes without saying that the true cause of the precession, namely, the nutation of the axis of the earth, could not be known to the Chinese.

Chu Hsi registers the following facts : " At the time of *Yao* at early dawn *Cor Hydra* culminated in Wu (S.), at the time of the *Yüeh-ling* (*m*) it had deviated as far as Wei (S.S.W.$\frac{3}{4}$W.), and since the *Han* and *Chin* time the deviation is still greater. At present the deviation from the position in the time of Yao probably measures up to one quarter (of the horizon?). In ancient times the sun at the winter solstice stood in *Niu* (301°), at present in *Tou* (277°) " (*n*).

Wang K'o-ta says : " As regards the deviation of the year (precession) at the time of *Yao* (*o*), the sun at the winter solstice stood in *Hsü* (320°) (*p*) + 1°, at the summer solstice in *Liu* (127°) + 14°, at the spring equinox in *Wei* (44°) + 12°, and at the autumn equinox in *Ti* (220°) + 10°. According to the *Ta-yen* calendar of the *K'ai-yüan* (*q*) period in the T'ang dynasty the sun at the winter solstice stood in *Tou* (277°) + 10°, at the

---

(*l*) *Hsü Hsing-li hui-t'ung, Wang K'o-ta* 象緯新篇。天運常外平而舒日道常內轉而縮其勢不得不然也由是天漸差而西歲漸差而束.

(*m*) During the *Chou* dynasty.

(*n*) *Chu Hsi* 50, 7 r. 天度。堯時昏旦星中于午月令差于未漢晉以來又差今比堯時似差及四分之一古時冬至日在牽牛今却任斗.

(*o*) Yao's traditional reign is from 2357-2255 B.C.

(*p*) The exact longitudes of the twenty-eight constellations here referred to may be looked up in Giles's Dictionary.

(*q*) 713-742 A.D.

summer solstice in *Ching* (12°) + 10°, at the spring equinox in *K'uei* (17°) + 7°, and at the autumn equinox in *Chên* (187°) + 14°. According to the T'ung-yüan calendar of the Sung dynasty the sun at the winter solstice was in *Tou* (277°) + 2°, at the summer solstice in *Ching* (92°) + 16°, at the spring equinox in *K'uei* (17°) + 1°, and at the autumn equinox in *Chên* (187°) + 7° (*r*). *Lo Hsia-hung* (*s*), was the first man during the Han time who took pains to calculate the precession, and he said that every 800 years it amounted to 1°. This was far from the mark. The astronomers of his time also found out that there was already a deviation of 5° from the *T'ai-ch'u* (*t*) calendar. *Yü Hsi* (*u*) of the *Chin* dynasty using a better method discovered that in fifty years the sun retrograded 1°. *Ho Ch'êng-t'ien* (*x*) (*Sung* period) doubled this figure and made it one hundred years. *T'ang Liu-ch'o* (*y*) (*Sui* period) took the average of these two numbers, fifty and one hundred, and made seventy-five

---

(*r*) *Wang K'o-ta, loc. cit.* 歲差法堯時冬至躔在虛一度夏至在柳十四度春分在胃十二度秋分在氐十度至唐開元大衍曆冬至日躔在斗十度夏至在井十度春分在奎七度秋分在軫十四度宋統元曆冬至在斗二度夏至在井十六度春分在奎初度秋分在軫七度.

I wonder whether these figures are correct and consistent. In A.D. 730 (K'ai-yüan) the retrograde movement of the sun would amount to 34°, 39°, 32°, 31° at the solstices and equinoxes from the time of Yao. A precession of 31° would fix the time of Yao at about 1455 B.C., and 39° at 2021 B.C. Both figures are in conflict with tradition and other astronomical data.

(*s*) 洛下閎.

(*t*) 104 B.C.

(*u*) 虞喜.

(*x*) 何承天.

(*y*) 唐劉焯.

years equal to 1°. *Sêng I-hsing* (*z*) (*T'ang* time) calculated eighty-three years, and *Kuo Shou-ching* (*a*) (*Yuan* dynasty) sixty-six years. Subsequently it was found that this number was not quite correct either, but it comes very near to the truth (*b*). The axis of the earth spinning like a top makes one complete nutation in 25,730 years. During this time it describes a full circle of 365° of Chinese computation, ergo 1° is equivalent to about 70½ years.

(*z*) 僧 一 行.
(*a*) 郭 守 敬.
(*b*) *Wang K'o-ta loc. cit.*

Book II.

HEAVEN.

BOOK II.

HEAVEN.

HAVING dealt already with natural heaven as the principal part of the universe and the correlate of earth in the first book, we have not much to add. But in Chinese philosophy and religion heaven plays a much more important rôle than earth. Its anthropomorphosis has advanced much farther than that of earth, and just this aspect apart from the physical one is to be considered.

A. PHYSICAL VIEWPOINT.

What the Chinese have to say about the qualities of heaven, its division and its nature, is far from being scientific and more or less mythological.

I. SUBDIVISIONS OF PHYSICAL HEAVEN.

(a) *According to seasons.*

In the Classics the vernal heaven is said to be styled the *blue heaven*, the summer heaven the *luminous heaven*, the autumnal heaven the *gloomy heaven*, and the winter heaven *high heaven* (a). The two first terms refer no doubt to the aspect of heaven, blue in spring and resplendent in summer. The explanation in the *Erh-ya* that in spring all plants come out green, which is repeated by other expositors, is very unsatisfactory. One cannot call heaven

---

(a) *Erh-ya* 釋天。春爲蒼天夏爲昊天秋爲旻天冬爲上天. See also the 劉熙釋名, 釋天.

blue because plants are green, even if the word for blue and green in Chinese is the same. The gloomy or mourning heaven is a very appropriate term for the melancholy autumnal sky, mourning, as the commentators say, at the dying and fading away of vegetation. High heaven is supposed to convey the idea that in winter heaven is higher than during the other seasons, for then the Yang fluid ascends, while the Yin essence sinks down. This is certainly the most plausible explanation.

However, it seems doubtful whether this entire distinction of the old dictionary is tenable after all. In the classical texts the afore-mentioned epithets of heaven, notably blue and luminous, occur also without any relation to a certain season (*b*), and the Erh-ya may well have misinterpreted these expressions.

(b) *Regions of Heaven.*

Huai-nan-tse and the *Po-ya* (Wei dynasty), probably in imitation of the former, distinguished nine regions of heaven, one in the centre and the other eight round about, corresponding to the eight quarters. For each region Huai-nan-tse gives the solar mansions included therein as follows.

(1) Centre, the *Lathe Heaven* with Horn, Neck, Bottom.

(2) E., the *Blue Heaven*; Room, Heart, Tail. *Po-ya:* the *Luminous Heaven.*

(3) N.E., the *Changing Heaven*; Sieve, Bushel, Ox. *Po-ya:* the *Barbarian Heaven.*

(4) N., the *Black Heaven*; Girl, Emptiness, Danger, House.

(5) N.W., the *Dark Heaven*; Wall, Astride, Mound.

(*b*) Cf. *Couvreur's* Dict.

(6) W., the *Luminous Heaven*; Stomach, Pleiades, End. *Po-ya:* the *Completed Heaven.*

(7) S.W., the *Vermilion Heaven*; Horn, Needle, Orion, Well.

(8) S., the *Burning Heaven*; Devil, Willow, Seven Stars. *Po-ya:* the *Red Heaven.*

(9) S.E., the *Yang Heaven*; Bow, Wing, Cross-bar (*c*).

These designations of the various divisions of heaven seem to have been given in conformity with the presumed relations between the five directions of heaven and the five elementary colours, which we will have to consider later. Accordingly E. = green (blue), N. = black, W. = white, S. = red, and the Centre = yellow. But in our case, with the centre of heaven, colour has been dropped altogether, and it is very suitably compared with a potter's lathe, for the entire heaven whirls around it. As to the rest, the eastern heaven is blue, the northern and north-western black, the western heaven is brilliant white, the south-western and southern heavens red, and the south-eastern heaven is luminous = yang. Why the north-eastern heaven is called changing, or by the *Po-ya* barbarian, is hard to guess. With the real colour of

---

(*c*) *Huai-nan-tse* III., 3 天文訓。何謂九野中央曰鈞天其星角亢氐東方曰蒼天其星房心尾東北曰變天其星箕斗牽牛北方曰元天其星須女虛危營室西北方曰幽天其星東壁奎婁西方曰昊天其星胃昴畢西南方曰朱天其星觜巂參東井南方曰炎天其星輿鬼柳七星東南方曰陽天其星張翼軫.

Po-ya, 魏張揖, 博雅, 釋天。東方昦天東南陽天南方赤天西南朱天西方成天西北幽天北方元天東北蠻天中央鈞天.

heaven all these denominations have very little in common, and they appear to be a mere play of fancy. Apart from that this empty schematism is of no consequence.

Yang Hsiung (first century B.C.) offers a list of names of the *Nine Heavens* differing completely from the foregoing. He distinguishes (1) the *Central Heaven*; (2) the *Heaven of Desire*; (3) the *Compliant Heaven*; (4) the *Changing Heaven*; (5) the *Bright Heaven*; (6) the *Vast Heaven*; (7) the *Universal Heaven*; (8) the *Foundering Heaven*; (9) the *Complete Heaven* (d).

It is not clear what Yang Hsiung understood by these names. Apparently they refer to various activities and attributes of heaven in the widest sense, the natural as well as the mythological.

(c) *The Nine-storied Heaven.*

In the *T‘ien-wên Ch‘ü Yuan* says : "The vault of heaven has the shape of *nine stories.* Who planned them? Who's work are they? Who was it that first built them?" and further, "On what does the edge of the nine heavens repose and on what depend? It has many corners and sinuosities; who knows their number?" (e). From this it is evident that even in the fourth century B.C. the idea of nine heavens rising story like one upon another was familiar to the Chinese. We do not learn what purpose these nine stories were to serve. Later they were adopted by the Taoists, and we saw how Chu Hsi incorporated them

---

(d) *Yang Hsiung, T‘ai-hsüan ching* IX., 8 r. 九 天。有 九 天 一 爲 中 天 二 爲 羨 天 三 爲 從 天 四 爲 更 天 五 爲 晬 天 六 爲 廓 天 七 爲 咸 天 八 爲 沈 天 九 爲 成 天.

(e) *Ch‘u-tse* III., 1 r. 天 問。圜 則 九 重 孰 營 度 之 惟 茲 何 功 孰 作 之 . . . . 九 天 之 際 安 放 安 屬 隅 隈 多 有 誰 知 其 數.

into his system, identifying them with nine strata of air of different density.

(d) *Buddhist and Taoist Heavens.*

The Buddhist Heavens are not of Chinese origin, but they became known to the Chinese from translations of Buddhist books and passed into Chinese literature. Moreover they were eagerly seized upon and imitated by later Taoists.

The Buddhists divide the universe into three worlds, *Trailokya* 三 界, but whereas the Brahmans take these terms to connote *earth*, the *atmosphere*, and *heaven* and thus have a division on a purely physical basis, the Buddhist division is metaphysical. Their three world regions are : *Kāmadhātu* 欲 界, the region of desires, *Rūpadhātu* 色 界, the region of form, and *Arūpadhātu* 無 欲 界, the region of formlessness, the anteroom to *Nirvāṇa.* Conformably to the *Ju-p‘o-sha-lun* (*f*), to the Kāmadhātu belong ten worlds or heavens, to Rūpadhātu eighteen, and to Arūpadhātu four (*g*).

The thirty-two heavens of the *Ju-p‘o-sha lun* are the following :

I. KĀMADHĀTU.

(1) *Karoṭapāṇi* 于 手 天, the Heaven of Bowl Bearers.

(2) *Mālādhara* 持 華 鬘 天, the Heaven of Garland Bearers.

(*f*) 如 婆 沙 論 (Upaśāka śāstra ?) quoted by the *Fa-yuan chu-lin* 法 苑 珠 林 in *T‘u-shu chi-ch‘êng* 乾 象 典, chap. 14, 天 部 外 篇 p. 10 r.

(*g*) According to *Eitel, Handbook*, Kāmadhātu comprises seven worlds, viz., earth and six Devalokas. To the *Ch‘i-shih ching* and the *Li-shih a-p‘i-t‘an lun* the first four worlds of Kāmadhātu are unknown likewise.

(3) *Sadāmada* 常 放 逸 天, the Heaven of the Ever Dissolute (*h*).

(4) 日 月 星 宿 天 the Heaven with the Sun, the Moon and the Stars.

(5) *Catur-mahārāja-kāyika* 四 天 王 天, the Heaven of the Four Kings of Heaven, the four guardians of the world living with their suite on the four slopes of the sacred mountain *Sumeru*. According to the *Li-shih a-p'i-t'an lun* 4,000 Yocana above India.

(6) *Trayastriṃśat* 三 十 三 天 or 忉 利 天, *Indra's* Heaven, between the summits of Sumeru, 8,000 Yocana above the earth, inhabited by Indra and thirty-two other gods.

(7) *Yama-devaloka* 夜 摩 天, *Yama's* Heaven, 160,000 Yocana above the earth.

(8) *Tushita* 兜 率 陀 or 喜 樂 天, the Heaven of the Bodhisattvas, 320,000 Yocana above earth.

(9) *Nirmāṇirati* 化 樂 天, the Heaven of Blessed Gods enjoying self-prepared delights, 640,000 Yocana high.

(10) *Paranirmita-vaśavartin* 他 化 自 在 天, Heaven of Gods permanently enjoying delights prepared by others. Seat of *Māra*, 1,280,000 Yocana high.

5 to 10 are the six *Devalokas* 天 宮, the six heavens in which the old Brahmanic gods and the *Bodhisattvas*

(*h*) There is no doubt that the first three heavens are identical with the three regions on the slopes or terraces of Mount Sumeru, which the *Ch'i-shih-ching* assigns to three classes of *Yakshas*, viz., the Bowl Bearers 鉢 手, the Garland Bearers 持 鬘 and the " *Ever Intoxicated* " 常 醉 其 下 級 中 有 夜 叉 住 名 曰 鉢 手 其 中 級 中 有 諸 夜 叉 名 曰 持 鬘 其 上 級 中 有 諸 夜 叉 名 曰 常 醉. The Sanscrit names, taken from the Buddhist Cosmogony of *L. de la Vallée Poussin* (Hastings IV., p. 134), correspond to the Chinese names of the *Ch'i-shih-ching*. The chariots of the Sun, the Moon, and the Stars forming the fourth heaven, for which I cannot supply the Sanscrit name, are believed to stop at half the height of Sumeru.

are lodged. The distance of these heavens from earth increases in geometric progression from 4,000 Yocana. In these heavens the gods live in palaces, as shown by the Chinese term. The palace of Indra is minutely described in the *Ch'i-shih-ching.*

II. RŪPADHĀTU.

The eighteen heavens constituting the world of form are called the eighteen *Brahmalokas* 梵 天, the worlds of the Brahmās, so named from the first three heavens in which Brahmās and their attendants reside :

(1) *Brahma-pārṣadya* 梵 衆, the Heaven for the attendants of the Brahmās.

(2) *Brahma-purohita* 梵 輔, the Heaven of the Brahma priests.

(3) *Mahā-brahma* 大 梵 天, the Heaven of the Great Brahmās.

(4) *Parīttabha* 少光, the Heaven of Minor Splendour.

(5) *Apramāṇabha* 無 量 光, the Heaven of Endless Splendour.

(6) *Ābhāsvara* 光 音, the Heaven of Splendour, or of Splendour and Sounds = *ābhā-svara* as in Chinese.

(7) *Parīttaśubha* 少 淨 the Heaven of Minor Purity.

(8) *Apramāṇaśubha* 無 量 淨, the Heaven of Endless Purity.

(9) *Śubhakṛtsna* 遍 淨, the Heaven of Universal Purity.

(10) *Puṇyaprasava* 福 生, the Heaven of Felicitous Birth.

(11) *Anabhraka* 福 慶, the Heaven of Greatest Bliss. A better rendering of Anabhraka is 無 雲 天, the Cloudless Heaven (*Li-shih a-p'i-t'an-lun*).

(12) *Vṛhatphala* 廣 果, the Heaven of Rich Fruits of **Virtue.**

(13) *Asaṃjñisattva* 無 熱, the Heaven without Burning Passions.

(14) *Avṛha* 無 想, the Heaven without Thought (Speech).

(15) *Atapa* 無 煩, the Heaven without Annoyance.

(16) *Sudṛś* 善 現, the Heaven of Beautiful Aspect.

(17) *Sudarśana* 善 見, the Heaven of Noble Views.

(18) *Akaniṣṭa* 色 究 竟, the Heaven without the Least Desire.

III. ARŪPADHĀTU.

(1)*Ākāśānantyāyatanam* 空 處 or 空 無 邊 處, the Heaven of the Endless Void.

(2) *Vijñānānantyāyatanam* 識 處 or 識 無 邊 處, the Heaven of Unlimited Knowledge.

(3) *Ākiṃcanyāyatanam* 無 所 有 處, the Heaven of Non-existence.

(4) *Naivasaṃjñānāsaṃjñānāyàtanam* 非 想 非 非 想 天, the Heaven in which there is no thinking and no non-thinking.

In the uppermost heavens existence evaporates more and more, in the last there is, so to speak, less than nothing (*i*) and the entrance into Nirvāna sufficiently prepared.

From the above outline there are many discrepancies in other Buddhist texts (*k*). Many heavens are either omitted altogether or placed differently. The *Ch'i-shih-ching*, e.g., has a special heaven for the god of demons, *Māra*, situated between *Paranirmita-vaśavartin* and the Brahma Heavens. In addition it mentions a heaven 不 粗 天, the "Heaven without Coarseness" above *Vṛhatphala*.

(*i*) It is true that Buddhist writers hold that the name of the last heaven does not imply an absolute negation of all mental processes, which still exist, though in a much reduced state.

(*k*) In the Cosmogony of *de la Vallée-Poussin* as well.

As an illustration of the enormous distance from the Brahma Heaven to earth the *Li-shih a-p'i-t'an lun* narrates the following story : " The monks inquired of Buddha, the Illustrious, how far distant Jambudvipa was from the Brahma World. Buddha said, ' Monks, from Jambudvipa to the Brahma World the distance is very great. If for instance on the 15th day of the 9th month at full moon a man in the Brahma World should throw down a square stone a thousand feet long and broad, it would do no harm for some time, for only in the following year in the 9th month on the day of full moon, would the stone reach Jambudvipa ' " (*l*).

It is well known that later Taoism copied not only the cult, but also the mythology of Buddhism. Thus *Taoist Heavens* were invented, numbering precisely 32 (*m*), though some sources mentioned have even 36. The *Yün-chi-ch'i-ch'ien* (*n*) gives the names of 36 heavens along with the heavenly kings residing therein, which are merely clumsy inventions from Buddhist reminiscences. Thus the second heaven is connoted as " the heaven of formlessness and marvellous purity with the changing and ascending celestial king, whose surname is Fêng and whose personal name, *Ti-a-sha* "; *Ti-a-sha* is intended to sound like a foreign name. The third heaven is styled " the extremely fine *Po-lo-ju* heaven with the deep dark

---

(*l*) 立世阿毗曇論 in *T'u-shu chi-ch'êng* 乾象典 chap. 14 天部外編 p. 11 r: 有比丘問佛世尊從閻浮提至梵處近遠如何佛言比丘從閻浮提至梵處其遠甚高譬如九月十五日月圓滿時若有一人在彼梵處放一百丈方石墜向下界中間無礙到于後歲九月圓滿時至閻浮提地.

(*m*) Cf. the *Chu-t'ien ling-shu ching* 諸天靈書經.

(*n*) 雲笈七籤, written in the first half of the eleventh century A.D.

celestial king *Yün* (Cloud), personal name *Kuei-ling.*"
Po-lo-ju means nothing, but it sounds like the Chinese
rendering of some Sanscrit name. A copious use is made
of the character 梵 Brahmā, although for Taoism it is
absolutely meaningless. In order to give to the whole a
somewhat archaic touch, some characters are frequently
omitted purposely, as if the text had been mutilated,
which, for the author has still another advantage, obviating
as it does the necessity of inventing still more fanciful
names for the lacunae.

(e) *Heaven in Other Countries.*

Men have seldom been satisfied with only one heaven;
most people, like the Chinese, have quite a number.

The *Babylonians* starting from the pole divided heaven
into three regions : (1) that of *Anu*, the ruler of heaven,
embracing the zodiacal signs *Taurus*, *Gemini*, *Cancer*, and
Leo ; (2) that of *Bel*, the son of *Anu* with the signs *Virgo*,
Libra, *Scorpio* ; (3) that of *Ea*, the god of the ocean with
the zodiacal signs from *Sagittarius* to *Aries* (o). This
division reminds one very much of *Huai-nan-tse*, including
the Solar Mansions in his Nine Heavens (p).

The *Pythagoreans* (*Philolaos*) distinguished three world
regions one above the other. The exterior region was the
circle of fire called *Olympos*; the intermediate, the circle
of stars, *Kosmos*, in which were moving the sun, the
moon, and the planets; and the interior region below the
moon and above the earth was called *Uranos* (q).

(o) *F. K. Ginzel*, Die astronomischen Kenntnisse der Babylonier,
1901, p. 3.

(p) *Vid.* p. 134.

(q) *Zeller* I., 409. Stob. I., 488 : τὸ μὲν οὖν ἀνωτάτω μέρος τοῦ
περιέχοντος, ἐν ᾧ τὴν εἰλικρίνειαν εἶναι τῶν στοιχείων ᾿Ολυμπον καλεῖ [Φιλολάος]
τὰ δὲ ὑπὸ τὴν τοῦ ᾿Ολύμπου φορὰν, ἐν ᾧ τοὺς πέντε πλανήτας μεθ᾿ ἡλίου καὶ
σελήνης τετάχθαι, κόσμον, τὸ δ᾿ὑπὸ τούτοις ὑποσέληνόν τε καὶ περίγειον μέρος,
ἐν ᾧ τὰ τῆς φιλομεταβόλου γενέσεως, οὐρανόν.

With the *Peruvians* four superimposed heavens rise above the earth (*r*). The modern *Maya* in *Yucatan* believe in the existence of seven heavens rising in stories one upon another. Each heaven has a hole in the centre through which grows a tree on which the souls of the deceased climb up, until they reach the heaven destined for their residence. That probably depends on their dignity. The upper stories are the most desirable. In the uppermost now is enthroned the *Gran Dios* of the Spaniards, the old Maya gods had to retreat before him and climb down into the lower stories (*s*). They have shared the fate of the old gods of India who at present must inhabit the lower of the 82 Buddhist heavens.

In the *Upanishads* ten worlds are mentioned, namely the air, wind, the sun, the moon, the Five Planets and the fixed stars. In other passages, seven or fourteen worlds are alluded to, viz., seven upper and seven lower ones (*t*). In the *Bible* we read almost as often about heavens as about heaven. The three or seven heavens of later *Judaism* and of the *New Testament* are said to be of Babylonian origin (*u*).

The *Greeks* were accustomed to regard the various worlds as spheres with peculiar motions, and in this way endeavoured to explain the manifold movements of the stars. These spheres were commonly regarded as being nine in number.

The later *Pythagoreans* had ten, having invented an additional "counter-earth." The number twelve also occurs (*x*). *Eudoxos* first assumed three homocentric spheres turning in different directions, for the purpose of

---

(*r*) *Beuchat*, Manuel, p. 630.
(*s*) *R. L. Lowie*, in Hastings IV., p. 170.
(*t*) *H. Jacobi*, Hastings IV., 157.
(*u*) *Schiaparelli*, p. 51.
(*x*) *Bouché-Leclercq*, p. 8.

explaining the revolution of the sun, and besides three for the moon and four for the planets. *Kallippos* added two spheres for the sun and two for the moon, and one sphere each for *Mercury*, *Venus* and *Mars* (*y*). The fixed stars, according to the Greek view, were in the eighth heaven (*z*). The number of these spheres was increased in the progress of time. Aside from the sphere of the fixed stars moved by God, *Aristotle* is said to have assumed 47 spheres, or, as some say, as many as 55 (*a*).

(f) *Heaven as Paradise.*

Heaven has always been considered the seat of *Shang-ti*, the Supreme God and of his attendants. He keeps court in his palaces as a celestial emperor. Other gods are to be found there also. However, to the Chinese, heaven is not paradise where the souls of the departed live after their death. Only some few select are allowed to stay at the court of Shang-ti. We read in the *Shiking* that the emperor *Wên-wang* is in heaven (*b*), together with his two ancestors *T'ai-wang* and *Wang-chi* (*c*). Subsequently deceased emperors were universally believed to share the throne of Shang-ti. Taoist immortals have often ascended to heaven, and we have poems descriptive of journeys in heaven, of which the *Li-sao* is the best known. But these were exceptional men, who by special favour were admitted to heaven. The Chinese heaven never became a real paradise, like the various Buddhist heavens or the heaven of the Christian religion, which is open to all mankind.

(*y*) *Hoppe*, pp. 176, 179.

(*z*) *Troels-Lund*, p. 103.

(*a*) *Bouché-Leclercq*, p. 26.

(*b*) *Legge*, *Shiking*, II., 427. 大 雅 文 王 篇. 。 文 王 在 上 於 昭 于 天.

(*c*) *Shiking*, II., 458. 下 武 篇。 三 后 在 天 王 配 于 京.

(g) *The Gates of Heaven.*

From the *Pên-ts'ao ching* we learn that heaven has nine gates. The central entrance is the broadest; the sun and the moon issue from this (*d*). The principal gate of heaven *Ch'ang-ho* is already known to *Huai-nan-tse* (*e*), and the *Shuo-wên* mentions it. The commentary adds that it is the gate of the *Tse-wei* palace near the north pole where Shang-ti has his residence (*f*).

The gate of heaven is open at times. The emperor *Hsüan-ti* (550—560 A.D.), of the Northern *Ch'i* dynasty, is said to have seen the gate of heaven open, when passing near the *Liao-yang* mountain (*g*). For others it was not visible, so it may have been an halluncination.

The *Negroes* of the *Gold Coast* believe that every morning heaven throws open a big gate to let the sun out (*h*). *Varro* reports concerning three gates of heaven, one near the sign of Scorpio, one between Leo and Cancer, and one between Aquarius and Pisces (*i*). We all know the gate of heaven of the Christian legend, for which *Peter* has the key.

II. QUALITIES OF PHYSICAL HEAVEN.

The purely physical qualities of heaven have already been dealt with. To the Chinese heaven appears *round, high, blue, atmospheric*—qualities, it is true, against which many doubts have been uttered.

(*d*) 本 草 經, work of the Han epoch.

(*e*) 淮 南 子。排 閶 闔 鑰 天 門.

(*f*) 天 門 上 帝 所 居 紫 微 宮 門 也 *Tse-wei* is the name of a star near the North Pole, so the Polar Star has been described as the gate of heaven also. Others say that the gate of heaven are two stars in the constellation 角 Horn. According to *Giles's Dict.* these two stars are between *Spica* and γ *Hydrae*.

(*g*) *Pei Ch'i-shu*, chap. 4, p. 1 r.
(*h*) *Tylor* I., 347.
(*i*) *Bouché-Leclercq*, p. 23, Note 1.

A *Yiking* commentary characterises the nature of heaven as follows :—" How great is Ch'ien ;—*hard, strong, well-balanced, correct, pure, unalloyed, excellent* ! " (*k*).

Hard refers to the substance of heaven, which though air is yet supposed to be hard (*l*); strong to the inherent force of heaven, displayed in its rotation, which is perfectly uniform, so that heaven never loses its equilibrium. It consists of pure *Yang* fluid, not alloyed with *Yin*.

Thus far the physical viewpoint has not been departed from. But it becomes somewhat metaphysical, when *Kuan-yin-tse* says that heaven covers everything and, whether creatures live or are killed, manifests neither love nor hatred (*m*); or when *Shên-tse* avers that heaven in its actions is unselfish, therefore so regular and correct and being so correct, so pure and bright (*n*); or when *Kuan-tse* even goes the length of declaring that heaven is just and disinterested, because it spreads itself over the beautiful and the ugly in the same manner (*o*). A being absolved of love and hatred in a special case and considered just and unselfish, cannot be merely material, and there must be spiritual forces at work within it.

Tung Chung-shu makes the interesting attempt to deduce the feelings of heaven from its natural qualities. We saw that the *Liki* already simply identified the justice and benevolence of heaven and earth with cold and warm air. Tung Chung-shu proceeds in a very similar way. *Pleasure, joy, anger* and *sorrow* are said to be essentially the same

---

(*k*) *Yiking*, App. IV., 415. Cf. p. 48.

(*l*) See above, p. 104.

(*m*) *Kuan-yin-tse*, p. 6 r. 關尹子三極篇。天無不覆有生有殺而天無愛惡.

(*n*) *Shên-tse* 申子。天道無私是以恆正天道恆正是以清明.

(*o*) Cf. above, p. 72, Note (*f*).

as *warmth, heat, clearness,* and *cold.* Heaven possesses these feelings in common with man, in whom the same forces are active as in heaven. Thus we obtain the following equations : (1) *Pleasure* = *warmth* = *spring,* (2) *Joy* = *heat* = *summer,* (3) *Anger* = *clearness* = *autumn,* (4) *Sorrow* = *cold* = *winter.* For pleasure love may be substituted, and for anger seriousness. With the warm spring fluid heaven loves and produces vegetation, and with the hot summer fluid it displays its joy and develops the plants, with the clear autumn fluid it shows its seriousness and causes everything to mature, and with the cold winter fluid it mourns and conceals its produce in the earth (*p*). A certain poetry cannot be denied to these physico-philosophical speculations recalling similar productions of western philosophers.

Thus the bridge is laid joining the material heaven with heaven as an object of religious worship. We have no more the blue celestial dome, but a being formed of the very finest substance, which feels as we do ourselves.

B. RELIGIOUS-PHILOSOPHICAL VIEWPOINT.

I. NATURE OF HEAVEN.

(a) *Heaven the origin of all things.*

Heaven is the source of all existence and the " ancestor of all things " (*q*). Heaven comprises everything, the earth

---

(*p*) *Ch'un-ch'iu fan-lu* XI., 10 v. 天辯在人。春愛志也夏樂志也秋嚴志也冬哀志也 …… 天無喜氣亦何以煖而春生育陽無怒氣亦何以清而秋殺就天無樂氣亦何以疎陽而夏養長天無哀氣亦何以激陰而冬閉藏故曰天乃有喜怒哀樂之行人亦有春秋冬夏之氣者合類之謂也.

(*q*) 董膠西集。天者羣物之祖也. The *Tung Chiao-hsi chi* is by *Tung Chung-shu,* second century B.C.

reposing in its centre included; everything that is, is a part of heaven, and everything that lives has been produced by heaven. " Men," says the *Shi-chi*, " have their origin in heaven and descend from their parents. When they are in trouble, they return to their stock. Consequently, when their sufferings have reached the highest degree, every one implores heaven just as, when pains have become unbearable, every one calls for his parents " (*r*).

Men have the feeling of children towards heaven, especially the emperor who reveres heaven as his father, and therefore is called the son of heaven (*s*). The *Liki* ordains that the virtuous man shall honour heaven like his parents (*t*).

(b) *Heaven governs the world.*

The notion of heaven as the ruler of the world is very old. We meet with it in numerous utterances of the *Shuking*, therefore it must reach back into the primeval times of Chinese civilization.

Heaven enjoins virtue as a duty of mankind (*u*), establishes laws, gives commands, honours the virtuous and punishes the depraved (*x*), rewards the good and

---

(*r*) *Shi-chi* 84, 1 r. 屈原傳。天者人之始也父母者人之本也人窮則反本故勞苦倦極未嘗不呼天也疾痛慘怛未嘗不呼父母也.

(*s*) *Ch'ien Han-shu* 25 b, 8 r. 郊祀志。王者父事天故爵稱天子.

(*t*) *Liki* II., 269, 哀公問。仁人之事親也如事天事天如事親.

(*u*) *Legge, Shuking* II., 294. 泰誓下。天有顯道厥類惟彰.

(*x*) *Eod.* I., 73, 74.

inflicts penalties on the wicked (*y*). In an unpretentious way he transmits to the people his own nature and promotes their development (*z*). He obtains this end by giving them princes and teachers to lead them the right way (*a*). Heaven does not always administer the government of the world directly, but he also rules through the emperor, whom he invests, as his substitute (*b*). This is the divine right in its most complete form. And not only the emperor, but the feudatory princes also are directly appointed by heaven. It is not advisable to try issues with such a representative of heaven. Thus we read in the *Tso-chuan*, "Heaven has invested *Ch'u*, and one must not fight against it. Can the power of *Chin*, be it ever so great, resist Heaven?" (*c*)

Sometimes heaven intervenes in the regular course of events. In the *Shiking*, e.g., it is said that "Heaven ordered a swallow to fly down, and thus Shang was born" (*d*), and in another passage, "Heaven commanded all the princes to build their capitals in the sphere of Yü's labours" (*e*).

(c) *Heaven as Providence*.

By directing the destinies of the world heaven becomes fate or providence. His power is so great that it would

---

(*y*) *Kuo-yü* : 先王之令有之曰天道賞善而罰淫.

(*z*) *Shuking* II., 320.

(*a*) *Eod.* II., 286. 泰誓上。天佑下民作之君作之師惟其克相上帝寵綏四方.

(*b*) *Shuking* II., 290, 291. 泰誓中。天乃佑命成湯 . . . . 天其以予乂民.

(*c*) *Tso-chuan, Duke Hsüan*, 15th year. 天方授楚未可與爭雖晉之彊能違天乎.

(*d*) *Shiking* II., 636. 玄鳥篇。天命玄鳥降而生商.

(*e*) *Eod.* II., 645. 殷武篇。天命多辟設都于禹之績.

be presumptuous to oppose it. Heaven pities the people
and fulfils their wishes (*f*). Virtue touches him, therefore
he looks down upon the people, scrutinises their justice
and accordingly bestows upon them a longer or a shorter
life (*g*). When heaven exalts anybody, as, for example,
Ch'ung-êrh, prince of *Chin*, no one can destroy him, and
the attempt to withstand heaven would be a serious
crime (*h*).

But heaven is not only the donor of happiness, he also
may send misfortune and is often unkind. If the people
are miserable, it is his doing. In his wrath heaven
frequently sends diseases, misery, famine and perdition, as
we gather from many remarks of the *Shiking* (*i*). Often-
times he brings about great catastrophes, as *e.g.*, when he
overthrew the *Yin* dynasty (*k*). Like a great potentate,
heaven sometimes alters his inclinations, so that one can
never be quite certain of his favour (*l*).

The Chinese never were absolute fatalists and besides
the fate of heaven they always took human activity into
account. This is emphasised by *Hsün-tse*, who says that
reasonable actions in conjunction with the activity of

(*f*) *Shuking* II., 288. 泰誓 上。天 矜 于 民 民 之 所 欲 天
必 從 之.

(*g*) *Shuking* I., 264. 高宗 肜 日。惟 天 監 下 民 典 厥 義
降 年 有 永 有 不 永.

(*h*) *Tso-chuan, Duke Hsi*, 23rd year : 天 將 與 之 誰 能 廢 之
違 天 必 有 大 咎.

(*i*) *Shiking* II., 312. 小 雅。昊 天 不 傭 降 此 鞠 訩 昊 天
不 惠 降 此 大 戾, and II., 325. 雨 無 正 篇。浩 浩 昊 天 不
駿 其 德 降 喪 饑 饉 斬 伐 四 國 昊 天 疾 威 弗 慮 弗 圖

(*k*) *Shuking* II., 474. 君 奭。弗 弔. 天 降 喪 于 殷.

(*l*) *Loc. cit.* II., 476—477. 天 命 不 易. 天 難 諶 . . . . 天 不
可 信.

heaven are productive of happiness, unreasonable ones of mishap. If anybody has sufficient money and makes an economic use of it, then heaven cannot render him poor, and if he cultivates his body, giving it the necessary exercise, then heaven cannot make him sick (*m*). Accordingly heaven would not be an absolute monarch whose sole will determines the weal and woe of his creatures, but these would have an extensive co-operation and be able in a great measure to shape their own destiny.

(d) Heaven acts like man.

Heaven is not a man, but he acts like one. In the *Shiking* he is introduced *walking* (*n*), and we are often told that he *looks down*. He *sees* and *hears*, says the *Shuking* (*o*). Heaven *loves* the people (*p*), he helps his friends and injures his enemies. Those who in their dealings follow his will he assists, and he opposes those who are against him (*q*). So we read in the *Tso-chuan* that heaven lent his hand to *Ch'u* to slay the prince of *Ts'ai*, who by the assassination of his sovereign had offended against heaven.

(*m*) *Hsün-tse* XI., 12 r. 天 論 篇。强 本 而 節 用 則 天 不 能 貧 養 備 而 動 時 則 天 不 能 病.

(*n*) *Shiking* II., 416. 白 華 篇。天 步 艱 難 之 子 不 猶.

(*o*) *Shuking* I., 74; I., 255; II., 292. 皐 陶 謨。天 聰 明 自 我 民 聰 明 天 明 畏 自 我 民 明 威 達 於 上 下 敬 哉 有 土. 說 命。惟 天 聰 明 惟 聖 時 憲 維 臣 欽 若 惟 民 從 乂 泰 誓 中。天 視 自 我 民 視 天 聽 自 我 民 聽.

(*p*) *Shuking* II., 290.

(*q*) *Kuan-tse* I., 8 v. 形 勢 篇。其 功 順 天 者 天 助 之 其 功 逆 天 者 天 違 之 天 之 所 助 雖 小 必 大 天 之 所 違 雖 成 必 敗.

Sometimes heaven is in an *angry* mood. An ill-fated man exclaims in the *Shiking*, " I was born in an unlucky hour, when heaven was at the moment in great anger " (r). In *Wang Ch'ung's* time it was the common belief that thunder is the *angry voice* of heaven, and that with his lightning he strikes people guilty of some secret offence (s). *Huai-nan-tse* relates a special incident, when heaven, implored by a woman from the people, sent down his thunderbolt (t). The commentary adds that this refers to a widow in *Chi*, who had taken her mother-in-law and her daughter into her house to care for them. The daughter had killed her own mother out of greed, and then charged the widow with the murder. To prove her innocence the widow invoked heaven, who then replied with his lightning.

It cannot be a matter for surprise that it occurred to some thinkers to ascribe to heaven, who thinks, feels and acts exactly like a human being, a human body as well. We find this idea discussed in a colloquy between a certain *Ch'in Pi* and *Chang Wên* in the *San-kuo-chih* (u). " Chang Wên asked again, ' Has heaven a head ? ' Ch'in Pi returned : ' Yes.' Chang Wên : ' Where ? ' Ch'in Pi : ' In the West, for it is said in the Shiking : " he turned his

---

(r) *Shiking* II., 521. 大雅。桑柔. 我生不辰逢天僤怒.

(s) *Lun-hêng* I., 285.

(t) *Huai-nan-tse* VI., 1 r. 覽冥訓。庶女叫天雷電下擊.

(u) *Shu-chih* VIII., 6 r. 蜀志秦宓傳。〔張〕溫復問曰天有頭乎宓曰有之溫曰在何方也宓曰在西方詩曰乃眷西顧以此推之頭在西方溫曰天有耳乎宓曰天處高而聽卑詩曰鶴鳴九皋聲聞于天若其無耳何以聽之溫曰天有足乎宓曰詩云天步艱難之子不猶若其無足何以步之溫曰天有姓乎宓曰有溫曰何姓宓曰姓劉溫曰何以知之答曰天子姓劉故以此知之答問如響應聲而出.

kind regards to the west" (x). Consequently the head must be in the West.' Chang Wên : 'Has heaven ears?' Ch'in Pi : 'Heaven is high, but he hears what is down below. The Shiking says : "When the cranes cry in the nine marshes, their cries are heard by heaven" (y). If he had no ears, how could he hear?' Chang Wên : 'Has heaven feet?' Ch'in Pi : 'The Shiking says : "Heaven walks on hard and difficult ground. This man does not act in the proper way" (z). If he had no feet, how could he walk?' Chang Wên : 'Has heaven a surname?' Ch'in Pi : 'Yes.' Chang Wên : 'Which?' Ch'in Pi : 'Liu.' Chang Wên : 'How do you know?' Ch'in Pi : 'The Son of Heaven has the surname Liu, thence I know it' (a). Thus question and reply followed each other like sound and echo."

From various celestial phenomena and heavenly bodies *Huai-nan-tse* formed the court of heaven. The four seasons are his officials, the sun and the moon his messengers, the stars his time, the rainbow and the comets his unpropitious omens. The directions of heaven are considered his ministers. Moreover there are heavenly palaces : in the *T'ai-wei* palace and in the *Tse-kang* resides *T'ai-i*, the Great Monad, in the *Hsien-yuan*, the wife of the emperor of heaven, and in *T'ien-a* the various spirits (b).

(x) *Shiking* II., 449.

(y) *Shiking* II., 297. Legge translates "in the sky," but that would not do for our text.

(z) See above, p. 151, note (n), Legge translates : "The way of heaven is hard and difficult."

(a) The emperors of the Han dynasty were from the *Liu* family.

(b) *Huai-nan-tse* III., 3 r., 6 r., 6 v. 天文訓。四時者天之吏也日月者天之使也星辰者天之期也虹蜺彗星者天之忌也 .... 何謂五官東方爲田南方爲司馬西方爲理北方爲司空中央爲都 .... 太微者太乙之庭也紫宮者太乙之居也軒轅者帝妃之舍也 .... 天阿者羣神之闕也.

(e) Heaven according to Lao-tse and Wang Ch'ung.

With *Lao-tse* heaven is scarcely distinguishable from Tao, a sort of mundane spirit manifesting itself in the material sky. He does not act and remains in a state of quietism and passivity, but though never disputing, nor speaking, nor calling, he obtains everything (*c*). Heaven does not show preference for anyone; but he sides with the good (*d*). Differing from men, who like to consort with those who are successful, heaven humbles the exalted and raises the lowly, he takes from those who have plenty and gives to those who are destitute (*e*). We have here a kind of world government or providence.

Wang Ch'ung knows no other than the physical heaven, which, as he points out, in the Classics is anthropomorphised and endowed with human features (*f*). It cannot have such, being devoid of the indispensable sense organs, ears, eyes, etc. (*g*). The fluid of heaven constitutes the formless empyrean (*h*). Its movements, the emission of this fluid, take place spontaneously, and are not intentional (*i*). Heaven does not speak nor act, nor is it affected by the prayers of mankind; it has no sensations, no wisdom (*k*), no consciousness, for it is nothing but air with some matter contained in the heavenly bodies. In

---

(*c*) *Tao-tê-king*, chap. 73. 任爲篇。天之道不爭而善勝不言而善應不召而自來.

(*d*) *Tao-tê-king*, chap. 79. 任契篇。天道無親常與善人.

(*e*) *Tao-tê-king*, chap. 77. 天道篇。高者抑之下者舉之有餘者損之不足者補之天之道損有餘而補不足人之道則不然損不足以奉有餘.

(*f*) *Lun Hêng* I., 128, 134.
(*g*) *Lun Hêng* I., 92.
(*h*) *Eod.* I., 113.
(*i*) *Eod.* I., 92.
(*k*) *Eod.* I., 101, 127.

humanity and particularly in the sages, heaven or the world reaches its highest development. The heart of heaven is the heart of the sages (*l*). Therefore the intelligence of mankind is the intelligence of heaven—an idea which, perhaps, was already conceived in the *Shuking* (*m*).

(*f*) *Heaven according to Chang-tse, Ch'êng-tse, and Chu Hsi.*

The arguments of the philosophers *Chang Ming-tao* and *Ch'êng I* conform more or less to the Taoist line of thought. Of the former are the following apophthegms :

"The unscrutable in heaven is called spirit, and that which is regular in the spirit is called heaven." Accordingly there is a spiritual force at work in heaven— we would say nature—producing all the wonderful transformations, the inner nature of which we are unable to explain. One speaks of heaven (nature) in so far as the regularity and order of these processes is taken into consideration.

"To create the myriads of things without worrying like the sages, is the way of heaven. A sage cannot understand this, for the wonderful faculty of creating without a plan cannot be grasped by a being acting deliberately" (*n*). This is the Taoist *Wu-wei*.

(*l*) *Eod.* I., 129.

(*m*) *Vid.* p. 151, note (*o*), and *Mencius* (Legge), p. 357, where it is said that Heaven hears and sees through the people. *Chu Hsi* says that Heaven has no body and cannot hear or see except through the people : 自 從 也 天 無 形 其 視 聽 皆 從 於 民 Legge incorrectly translates 自 with " according as."

(*n*) *Hsing-li ta-ch'üan* V., 19 v. 張 子 正 蒙. 天 道 篇。鼓 萬 物 而 不 與 聖 人 同 憂 天 道 也 聖 不 可 知 也 無 心 之 妙 非 有 心 所 及 也.

"Heaven does not perceive things with ears, eyes, and thoughts, his perceptive faculty transcending sense perceptions by far. Heaven sees and hears through the people and displays his majesty through the people. Therefore, the Shiking and Shuking say that the commands of God and of Heaven repose in the hearts of the people " (*o*).

This is a Confucian construction put on the Taoist intuitive knowledge, and at the same time humanity takes the place of heaven or Tao as in the Shiking and in Wang Ch'ung.

Ch'êng-tse gives utterance to the following sentiments : "The principle of heaven is to create, and that this creation goes on without ceasing comes from the indeliberate activity (Wu-wei). If in creating, intelligence and ability were used up, it could not go on uninterruptedly " (*p*).

Ch'êng-tse distinguishes clearly between the physical and metaphysical heaven. He says, "Wherever in the Shiking and Shuking a ruling power is mentioned, God is meant, and where they speak of an encircling and arching over, heaven is intended " (*q*).

When somebody inquired about the difference between heaven and God, he made this reply : "The material

---

(*o*) *Eod.* V., 19 v. 天之知物不以耳目心思然知之之理過於耳目心思天視聽以民明威以民故詩書所謂帝天之命主於民心而已焉.

(*p*) *Hsing-li ta-ch'üan* XXVI., 10 v. 天地。程子曰。天理生生相續不息無爲故也使竭智巧而爲之未有能不息也.

(*q*) *Hsing-li ta-ch'üan, eod.* XXVI., 10 v. 詩書中凡有箇主宰意思者皆言帝有一箇包含徧覆底意思則皆言天.

substance is called heaven, the ruling power God, the
wonderful creative forces are the spirits, nature is Ch'ien
(heaven). As a matter of fact all this is one, the
divergence is merely owing to the names given from
different points of view. If we wish a special designation
for heaven we must call it Tao " (r).

Ergo heaven is only something material, but controlled
by a superior, spiritual power, called God. The wonderful
forces living in nature are spirits.

Chu Hsi holds that the word " heaven " in the Classics
is used in three acceptations—(1) as the blue sky, (2) as a
superior power, (3) as connoting a principle. This superior
power is not a being like man, who as judge, lives in
heaven, yet it is necessary that such a ruler exist. " By
the blue heaven one understands the continually revolving
sky. Now, should anybody pretend that in heaven there is
a man who there judges the sinners and evil-doers, this
could not be maintained. Neither is it possible that there
should be no ruler at all. It is important to keep this in
view " (s).

Someone inquired of Chu Hsi what the ruling power
was which Ch'êng-tse called God. Chu Hsi replied : " Of
course there must be a ruling power. Heaven is a perfectly
hard body, consisting entirely of Yang, revolving of its
own accord without ceasing. Therefore, there must be a

(r) *Loc. cit.* XXVI., 11 r. 或 問 天 帝 之 異 曰 以 形 體 謂
之 天 以 主 宰 謂 之 帝 以 至 妙 之 功 用 謂 之 鬼 神 以
性 情 謂 之 乾 其 實 一 而 已 所 自 而 名 之 者 異 也 夫
天 專 言 之 則 道 也.

(s) *Chu Hsi* 49, 25 r. 天 地 。蒼 蒼 之 謂 天 運 轉 周 流
不 己 便 是 那 箇 而 今 說 天 有 箇 人 在 那 裏 批 判 罪
惡 固 不 可 說 道 全 無 主 之 者 又 不 可 這 裏 要 人 見
得.

ruling power causing this. Men must come to a clear understanding on this point. With mere words nothing is gained " (*t*).

Consequently there is a superior power—a God in heaven, but he must not be conceived as similar to man. " God is a principle as superior power " (*u*). The God of Chu Hsi, therefore, is something quite abstract—no personality, but merely a principle.

II. THE INVOCATION OF HEAVEN.

Since heaven is thought of as the ruler of the world and the disposer of human destinies, it is natural that people should have turned to him with *prayers* and *offerings*, when desirous of obtaining his assistance or acknowledging their indebtedness for favours received.

We have in the *Shiking* several instances of the invocation of heaven. One paragraph runs thus : " Blue heaven, blue heaven ! behold those arrogant men and have compassion on these miserable ones !" (*x*). And elsewhere we read : " Bright high heaven ! look down on earth below " (*y*). It is worthy of notice that in both cases the prayer is addressed directly to the visible heaven.

Not seldom the prayer takes the form of a complaint, nay almost a reproach of heaven, *e.g.*, when some one exclaims : " What offence have I committed against heaven,

---

(*t*) *Chu Hsi eod.* 49, 27 v. 或 問 伊 川 說 以 主 宰 謂 之 帝 孰 爲 主 宰 曰 自 有 主 宰 蓋 天 是 箇 至 剛 至 陽 之 物 自 然 如 此 運 轉 不 息 所 以 如 此 必 有 爲 之 主 宰 者 這 樣 處 要 人 自 見 得 非 言 語 所 能 盡 也.

(*u*) *Chu Hsi eod.* 49, 25 r. 帝 是 理 爲 主.

(*x*) *Shiking* II., 348. 巷 伯 篇。蒼 天 蒼 天 視 彼 驕 人 矜 此 勞 人.

(*y*) *Shiking* II., 363. 小 明 篇。明 明 上 天 照 臨 下 土.

and how have I sinned against him?" (z) or "Oh, why does that exalted and resplendent heaven have no pity on me?"

Some historic instances of the invocation of heaven are known to us also. When General *Lü* was to be put to death by order of the emperor *Erh-shih-huang-ti*, he looked up to heaven and invoking him thrice with a loud voice he said, "Heaven! I am innocent" (a). *Hsiang Yü* is reported after his arrival in Tung-ch'êng to have said to his horsemen : " In more than seventy battles I have conquered the world. That now I am suddenly surrounded here is because heaven wishes to destroy me. I have not made any mistake in strategy " (b). Every time when *Liu Tsan*, a general, went into action, he was wont to loosen his hair and to implore heaven. Upon this he intonated a song, in which his companions joined, and only then he took the field (c).

About the sacrifices offered to heaven by the emperor we have spoken above (p. 79).

III. THE PERSONIFICATION OF HEAVEN.

From remotest antiquity, of which the *Shuking* and the *Shiking* inform us, heaven had been already humanised. No matter whether one spoke of the " blue sky " or of the ruler of heaven, in both cases one would employ the same word, 天 *t'ien*. For heaven as a person, however, the

---

(z) *Eod.* II., 336. 小弁篇. 何辜于天我罪伊何.

(a) *Shi-chi* 6, 13 v. 將閭乃仰天大呼天者三曰天乎吾無罪昆弟三人皆流涕拔劍自殺.

(b) *Shi-chi* 7, 13 r. 項羽本紀。項王至東城 .... 謂其騎曰吾 .... 七十餘戰 .... 霸有天下然今卒困于此乃天之亡我非戰之罪也.

(c) 聞奇錄。留贊爲將臨敵必先被髮叫天因抗音而歌左右應之歌畢乃進戰.

term *Shang-ti,* or *Ti* alone, meaning the "august Sovereign," commonly translated as "God," was usual. The Chinese pictured to themselves a sovereign governing in heaven, even as his representative, the emperor of China, on earth. Like a prince he lives in his palaces, has his ministers and functionaries, as well as multitudes of ghosts and spirits, all carrying out his commands. But the Confucianists have ever preferred the term "heaven," even where the spirit of heaven is intended, and given to the word *Shang-ti* an abstract meaning as far as possible. With *Chu Hsi,* as we saw, God is nothing more than a ruling principle. Still, at the present day we have a temple of heaven in Peking, but no Shang-ti temple. In cult, Shang-ti is considered as entirely identical with heaven.

From times of yore the imperial ancestors were worshipped along with *Shang-ti,* for, says the *Liki,* the multitudinous things take their origin from heaven, as men from their ancestors (*d*).

Still another name is sometimes applied to God, namely, *T'ien-kung* (*e*), the "Master of Heaven," mentioned already in the Han epoch. The *Han-shu* narrates a dream of a village elder, Hsing-tang, in Lin-tse-hsien. In this dream a messenger of the Master of Heaven appeared to him, and transmitted to him an order for the then regent, *Wang Mang,* who was called upon to ascend the throne (*f*).

A popular name for God is "*Lao t'ien-yeh*" (*g*), the Old Gentleman of Heaven, which is especially in vogue in the north of China.

(*d*) *Liki* I., 430. 郊特牲。萬物本乎天人本乎祖所以配上帝也.

(*e*) 天公.

(*f*) *Ch'ien Han-shu* 99 a, 17 r. 王莽傳.

(*g*) 老天爺.

Book III.

YIN AND YANG.

BOOK III.

YIN AND YANG.

A. ANCIENT TIMES.

I. THE OLDEST SOURCES.

WE have already become acquainted with the main features of the theory of the primary elements, Yin and Yang, of which the universe is believed to be formed. Now the question arises from what time this theory dates, and how far back into antiquity we are able to trace it. The oldest texts in which we find references are the *Shiking*, the *Chou-li*, and the *Tso-chuan*.

In the *Kung-liu* Ode of the *Shiking* it is said of the Duke of Lu : " He examined the Yin and the Yang " (a). The commentators and *Legge* take this to mean " light and shade." This does not give a good sense, for there is no question of fields, to which light and shade are said to refer, nor does one see why the prince should examine the sunny and shady sides of fields. Yin and Yang must here refer to the primogenial forces of nature, by which the sovereign, as well as the sage, have to order their activities, taking them as their model, and in turn regulating them themselves, as we shall see later. Just so the oneirocritics in the *Chou-li* would observe the Yin and Yang fluids, the handle of the " Bushel " showing them the temporary seat of the Yang in the sky, and the position of the sun indicat-

---

(a) *Shiking* II., 488. 大雅篤公劉篇。相其陰陽.

ing the seat of the Yin (*b*). From the preceding verse, in which the prince determines the four quarters from the shade (*c*), we infer that some observations of the sky are alluded to. According to Legge, this ode would have been composed in the time from 1114—1076 B.C.

The *Tsai-wei* Ode has the following verse : " When do we return, when do we return? The year will have reached the *Yang month* already " (*d*) ; and, similarly, the *Ti-tu* Ode says : " The sun and the moon are already in the *Yang month*, my heart is afflicted " (*e*).

The Yang month (*f*) is the tenth month. This expression involves a knowledge of the theory of the alternation of Yin and Yang. We would not be surprised if the Chinese had dubbed July or August the " Yang " or " Sun Month," but how is it that they just chose November? *Kuo P'o*, in his commentary to the *Erh-ya*, says, because in the tenth month the pure Yin fluid prevails, and one regrets the complete absence of the Yang. That means to say one calls it the Yang month because it does not contain any Yang. The various names for the tenth month indicate that in this month already, in the opinion of the Chinese at least, the beginning of spring takes place, for it is also styled 小陽月 " small Yang month," 陽春 " Yang spring," and 小陽春 " small Yang spring." The Yang fluid, bringing about spring, commences already in the tenth month slightly to stir. It is significant that this month has also been called the " Plum month," 梅月 because in it, as the first blossoms, those of the plum tree come forth. " The early plums blossom already before the

---

(*b*) Cf. p. 64.

(*c*) 既景廼岡.

(*d*) *Shiking* II., 259. 小雅采薇篇。曰歸曰歸歲亦陽止.

(*e*) *Shiking* II., 265. 杕杜篇。日月陽止女心傷止.

(*f*) 陽月.

winter solstice," remarks *Ch'êng-tse.* " If then the Yang had not yet been awakened, which force could cause them to burst forth ? " (*g*). Wood is considered to be the specific element of spring. As we shall see later, *Huai-nan-tse* lets it be born in the tenth month; consequently spring must originate in the tenth month already.

In accordance with the common view advocated by *Tung Chung-shu, e.g.,* and expressed by the term 新 陽 " New Yang " for the eleventh month, the Yang fluid does not come into being but one month later, whence Kuo P'o's perplexity. This, after all, is tantamount to what Legge says, viz., that even in the tenth month Yang is already extant in an embryonic state, for it never disappears completely. At all events, when the *Tsai-wei* Ode was written, which was between 1121—1076 B.C., according to Legge, the peculiar hypothesis of the increase and the decrease of the Yang fluid must have been known.

In the *Chou-li* (eleventh century B.C.) the following passages are of moment : " The herdsman uses russet animals for the *Yang* sacrifices and determines the colour of their hair, and black animals for the *Yin* sacrifices, whose hair is determined likewise " (*h*). The Yang sacrifice is that offered to heaven, and the Yin sacrifice that to earth. The russet colour of the victims corresponds to the colour of fire, the Yang fluid, the black colour to that of the Yin essence.

" The director of sacred ceremonies uses the products of heaven to produce the *Yin* force and he checks it by moderation and rites, and he uses the products of earth to

---

(*g*) *Hsing-li ta-ch'üan,* 27, 16 r. 程 子 曰。早 梅 冬 至 已 前 發 方 一 陽 未 生 然 則 發 生 者 何 也.

(*h*) E. Biot, *Chou-li* I., 270. 地 官。牧 人 凡 陽 祀 用 騂 牲 毛 之 陰 祀 用 黝 牲 毛 之.

excite the *Yang* force and checks it by harmony and music " (*i*). According to the commentary, by the products of heaven living creatures, here animals, are intended, and by the products of earth, plants. When the Yin fluid in man is too empty, it deteriorates, therefore, with a view to supplementing it, he must eat meat. But if he has too much motion, it injures his constitution, therefore he is kept within the necessary bounds by the aid of moderation and rites, which are regarded as Yin. When, contrariwise, the Yang fluid in man is superabundant, he becomes too much excited, therefore he must be placed on vegetable diet, whereby the fluid is regulated. If, however, he becomes too quiet, this also proves hurtful to his constitution, then he must be stirred up a little by harmony and music. Music is Yang (*k*).

" The oneirocritics are concerned with the year and the seasons, they observe the union of heaven and earth and distinguish between the Yin and the Yang fluids " (*l*). The commentary says that the union of heaven and earth is effected by the position of the " Bushel " in one of the " Ten Heavenly Stems," 天 幹 and of the sun in one of the " Twelve Earthly Branches," 地 支. Both series of cyclical signs are employed to connote the directions, the

---

(*i*) *Chou-li* I., 435. 春 官。大 宗 伯 以 天 產 作 陰 德 以 中 禮 防 之 以 地 產 作 陽 德 以 和 樂 防 之.

(*k*) 注。天 產 者 動 物 地 產 者 植 物 陰 德 陰 氣 在 人 者 陰 氣 虛 純 之 則 劣 故 食 動 物 作 之 使 動 過 則 傷 性 制 中 禮 以 節 之 陽 德 陽 氣 在 人 者 陽 氣 盈 純 之 則 躁 故 食 植 物 作 之 使 靜 過 則 傷 性 制 和 樂 以 節 之.

(*l*) *Chou-li* II., 82. 春 官。占 夢 掌 其 歲 時 覯 天 地 之 會 辨 陰 陽 之 氣.

celestial as well as the terrestrial. The direction in which the handle of the Bushel points, is Yang (see above, p. 64). The handle of the Bushel (Great Bear) in the sky turns from the left to the right like a clock, and indicates the seasons. The station in which the sun stays is Yin. The sun proceeds on the sky from right to left. In the first month, at the beginning of spring, the Bushel points to the sign Yin=E.N.E.$\frac{3}{4}$N., and the sun stands on the opposite side in the sign Hsü=W.N.W.$\frac{3}{4}$N. Consequently Yang stays in the sign Yin and Yin in Hsü. This distinction between Yin and Yang serves the purpose of forecasting lucky and unlucky events (*m*).

These passages of the Chou-li initiate us into the mysteries of the Yin-yang theory, and in the absence of this theory would remain inexplicable. From other paragraphs of the same text we see that, as early as in the eleventh century B.C., Yin and Yang were used in the following meanings :

(1) Yang=*male*; yin=*female*. Yang-li, an archery match with a banquet, was a festival for men exclusively; Yin-li=marriage, a ceremony in which women were primarily interested (*n*).

(2) Yang=*above*; yin=*below*. The six upper tones for which, as some say, bamboo tubes were employed, were

---

(*m*) 注。天地之會陰陽之氣年年不同故云今歲四時也建謂斗柄所建謂之陽建故左還于天厭謂日前一次謂之陰建故右還于天故堪輿天老日假令正月陽建于寅陰建在戌日辰者日據幹辰據支觀此建厭所在辨陰陽之氣以知吉凶也.

(*n*) *Chou-li* I., 196. 地官大司徒。二曰以陽禮敎讓則民不爭三曰以陰禮敎親則民不怨.

considered as yang, the lower six, for which they used copper tubes, as yin (*o*).

(3) Yang=*anterior*; yin=*posterior*. The anterior aperture of a turtle used for divination was called yang, the posterior yin (*p*).

(4) Yang=*hard*; yin=*soft*. Hard wood, which had received plenty of sunshine, was regarded as yang; soft wood, which had grown mostly in the shade, as yin. The latter, in order to be wrought in wheels together with hard wood, had to be hardened with fire (yang) by the cartwright (*q*).

(5) Yang = *light*; yin = *heavy*. The arrow makers examined the equilibrium of an arrow by putting it into water and letting it swim. Then the heavier parts turned downside and the lighter floated above. The commentator *Chao* assumes that two pieces of bamboo of different weight were used, others speak only of one piece (*r*).

All these terms are secondary, and involve the existence of the Yin-yang theory. That this doctrine was well known

---

(*o*) *Chou-li* II., 55. 春官。典同掌六律六同之和以辨天地四方陰陽之聲以爲樂器. See also *Mayers*, Reader, Pt. II. Nos. 199, 200.

(*p*) *Loc. cit.* II., 75. 春官。卜師凡卜辨龜之上下左右陰陽以授命龜者而詔相之。注。陰後弇也陽前弇也.

(*q*) *Eod.* II., 468. 冬官。輪人凡斬轂之道必矩其陰陽陽也者稄理而堅陰也者疏理而柔是故以火養其陰而齊諸其陽則轂雖敝不蔽.

(*r*) *Eod.* II., 534. 冬官。矢人水之以辨其陰陽夾其陰陽以設其比。趙氏曰陽竹輕清陰竹重濁然生而混成不可辨也惟水隨物輕重而應之以浮沉所以辨其陰陰者欲以設其比須使輕重均方可也.

in the seventh and sixth centuries B.C. is attested by the *Tso-chuan.*

In the *sixteenth year* of *Duke Hsi* (642 B.C.) five meteors fell in Sung and six sea-eagles flew backwards, a phenomenon explained by the Tso-chuan as a consequence of a strong gale. Duke *Hsiang* of Sung inquired of *Shu-hsing* what this signified. When the latter came back from his audience he said, " The prince put his question wrongly. This is merely a case of Yin and Yang—we would say it is but a natural phenomenon—and has not been caused by lucky or unlucky circumstances. Happiness and misfortune depend only on men " (*s*).

A propos of a violent hail-shower in the *fourth year* of *Duke Chao* (538 B.C.), *Chi Wu-tse* questioned *Shên Fêng* how such a catastrophe could be averted. In a lengthy discussion on ice and cold, and the methods to regulate them, Shên Fêng said (*inter alia*) : " There was no extraordinary Yang (heat) in winter and no hidden Yin (cold) in summer " (*t*). Such a state, when there was no extraordinary heat in winter and no exceptional cold in summer, was held to be the natural one, Yin and Yang being in harmony.

On June 3 of the year 520 B.C., according to the *Ch'un-ch'iu*, there was an *eclipse of the sun*, on which the *Tso-chuan* comments as follows : " The duke asked *Tse Shên* saying, ' What does that mean? Does it bring happiness or misfortune? ' The other rejoined, ' At the time of the two solstices and equinoxes an eclipse of the sun does not portend a calamity. The sun and the moon in their courses take the same road at the equinoxes and pass each other at the solstices. In other months an eclipse of the sun

---

(*s*) *Legge, Ch'un-ch'iu*, Vol. I., p. 170. 退 而 告 人 曰 君 失 問 是 陰 陽 之 事 非 吉 凶 所 生 也 吉 凶 由 人.

(*t*) *Ch'un-ch'iu* II., 596. 冬 無 愆 陽 夏 無 伏 陰.

is a calamity, for then the Yang cannot get the better, therefore there will always be an inundation'" (u). The Yang principle represented by the sun cannot withstand the Yin principle embodied in the moon; consequently Yin = water for the time being is more powerful than Yang = fire, and as a concomitant phenomenon we have an inundation.

Yet this view was not universal, and an eclipse of the sun might eventually be assumed as forecasting a drought. On April 1, 517 B.C. the *Ch'un-ch'iu* again announces an eclipse of the sun. "*Tse Shên*," says the *Tso-chuan*, "declared, there will be high water," but *Chao-tse* was of opinion that it meant a drought, for, quoth he, "the sun has passed the equinox and the Yang has not yet obtained preponderance. When it does, the victory will be the more crushing, and we must expect a drought. The Yang cannot expand and then will be highly concentrated" (x). In this case the drought is a consequence of an excessive accumulation of the hot Yang fluid.

As the result of our investigation we may summarise and state that already in the twelfth and the eleventh centuries B.C., not only the words Yin and Yang, but also the entire theory built thereon, was known in all its details.

(u) *Ch'un-ch'iu* II., 688. 昭 公 二 十 一 年 秋 七 月 壬 午 朔 日 有 蝕 之。公 問 於 梓 慎 曰 是 何 物 也 禍 福 何 爲 對 曰 二 至 二 分 日 有 蝕 之 不 爲 災 日 月 之 行 也 分 同 道 也 至 相 過 也 其 他 月 則 爲 災 陽 不 克 也 故 常 爲 水.

(x) *Ch'un-ch'iu* II., 702. 昭 公 二 十 四 年 夏 五 月 乙 未 朔 日 有 蝕 之 梓 慎 曰 將 水 昭 子 曰 旱 也 日 過 分 而 陽 猶 不 克 克 必 甚 能 無 旱 乎 陽 不 克 莫 將 積 聚 也.

II. The Original Meaning of Yin and Yang.

The meanings of Yin and Yang are so numerous that it is of interest to know the original signification from which the others are derived. The evolution of the Chinese language proceeded so logically that it is possible to indicate the fundamental meaning of most characters. In this respect the Chinese script is of inestimable service, for one mostly can recognise in some measure how the Chinese conceived their ideograms when they invented their characters, *i.e.,* at the beginning of their culture. As a principal maxim we must lay down the rule that, in the case of a character having several meanings, the concrete and simple ones always precede the more abstract and complicated, for, as in everything else, in language likewise the human mind starts from what is simple and easy.

The two modern characters, 陽 Yang and 陰 Yin, are both compounded with ß = 阜 *fou* = mound of earth; the meaning, therefore, must have something to do with a mound. Such a meaning exists in fact. The *Erh-ya* informs us that the *southern side of a mountain* is called Yang, *the northern* Yin (y). To judge by the phonetic elements of the two characters, 陽 must have been the *sunny side,* 陰 *the shady side of a hill,* which corresponds to the southern and northern sides (z). The radical ß however, was added to the characters only later, probably just to emphasise this special meaning of the bright and shady sides. In old script, according to *Kang-hsi,* both characters appear without a radical as 昜 and 侌.

昜, in old script 昜, depicts the sun above the horizon 日 and underneath 勿 = 彡, pennants or a staff with pennants. The sunbeams are compared to flying pennants,

---

(y) *Erh-ya*: 山 南 曰 陽 山 北 曰 陰.

(z) *Chalmers,* Structure of Chinese Characters, p. 154; and *Wieger,* Leçons Etymologiques, p. 265.

and the whole picture represents the sun with flaming rays. Since one had already an image of the sun in ||, in this compound most likely stress was laid upon the rays, and the whole character meant " sunbeams " or " sunlight " (a).

今 = 侌 = 霙 is composed of 今 " now," and 云, an old picture of a coiling cloud. Both together mean that, at the time being, there are clouds, i.e., *clouds covering the sun* (b). This notion has still been preserved in the acceptation : " cloudy," " overclouded." 陰 is the overclouded sky, 晴 the bright sky.

Thus we have found as the fundamental meanings of Yin and Yang *bright sunlight* and *dark, coiling clouds.* The sharp contrast between *clouds* and *sunshine* is evident.

III. Yin and Yang as Fluids and Primary Elements.

From the fiery solar fluid and the moist nebular masses forming clouds to *fire* and *water*, the primogenial elements from which we saw the world evolved, there is but one step. Yin and Yang conceived as substances are nothing else.

This conception is implied in the two cited paragraphs of the *Tso-chuan* dealing with eclipses of the sun (c). Accordingly, the Yang principle of the sun can produce a drought, being fire, and the Yin principle of the moon, being admittedly water, can cause a flood or an inundation.

We read in *Lieh-tse* : " The plenitude and emptiness of a body, its increase and decrease are in connection with heaven and earth and affected by kindred objects. Therefore, the Yin fluid being strong, one dreams of wading through a great water and is frightened, and the Yang

---

(a) *Chalmers,* p. 85 ; *Wieger,* p. 295.

(b) Cf. *Wieger,* p. 279 *Yinn,* Temps Couvert : 从今从云會意。 雲覆日也. *Chalmers,* p. 81.

(c) See above, pp. 169-170.

fluid being particularly vigorous, one dreams of being in a big fire and of being burned " (*d*). The different states of the human body, its strength and weakness, increase and decrease, are caused by the Yin and Yang fluids, the same forces as those active throughout nature. Why does the Yang fluid evoke dreams of fire and the Yin fluid dreams of water? Because both consist of these elements.

The *Su-wên* claims that with excessive Yang the body becomes hot without, however, being able to perspire, whereas with excessive Yin it becomes cold and perspires (*e*). What does that mean else but that Yang stands for heat and dryness, and Yin for cold and dampness?

Huai-nan-tse makes of Yin and Yang directly water and fire, stating that from the hot Yang fluid comes fire and the essence of fire becomes the sun, and the cold Yin fluid turns into water, and the essence of water forms the moon (*f*). And further he says : " The Yang fluid is fire and the Yin fluid water " (*g*). Similarly, *Kuan Tse-yang* asserts that the sun is the heavenly Yang, and fire the Yang on earth; and we may safely continue saying that moon is the heavenly Yin, and water the Yin on earth.

Wang Ch'ung denominates Yin and Yang the cold and the hot fluids (*h*), describing Yang as fire (*i*) and Yin as clouds or rain, i.e., water (*k*).

(*d*) *Lieh-tse* III., 5 r. 周 穆 王 篇。一 體 之 盈 虛 消 息 皆 通 於 天 地 應 於 物 類 故 陰 氣 壯 則 夢 涉 大 水 而 恐 懼 陽 氣 壯 則 夢 涉 大 火 而 燔 炳. The *Su-wên* has this same passage with almost identical words.

(*e*) *Su-wên*: 陽 勝 則 身 熱 . . . . 汗 不 出 . . . . 陰 勝 則 身 寒 汗 出.

(*f*) Cf. p. 38.

(*g*) *Huai-nan-tse* III., 7 v. 天 文 訓。陽 氣 爲 火 陰 氣 爲 水.

(*h*) *Lun Hêng* I., 111.

(*i*) *Eod.* I., 246, 294.   (*k*) *Eod.* I., 294, 284; II., 345.

Starting from the proposition that Yang is fire and Yin water, we obtain a series of attributes of these elements which are also ascribed to Yin and Yang.

Yang (fire) accordingly is *hot, dry, bright,* anxious to *expand,* tending *upwards* or *outwards,* is *pure* and *light.* Yin (water), on the other side, is *cold, moist, dark,* eager to *contract,* tending *downwards* or *inwards,* is *turbid* and *heavy.*

Lieh-tse narrates of a fabulous country, *Ku-mang,* where the Yin and the Yang fluid do not mix, and consequently heat and cold are not distinguished (*l*). *Tse-hua-tse* makes the Yin pole in the north produce cold, from which springs water, and the Yang pole in the south produce heat, whence comes fire (*m*). We learned already that Yin and Yang are held to be the causes of droughts and inundations, and are made responsible for the dryness and perspiration of the human body (*n*). *Huai-nan-tse* says that when Yin or water prevails in summer it is damp, and when winter is swayed by Yang or fire it is dry (*o*). *Kuang-ch'êng-tse* calls the seat of the most perfect Yang the Great Brightness above, and the seat of the most perfect Yin the Gate of Darkness.

The Yang fluid has the tendency to extend, to open and to escape upwards or outwards. The bearing of the Yin is just the reverse; it contracts and concentrates itself downwards or towards the centre. Even speaking and

---

(*l*) *Lieh-tse* III., 5 v. 周穆王篇。名古莽之國陰陽之氣所不交故寒暑無辨.

(*m*) *Tse-hua-tse.* 子華子。北方陰極而生寒寒生水南方陽極而生熱熱生火.

(*n*) Cf. pp. 170 and 173.

(*o*) *Huai-nan-tse* III., 7 v. 天文訓。水勝故夏至濕火勝故冬至燥.

silence are supposed to be brought about by Yin and Yang. *Kuei-ku-tse* (fourth century B.C.) says : " Expanding is equivalent to opening, to speaking and to Yang. Contracting is the same as closing, becoming silent and Yin " (p); and *Wên-tse* professes that the sage closes his mouth with Yin and opens it with Yang (q).

The fullest enumeration of these qualities is to be found in *Huai-nan-tse* : " The principle of heaven is round, that of earth is square. The square governs *darkness*, the round *brightness*. The bright *exhales* the fluid, therefore *fire* is called the *external appearance*. The dark *contracts* the fluid, therefore *water* is termed the *internal appearance*. That which exhales the fluid, pours out, that which contracts it, breeds. Thus the Yang pours out, and the Yin breeds " (r). These arguments are not very logical. The qualities alleged by Huai-nan-tse belong to the Yin and Yang in a quite natural way, but it is impossible to derive them one from another by force, as he does. As regards the production of all organisms by the dual forces of nature one may compare what has been said above (p. 55).

In the cosmological theories we saw how *Lieh-tse* and *Huai-nan-tse* made the *pure* and *light* Yang substances rise and form heaven above, while they made the *turbid* and *heavy* Yin particles sink down and produce earth. Fire always will rise up, and water sink down.

(p) *Kuei-ku-tse*, chap. 1, p. 1 v. 捭闔篇。捭之者開也言也陽也闔之者閉也默也陰也.

(q) *Wên-tse* III., 9 r. 守弱篇。聖人與陰俱閉與陽俱開.

(r) *Huai-nan-tse* III., 1 v. 天文訓。天道曰圓地道曰方方者主幽圓者主明明者吐氣者也是故火曰外景幽者含氣者也是故水曰內景吐氣者施含氣者化是故陽施陰化.

IV. YIN AND YANG THE SUBSTANCES OF HEAVEN AND EARTH, THE SUN AND THE MOON.

The universe was evolved from the primogenial elements Yin and Yang, the fiery ether becoming heaven and the moist fogs being condensed into earth. Consequently, as has been shown more in detail in Book I., p. 55, Yin and Yang are the substances of which heaven and earth consist. At the same time they are the elements from which the sun and the moon were shaped. The sun is Yang, the moon Yin (s).

" The principle of heaven and earth," says *Lieh-tse*, " is either Yin or Yang " (t). *Kuei-ku-tse* inverts this saying : " Heaven and earth are the principles of Yin and Yang " (u). The *Su-wên* states : " Heaven and earth are regarded as Yin and Yang " (x). Generally, Yin and Yang are all but identified with heaven and earth, and consequently the qualities which, strictly speaking, only belong to heaven and earth, and, applied to Yin and Yang, become partly contradictory, are nevertheless ascribed to both. Yang is considered to be *round, moved, masculine* and *fecundating*, because heaven is, and Yin passes as *square, calm, feminine* and *breeding*, because earth possesses these attributes. It goes without saying that the fiery Yang element can as little be round as the moist Yin element square; and it is senseless to declare Yin to be calm and motionless, since it has motion, which particularly manifests itself in producing the weather and the seasons, but Chinese scholars seem never to have entertained such doubts.

(s) *Vid.* above, pp. 83 and 89.

(t) *Lieh-tse* I., 3 v. 天 瑞 篇。天 地 之 道 非 陰 則 陽.

(u) *Kuei-ku-tse*, chap. 1, p. 2 r. 捭 闔 篇。天 地 陰 陽 之 道.

(x) *Su-wên* : 以 天 地 爲 之 陰 陽.

Chang Hêng states : " Heaven has its substance in Yang, therefore it is round and thereby moves. Earth has its substance in Yin, therefore it is flat and thereby motionless. The moved pours out and fecundates, the unmoved contracts and breeds " (*y*). If heaven is round and moved, because it consists of the Yang fluid, then this must be round and moved as well, and equally the Yin must be flat and unmoved. *Kuan-tse* directly asserts that " Yin is motionless " (*z*).

We read in the *Po-hu-t'ung* : " The Yang precedes and the Yin follows, the male acts and the female follows " (*a*). This means to say that the Yang is male and active, the Yin female and passive. Such a characterisation of the Yin and Yang is less objectionable. The idea to think of the warm sunshine as the genitor, and of the humidity of earth as the mother of all plants, is not so incongruous. The importance of seed was not yet known to the Chinese.

How it is possible that the moon consists of the Yin fluid, whereas the entire heaven is Yang, and how the fire on earth can be Yang, although earth itself belongs to the Yin element, we shall see later.

V. The Alternation of the Yin and Yang during the Seasons and According to the Points of the Compass.

The dual forces of nature are not immutable, but subject to a permanent change—sometimes the one prevails, sometimes the other. There is a regular growing and declining, both, as it were, fight for supremacy. The *Liki* speaks of

---

(*y*) *Chang Hêng* : 天 體 於 陽 故 圓 以 動 地 體 於 陰 故 平 以 靜 動 以 行 施 靜 以 合 化 煙 鬱 構 精 時 育 庶 類.

(*z*) *Kuan-tse* XIII., 3 v. 心 術 篇。陰 者 靜.

(*a*) *Po-hu-t'ung* : 陽 唱 陰 和 男 行 女 隨 也.

this antagonism in the second summer and the second winter months (*b*). As soon as one fluid has reached its climax, there is a reverse, and the other begins to grow until it obtains predominance, to be overthrown again in its turn. This is what *Wên-tse* has in mind when he says : " As soon as the Yang fluid has attained its highest development, there comes a reverse, and the Yin takes its place, and no sooner has the Yin fluid reached its acme, than a reverse sets in and the Yang again supplants it " (*c*). This climax for the Yang fluid is the *summer solstice*, and for the Yin the *winter solstice*. The change of the two fluids is connected with the seasons, and it is just the seasons that are produced by them. Spring and summer are more filled with the warm Yang fluid, autumn and winter with the cool Yin fluid. Therefore, according to the *Liki*, at the spring and summer sacrifices the Yang usages, and at the autumn and winter sacrifices the Yin rites were observed (*d*).

Kuan-tse describes how, by the movement of the Yin and Yang, the seasons are produced : " In spring the Yang fluid begins rising, and all products originate. In summer the Yang fluid ceases rising, and meanwhile all products grow. In autumn the Yin fluid begins descending, and the products are harvested, and in winter this descending of the Yin fluid reaches its limit, and all products are housed " (*e*). We have to conceive the Yang fluid as light, warmed air, and the Yin as heavy, atmospheric vapours.

(*b*) *Liki* : 月令。仲夏之月日長至陰陽爭死生分。仲冬之月日短至陰陽爭諸生蕩.

(*c*) *Wên-tse* VI., 30 r. 上德篇。陽氣盛變爲陰陰氣盛變爲陽.

(*d*) *Liki* II., 249. 祭統。礿禘陽義也嘗烝陰義也.

(*e*) *Kuan-tse* XX., 2 v. 形勢解。春者陽氣始上故萬物生夏者陽氣畢上故萬物長秋者陰氣始下故萬物收冬者陰氣畢下故萬物藏.

At the *winter solstice* the " Bushel " points direct north, the Yin fluid has reached its climax, and the Yang fluid begins to grow. The Yin fluid advances northward as far as the north pole, and beneath this descends to the lower world ; therefore one may not dig up the soil or bore wells (for the soil is frozen). The products are well stored away, and insects creep into their holes to hibernate. The winter solstice is attended by water, which in the eleventh month reaches its highest level. Then reigns the Yin fluid, and we have moisture (rain and snow). The gnomon, eight feet long, has a shadow of thirteen feet at noon. At the *summer solstice* the Bushel points direct south, the Yang fluid has reached its cynosure, and the Yin fluid starts growing. Progressing southward the former arrives at the south pole, where it rises up to the " red heaven." Therefore one does not level hills then, wishing to build a house (on the hills it is cooler than below). Plants grow luxuriantly, and the various kinds of grain yield abundant crops. The summer solstice is attended by fire, which in the fifth month reaches its highest level. Then the Yang fluid holds sway, and we have dryness. The gnomon at noon shows a shadow only one foot five inches long (*f*).

With the object of distinguishing between the quality of the two elements at the commencement and the close of their development, the Yang element in spring is

---

(*f*) *Huai-nan-tse* III., 7 v. 天文訓。冬至則斗北中繩陰氣極陽氣萌 .... 夏至則斗南中繩陽氣極陰氣萌 .... 陰氣極則北至北極下至黃泉故不可以鑿地穿井萬物閉藏蟄蟲首穴 .... 陽氣極則南至南極上至朱天故不可以夷丘上屋萬物蕃息五穀兆長 .... 日冬至則水從之日夏至則火從之故五月火正而水漏十一月水正而陰勝 .... 八尺之修日中而景丈尺 .... 八尺之景修徑尺五寸.

denominated *Shao-yang*, " scanty Yang," in summer *T'ai-yang*, " abundant Yang," and the Yin in autumn is called *Shao-yin*, " scanty Yin," and in winter *T'ai-yin*, " abundant Yin." Only 45 days after the winter solstice the Yang is said to begin to rise and the Yin to descend somewhat; 45 days after the summer solstice it is reversed : the Yin then ascends and the Yang descends.

When in the second month of the year 134 B.C. the capital was visited by a violent hail shower, *Tung Chung-shu*, upon being consulted about it, gave as a reason that the Yin fluid had overwhelmed the Yang fluid, and on this occasion discoursed on the co-operation of the two forces as follows (*g*) : " The fluid of heaven and earth consists half of Yang and half of Yin. The harmonious fluid circulates day and night without ceasing. When the Yang force rules, the harmonious fluid is entirely Yang. So it is in the month with the sign *sse*, which therefore is connoted as Chêng-yang, ' right Yang month ' (*h*). When

---

(*g*) *Tung Chung-shu chi* in *T'u-shu chi-ch'êng.* 乾 象 典 chap. 15,

陰 陽 部 總 論 I., 11 r. 董 仲 舒 集。雨 雹 對。天 地 之 氣
陰 陽 相 半 和 氣 周 廻 朝 夕 不 息 陽 德 用 事 則 和 氣
皆 陽 建 巳 之 月 是 也 故 謂 之 正 陽 之 月 陰 德 用 事
則 和 氣 皆 陰 建 亥 之 月 是 也 故 謂 之 正 陰 之 月 十
月 陰 雖 用 事 而 陰 不 孤 立 此 月 純 陰 疑 於 無 陽 故
謂 之 陽 月 詩 人 所 謂 日 月 陽 止 者 也 四 月 陽 雖 用
事 而 陽 不 獨 存 此 月 純 陽 疑 於 無 陰 故 亦 謂 之 陰
月 自 十 月 已 後 陽 氣 始 生 於 地 下 漸 冉 流 散 故 言
息 也 陰 氣 轉 收 故 言 消 也 日 夜 滋 生 遂 至 四 月 純
陽 用 事 自 四 月 已 後 陰 氣 始 生 於 天 上 漸 冉 流 散
故 云 息 也 陽 氣 轉 收 故 言 消 也 日 夜 滋 生 遂 至 十
月 純 陰 用 事 二 月 八 月 陰 陽 正 等 無 多 少 也·

(*h*) The fourth month, called the " right Yang month," and at the same time the Yin month.

the Yin force predominates, the harmonious fluid is all Yin. This is the case in the month with the sign *hai*, which therefore bears the name Chêng-yin, 'right Yin month '" (*i*).

" Although in the tenth month Yin reigns supreme, yet it is not quite alone. This month possesses pure Yin, but one doubts whether there is no Yang at all, and therefore calls it the Yang month. That is what the poet of the Shiking tried to express in the line : ' the sun and the moon are already in the Yang month.' Even though in the fourth month the Yang fluid is paramount, yet it is not alone either. This month has pure Yang, but one doubts that there should be no Yin left at all, hence one calls it ' the Yin month.'

" After the tenth month the Yang fluid begins growing on earth and gradually spreads, therefore one speaks of an increase. The Yin fluid in turn shrinks, and one speaks of a decrease. The growing goes on by day and night, until in the fourth month pure Yang prevails. From the fourth month forward the Yin fluid begins growing in heaven, gradually expanding, which is called increase. Meanwhile the Yang shrinks, which is termed decrease. The growing continues day and night, until in the tenth month pure Yin is all powerful. In the second and eighth months Yin and Yang are perfectly balanced, there being no plus and no minus on either side."

Neither of the two fluids ever disappears completely; even when the other has reached its greatest expansion, there is still a germ left from which it grows again. This is shown in the modern Yin-yang pictures, the white Yang spiral having a black spot, the Yin embryo, and the black Yin ornament a white spot representing the Yang embryo. During six months each fluid expands, and during six

---

(*i*) The tenth month, called the " right Yin month " and the Yang month.

months it shrinks. From the winter solstice in the eleventh month the Yang fluid begins to spread from earth, until it has displaced the Yin fluid almost completely, filling all heaven. With the summer solstice the growing of the Yin sets in, starting from heaven and descending on earth. Both fluids have the same quantities in spring and autumn, in the second and eighth months.

Yin and Yang at various times move up and down, expand and contract. Aside from this they are supposed to be localised in different quarters, nor do they stay there permanently, but they move round the entire horizon sideways. The South is regarded as the seat of the Yang element, and the North of the Yin. With a view to corresponding to the Yang, the emperor chooses his seat, so that he looks southward (*k*). The longest day is worshipped in the southern part of the city, the sun being considered the representative of the Yang fluid (*l*). When the ruler offers sacrifice to the Soil, which is governed by the Yin fluid, he also faces the South, but he stands at the northern wall to conform to the Yin (*m*). Then the tablet of the Soil on the altar was placed with the front to the North. The reason for these arrangements is easy to see: in the South there is the greatest heat, ergo the main seat of the Yang must be there; in the North there is the greatest cold, which can only be attributed to the Yin.

That the Yang fluid, however, is not stationary in the South, but travels around the horizon, we could infer already from those texts in which the rotation of the " Bushel " is mentioned, which points to the direction in

---

(*k*) *Liki* I., 423. 郊 特 牲。君 之 南 鄉 答 陽 之 義 也.

(*l*) *Liki* I., 427, *eod.* 大 報 天 而 主 日 也 兆 於 南 郊 就 陽 位 也.

(*m*) *Liki* I., 424, *eod.* 社 祭 土 而 主 陰 氣 也 君 南 鄉 於 北 牖 下 答 陰 之 義 也.

which the Yang is staying at a given time (*n*). We read in the *Liki* that at the east side of the courtyard dogs were cooked to propitiate the Yang fluid, because there it came out first in spring (*o*). With this statement an utterance of *Huai-nan-tse* to the effect that the Yang originates in the North, and the Yin in the South (*p*), seems to be at variance. However, Huai-nan-tse has the embryonic state of the two elements in view, when they do not yet manifest themselves externally. The Yang fluid is produced as early as the eleventh month in the North, but one does not perceive its working before spring, when it has advanced to the East. In a similar way the Yin fluid comes forth in the fifth month in the South, but displays its activity only in autumn and in the West. In accordance with this theory the two fluids would always be united and turn in the same direction. The view of *Tung Chung-shu* differs in that he makes both gyrate round the horizon, but in opposite directions. The Yang fluid issues in the N.E., moves thence to the S., where it has its seat, and then farther on to the W. and the N., where it disappears and rests. When it reaches the south pole there is great heat. The Yin fluid comes out in the S.E., moves on to the N., where it has its seat, and farther to the W. and the S., where it vanishes and hides. When it reaches the north pole, great cold prevails and it freezes. According to Tung Chung-shu, whose ideas, however, do not meet with universal approval, the Yang adheres to matter, whereas the Yin fills the empty space (*q*).

(*n*) *Vid.* p. 175.

(*o*) *Liki* II., 443. 鄉 飲。烹 狗 於 東 方 祖 陽 氣 之 發 於 東 方 也.

(*p*) *Huai-nan-tse* III., 10 r. 天 文 訓。陽 生 於 子 陰 生 於 午.

(*q*) *Ch'un-ch'iu fan-lu* XI., 12 r. 陰 陽 位。陽 氣 始 出 東 北 而 南 行 就 其 位 也 西 轉 而 北 入 藏 其 休 也 陰 氣 始

VI. Yin and Yang cause the Weather.

As the seasons so weather conditions depend on the dual forces Yin and Yang. One is agreed on the fact that the various meteorological phenomena are effected by Yin and Yang, but opinions differ with regard to the explanation of the diverse processes, although the fundamental conceptions are the same.

1. *Wind.*

The mythologising line of thought conceives of wind as being the angry breath of heaven (*Huai-nan-tse*), or a sighing (*Tung Chung-shu*), or the commanding voice of heaven and earth. According to the *Su-wên* it is merely the breath of the Yang. The *Ta-tai-li* maintains that wind as well as thunder, lightning, fog, and rain are produced by the interaction of Yin and Yang, viz., through deflection, the fluids striving asunder. *Wang Ch'ung*, who mentions the notion of wind as a commanding voice, himself regards it as air.

2. *Thunder and Lightning.*

This phenomenon is evoked by the intermingling of Yin and Yang, heaven and earth being strongly compressed. It is fire in water (*Chuang-tse*). At any rate, both elements are closely united and joined together. The mere union is said to produce thunder, the joggling lightning (*Ta-tai-li*). Thunder is believed to be the mutual excitation of the fluids, lightning their shooting to and fro (*Huai-nan-tse*).

出 東 南 北 行 亦 就 其 位 也 西 轉 而 南 入 屏 其 伏 也
是 故 陽 以 南 方 爲 位 以 北 方 爲 休 陰 以 北 方 爲 位
以 南 方 爲 休 陽 至 其 位 而 大 暑 熱 陰 至 其 位 而 大
寒 凍 ‥‥ 陽 出 實 入 實 陰 出 空 入 空.

Tung Chung-shu reduces thunder to the violent clashing of
the fluids and lightning to the light flashing up at this
collision. According to *Wang Ch'ung* thunder is nothing
else than the exploding Yang fluid. In the midst of
summer the fiery element rules, but the moist one attempts
to supersede it. This leads to frictions and explosions. A
very similar explosion takes place when a basin full of water
is thrown into a fire.

3. *Clouds, Fog, Rain, and Dew.*

Fog is the confusion and medley of the two elements
(*Ta-tai-li, Huai-nan-tse*), a notion easily derived from the
observation of clouds, fogs and nebular masses wildly
rolling and floating. On the other hand, rain is presumed
to be the harmonious union of Yin and Yang (*Ta-tai-li*),
or the harmonious fluid keeping earth together (*Huai-nan-
tse*). The *Su-wên*, from its medical viewpoint, declares
rain to be the " perspiration of Yang." Fogs are said to
rise, when the air is thin below, and rain, when it is thin
above (*Tung Chung-shu*). *Wang Ch'ung* considers clouds,
fog, rain, and dew as so many manifestations of the same
Yin principle. Water rises from earth as vapour, is condensed to clouds in the sky, and these change again into
rain and dew, which again fall down on earth.

4. *Rain, Dew, Frost (Ice), and Snow.*

When the Yang fluid reigns, it spreads and becomes
rain and dew; when the Yin fluid proves victorious, it
becomes congealed and turns into frost and snow (*Ta-tai-li,
Huai-nan-tse*). Snow is rain frozen in the upper regions of
the atmosphere, ice and hail freeze in the cooler, lower
strata, the upper being still warm (*Tung Chung-shu*). In
summer, through the influence of the heat, fogs and clouds
become rain and dew, in winter, through cold, snow and
ice (*Wang Ch'ung*).

5. *Hail and Sleet.*

Hail and sleet are sometimes regarded as something quite different from snow and ice. Hail is said to be a particular Yang fluid, and sleet a particular Yin fluid (*Ta-tai-li* and *Huai-nan-tse*). A reason for this distinction is not apparent (r).

VII. YIN AND YANG THE PRIMARY SUBSTANCES OF THE FIVE ELEMENTS.

By the differentiation of the two primary substances, moreover the Five Elements : metal, wood, water, fire, and earth are evolved. How the Chinese imagined this process in particular we shall see later, when speaking about the Five Elements. It is the general opinion that these elements are nothing but special modifications of Yin and Yang, proceeding from the concentration, the diffusion and mixture of these substances. We read especially in later writers a great deal about Yang in Yang, Yang in Yin, Yin in Yang, etc. Germs of this mode of viewing things are already to be found in ancient times. Thus *Kuan-yin-tse* says that the crane is a Yang bird, but walking about in Yin (s), which, of course, means water. Usually birds are classed as belonging to the Yang element. *Kuan-tse* states that pearls are Yang in Yin, and therefore overcome fire. Jade is Yin in Yin, and therefore vanquishes water. Presumably Kuan-tse means to say that pearls belong to the Yin element, for they come from water, but their splendour is Yang-like. Jade, however, by its mild

---

(r) *Su-wên* in *T'u-shu chi-ch'êng* 乾 象 典 chap. 17, 陰 陽 部 雜 錄 I, 8; *Ta-tai-li* 曾 子 天 圓; *Giles, Chuang-tse,* p. 353; *Huai-nan-tse* III., 2, r. 天 文 訓; *Tung Chiao-hsi chi* 雨 雹 對; *Lun Hêng,* I., 277, 294, 295; II., 173, 357.

(s) *Hsiang-hao-ching* 相 鶴 經.

brilliancy, seems to be perfect Yin, comparable to the light of the moon, which, as we know, passes as Yin.

Whereas, according to the common view, the Five Elements as a matter of fact are identical with Yin and Yang, *Tung Chung-shu* wishes to draw a sharp line between the two. Yin and Yang, he says, develop simultaneously with the Five Elements, co-operate with them and assist them, but are not the same. " The scanty Yang develops together with wood, and helps the growing in spring. The abundant Yang develops along with fire, and helps the ripening in summer. The scanty Yin develops along with metal, and helps the completion in autumn; and the abundant Yin develops along with water, and helps the storing away in winter " (t). Accordingly one might look upon the elements perhaps as the ever-changing phenomena, now growing, now decaying, of the eternal, undestructible primary substances.

VIII. Yin and Yang as Correlates.

By analogy one has transferred the words Yin and Yang also on things, qualities or notions which have some reference to the dual forces, or possess similar qualities. Correctly speaking, one ought to say merely that two things bear a similar relation to one another as Yin does to Yang, but, as so often is the case, this mere similarity has been transformed into complete equality, and the Chinese do not hesitate to connote things straightway as Yin and Yang. Needless to say that between two such notions there must be a contrast, as always exists between Yin and Yang, which, in all their manifestations, are regarded as opposite.

(t) *Ch'un-ch'iu fan-lu* XI., 8. 天辨在人。少陽因木而起助春之生也太陽因火而起助夏之養也少陰因金而起助秋之成也太陰因水而起助冬之藏也.

In a great many cases the reason for transferring the categories Yin and Yang on two correlate notions is easy of apprehension. In our oldest sources already they consider as Yin and Yang : *drought and inundation, summer and winter, upper and lower world, heights and depths, life and death, advancing and retreating, benevolence and justice, generosity and egoism, archery matches and marriages.*

Drought and inundation, summer. and winter are the effects of fire and water, heat and cold, ergo of Yin and Yang. The upper world is the region of the bright element, the lower world of the dark one. The Yang tends upwards, the Yin sinks down, therefore heights and things above are Yang, depths and things below are Yin. Life is motion like the active Yang principle, death is a standstill and a repose like the passive Yin. Advancing corresponds to the spreading and the expansion of the Yang, retreating to the contraction of the Yin. Benevolence is likened to warmth, and justice to coolness. A generous man is largehearted and in this respect comparable to the Yang fluid, the egoist on the other side thinks only of himself and is narrow-minded, his heart, so to speak, shrinks together like the Yin. An archery match, as we explained above, is something virile, therefore Yang; marriage is held to be a festivity primarily concerning women, therefore something feminine = Yin.

Heaven, high and imposing, overarches low earth. These purely physical qualities have been conceived in a figurative sense, as we saw, and in the Yiking commentary already heaven is thought of as *noble*, and earth as *base* (*u*). All the attributes of heaven and earth then simply are transferred upon their substances, Yin and Yang, and so Yang is regarded as *noble*, and Yin as *common*. This

---

(*u*) Cf. p. 71.

contrast : *noble—common, exalted—base*, by a further generalisation seems to have led to the opposition of *good* and *bad*. Everything good, beautiful, agreeable is Yang, everything bad, wicked, and disagreeable, Yin. This is a basic notion which gave rise to many new pairs of Yin and Yang, e.g., *left and right, anterior and posterior.* The left is the seat of honour for men, the right for women, therefore naturally left = Yang and right = Yin (x). Similarly, the front seat is generally considered preferable to a place behind.

Further contrasts are : *Virtue—vice, order—confusion, reward—punishment, cheerfulness—anger, joy—sadness, wealth—poverty. Kuei-ku-tse* adduces as belonging to Yang : *growth, life, peace, joy, wealth, honour and rank, celebrity, love, profit, obtaining one's wishes*, and as partaking of Yin : *death, sorrow, distress, poverty, misery, bitterness, ignominy, rejection, loss, not obtaining one's wishes, injury, punishment, decapitation* (y).

Similar considerations are probably responsible for the assignment of a notion to either class. One discovered some similarities with qualities of the Yin and Yang fluids or of heaven and earth, or had recourse to good and bad as a principle of division. Of course, it is not always possible to trace back the Chinese line of reasoning.

Pursuant to the *Liki, drinking* is conceived as Yang, and *eating* as Yin (z), the *head* of a victim as Yang, and

---

(x) *Liki* I., 479. 內 則。凡 男 拜 尚 左 手。注. 左 陽 也。凡 女 拜 尚 右 手。注. 右 陰 也.

(y) *Kuei-ku-tse,* chap. 1, p. 1 v. 捭 闔 篇 故 言 長 生 安 樂 富 貴 尊 榮 顯 名 愛 好 財 利 得 意 喜 欲 爲 陽 曰 始 故 言 死 憂 患 貧 賤 苦 辱 棄 損 亡 利 失 意 有 害 刑 戮 誅 罰 爲 陰 曰 終.

(z) *Liki* I., 418. 郊 特 牲。凡 飲 養 陽 氣 也 凡 食 養 陰 氣 也.

the *lungs* as Yin (*a*), *music* as Yang and *rites* as Yin (*b*). Food is more substantial and material than beverage, therefore food is probably placed on a level with the coarser Yin fluid, while beverage is likened to the finer Yang fluid. The head as the uppermost and most important part of the body is thought of as Yang, but wherefore must the lungs be Yin? A commentator contends that the lungs correspond to the element metal, which is a product of Yin. Music is said to be Yang, for enlarging and expanding the heart like the Yang principle, and rites to be Yin, because they check and restrain as the Yin principle gathers and preserves.

Bitter and *sweet* are supposed to be Yang, *sour* and *acrid* to be Yin (*c*). That sweet is considered Yang, and sour Yin can be understood, but why is bitter Yang and acrid Yin?

IX. Yin and Yang in Animals and Man.

All organisms of the vegetable and animal kingdom, the so-called "ten thousand things," being produced by the two primary elements, it is needless to say that animals and man must be so too. Accordingly we read in *Lü Pu-wei* : "Man and animals are the transformations of Yin and Yang, being produced by the action of the two forces in nature" (*d*). This natural viewpoint agreeing best with the Yin-yang theory, however, is abandoned by many

---

(*e*) *Ta-tai-li*,　郊 特 牲。祭 黍 稷 加 肺 祭 齊 加 明 水 報 陰 也 取 膟 膋 燔 燎 升 首 報 陽 也.

(*b*) *Liki* I., 420, *eod.* 樂 由 陽 來 者 也 禮 由 陰 作 者 也.

(*c*) *Su-wên.*

(*d*) *Lü-shih ch'un-ch'iu* XX., 8 r. 知 分 篇。凡 人 物 者 陰 陽 之 化 也 陰 陽 者 造 乎 天 而 成 者 也. It is doubtful, however, whether here 人 物 is to be taken as "man and animals" or as "human beings" only.

writers, who establish different laws for the different classes of living beings.

The haired and feathered creatures, i.e., animals and birds are said to be generated by the Yang fluid, the scaly and shell-covered, i.e., crustaceans and fish, by the Yin fluid, and only in man, the naked creature, the essences of Yin and Yang are blended (*e*). Since fish live in water, the Yin element, the idea to think them engendered by this element alone is not unnatural. Then for animals and birds remains the light Yang element, air. Less intelligible is the view of the *K'ung-tse chia-yü* that birds and fish are produced by Yin, but belong to Yang, and therefore are born from eggs (*f*). This source likewise assumes for man the co-operation of Yin and Yang.

Furthermore the *K'ung-tse chia-yü* states that female animals are governed by the extreme Yin and male animals by the extreme Yang (*g*). Consequently a female bird would be produced by Yin, and also be governed by it, but belong to Yang nevertheless, and conversely a male bird would be produced by Yin, but belong to Yang, and also be governed by it. It is impossible to form a clear conception of what that means. These are merely formalistic deductions without much sense.

With men a further distinction is made between the *spirit* and the *vital force*, the former being thought of as Yang essence and the latter as Yin (*h*). The *Liki* describes

---

(*e*) *Ta-tai-li,* 曾 子 天 圓。毛 羽 之 蟲 陽 氣 之 所 生 也 . . . . 介 鱗 之 蟲 陰 氣 之 所 生 也 唯 人 爲 倮 匈 而 後 生 也 陰 陽 之 精 也.

(*f*) 孔 子 家 語 VI., 4 r. 執 轡。鳥 魚 生 陰 而 屬 於 陽 故 皆 卵 生.

(*g*) *Loc. cit.* VI., 4 v. 至 陰 主 牝 至 陽 主 牡.

(*h*) *Ta-tai-li* 曾 子 天 圓. 陽 之 精 氣 曰 神 陰 之 精 氣 曰 靈.

man, the acme of creation, as the outgrowth of the connection of Yin and Yang, the union of ghost and spirit,
the finest essence of the Five Elements (*i*). To produce
this acme of creation Yin and Yang are requisite by any
means, the former producing the lower, the latter the
higher mental faculties. For the creation of animals one
primary element eventually is sufficient, a view, it is true,
in contradiction to the theory of the entire universe consisting of Yin and Yang. One wished to exalt man,
decrying all other creatures, an attempt in which western
philosophers have indulged likewise.

X. YIN AND YANG IN CULT.

The doctrine of Yin and Yang plays an important part
in the intellectual life of the Chinese. We meet with traces
of it in the older cult and in various sciences or pseudo-
sciences, which partly are based on this theory.

We saw already that they used to sacrifice a dog to the
Yang fluid in the east, because there the Yang first makes
its appearance. Generally speaking, it seems as if the two
fluids were not so much venerated directly, but more in
their manifestations, heaven and earth, or the sun and the
moon, which are less abstract and therefore more accessible
to the religious mind. The sacrifices offered to these were
eo ipso considered as destined for their substances Yin and

(*i*) *Liki* I., 381. 禮運。故人者其天地之德陰陽之交鬼
神之會五行之秀氣也. The commentator *Ch'ên* observes that
the *breath*, the *arteries*, the *head*, and the *upper part of the body* are
Yang, while the *blood*, the *body*, the *feet*, and the *lower part of the body*
are Yin. Similarly the *speaking* of the mouth, the *seeing* of the eye,
and the *expiration* of the nose are effects of the Yang; the *silence* of
the mouth, however, the *non-seeing* of the eye, and the *inpiration* of the
nose are caused by the Yin. Speaking of two fluids, the spirit is the
activity of the Yang, and the ghost the activity of the Yin; but considering both as one fluid, which is more correct, the spirit would
represent the Yang or the expansion of this fluid, and the ghost the Yin
or the contraction of this fluid.

Yang. The sun on the longest day of the year was worshipped in the southern part of the city, because the Yang has its seat there. The tablet for the Soil on the altar was turned to the north, the north side corresponding to Yin, by which the Soil is filled. The custom of the sovereign taking his seat, so that it faces the south, was also established out of regard for the Yang fluid residing in the south (*k*).

The prince was regarded as the representative of the Yang, the princess as representative of the Yin. Since the sun, the Yang orb, rises in the east, and the moon, the Yin orb, in the west, at the sacrifices offered to these two the prince takes his place on the eastern steps of the palace, and the princess in her western apartment. The prince sacrifices to the sun from a vessel shaped like an ox, corresponding to the Yin, turned westward, because the sun moves toward the west. The princess offers a libation to the moon from a vessel ornamented with thunder-clouds corresponding to the Yang, and turns to the east, because the moon takes this course (*l*).

At the spring and summer sacrifices the Yang rites, at the autumn and winter sacrifices the Yin rites used to be observed, because the first two seasons were dominated by the Yang fluid, the latter by the Yin fluid. We are not told in what these rites consisted, presumably in some actions which had some analogies with the dual forces. The *Liki* states in a general way of all rites that in their nature they equal heaven and earth, imitate the seasons and follow the Yin and Yang (*m*).

(*k*) Cf. p. 182.

(*l*) *Liki* I., 410. 禮器。君在阼夫人在房大.明生於東月生於西此陰陽之分夫婦之位也君西酌犧象夫人東酌罍尊.

(*m*) *Liki* II., 465.

Between the operation of the two fluids and the actions of the head of the State, the emperor, the empress, the ministers, and the sages, there are close connections, and they may influence one another. This must be the meaning of several passages in the classical texts referring to the regulation of the Yin and Yang by the rulers. Actions with a Yang character are believed to remove an excess of the Yin fluid, and in the same manner Yin actions may be taken advantage of to repress the Yang fluid. So it is said by *Wên-tse* that the emperors *Shên-nung* and *Huang-ti* regulated the seasons and harmonised the Yin and Yang (*n*).

The Son of Heaven, according to the *Liki*, has to order the working of the Yang principles, and the empress to do the same for the Yin (*o*). If, e.g., the male doctrines were not sufficiently observed, or if the Yang principles did not receive due attention, this might lead to an eclipse of the sun, which is a suppression of the Yang fluid by the Yin. Then the Son of Heaven would dress in white and take measures against the officials interfering with the Yang principles. When female submissiveness had not been practised and the Yin principles were violated, perhaps an eclipse of the moon might be seen in heaven, the overwhelming of the Yin by the Yang. Then the empress would come forward, as the representative of the female Yin principle, putting on white clothes likewise and removing the impediments which her attendants might have placed in the way of the Yin principles. Thus the emperor and his consort worked conjointly like the sun and the moon or ‚Yin and Yang (*p*).

(*n*) *Wên-tse* XII., 1 r. 上 禮 篇。神 農 黃 帝 覈 領 天 下 紀 綱 四 時 和 調 陰 陽.

(*o*) *Liki* II., 433. 昏 義。天 子 理 陽 道 后 治 陰 德.

(*p*) *Liki* II., 433. 昏 義。是 故 男 敎 不 修 陽 事 不 得 適 見 於 天 日 爲 之 食 婦 順 不 修 陰 事 不 得 適 見 於 天

The higher appreciation of the nobler Yang principle in comparison with the less esteemed Yin becomes evident by the endeavour to conform to the Yang and to neglect or disregard the Yin in some instances. When the Sage values the Yang, says *Wên-tse*, the empire is in harmony, but when he favours the Yin, the empire will go to ruin (q). The same is true of princes : As long as they hold the Yang principle in high esteem, everything grows and flourishes, but when they turn to the Yin principle, the State will perish (r). Yet under certain conditions a prince or a sage may also imitate the Yin principle. The people will gladly submit to his sway, if he is like the Yang in winter and the Yin in summer (s), i.e., like the warm sunshine during the cold and like coolness at a time of great heat.

XI. Yin and Yang in Divination.

It is a widespread view of Chinese scholars shared by many foreigners that the *Yiking*, the most important work for divination with the stalks of milfoil, is our oldest source for the Yin-yang theory. However, in the text of the

---

月爲之食是故日食則天子素服而修六官之職蕩天下之陽事月食則后素服而修六宮之職蕩天下之陰事故天子之與后猶日之與月陰之與陽相須而后成者.

(q) *Wên-tse* VI., 31 v. 上德篇。聖人俍陽天下和同俍陰天下溺沉. The character 俍 gives no sense, and should be changed into 依.

(r) *Loc. cit.* VI., 28 v. 王公尙陽道則萬物昌尙陰道則天下亡.

(s) *Têng Hsi-tse*, chap. 1, p. 4 r. 鄧析子。無厚篇爲君當若冬日之陽夏日之陰萬物自歸莫之使也. With almost the same words, Wên-tse II., 9 v. 精誠篇 and the *Chi-chung chou-shu* 汲冢周書.

Yiking no trace of such a doctrine can be found, although, as we have shown, at the time when this Classic is supposed to have been written, viz., in 1110 B.C., the doctrine was known, and only in the Yiking commentaries, which presumably were composed by the disciples of Confucius and originated between 450—350 B.C., does it confront us. Even this is disclaimed by *Legge,* who contends that the doctrine of Yin and Yang as active and passive, expanding and contracting substances, was not fully developed before the Sung dynasty (*t*). From our investigations based only on sources anterior to the Sung epoch the contrary is apparent. Legge is in opposition to nearly all Chinese commentators and many sinologists. He states that he has not discovered a trace of the said theory in the Yiking commentaries, but they are contained in it, notably in Appendix III.

There we read : " The regular sequence of Yin and Yang is what is called the course of nature " (*u*). Legge translates : " The successive movement of the inactive and active operations constitutes what is called the course of things." Here we have the two primary elements, which in a regular course replace one another, now the one being supreme, now the other, whereby the seasons are produced. Legge admits this in his note to p. 357.

For Yin and Yang in the Yiking mostly their manifestations, heaven and earth, are substituted. " Heaven is a Yang being, earth a Yin being. Yin and Yang combine their activity, and the Hard and Soft make their appearance " (*x*).

(*t*) *Legge, Yiking,* Introd., p. 44.

(*u*) *Yiking,* 繫辭上傳。一陰一陽之謂道.

(*x*) *Yiking,* p. 395. 繫辭下傳。乾陽物也坤陰物也陰陽合德而剛柔有體.

With the doctrine of the co-operation of heaven and earth, and the production of the myriad things through these, the commentators are well conversant. It involves the existence of the Yin and Yang fluids, for without these heaven and earth could not affect each other. How should heaven give things their external shape, and how should earth fill it with matter (*y*), if certain forces or fluids, just Yin and Yang, did not issue from both?

That Yin and Yang are not only conceived as *bright* and *dark*, *hot* and *cold*, or some other qualities in the Yiking, but as substances too, is evident from the following passages : " The dragon lies hidden. There is no time for action, for the *Yang fluid* keeps itself hidden and concealed " (*z*). According to the Chinese conception of nature, the active life-giving Yang fluid conceals itself in winter, when Yin prevails.

" He walks on hoar-frost. The ice coagulates. *The Yin begins to congeal*" (*a*). Legge translates, " the cold (air) has begun to take form," which amounts to the same. Cold air also is a fluid or a substance.

It must be admitted that the statements of the Yiking on the Yin and Yang are not very clear, which may be owing to the fact that the commentators have taken pains artificially to introduce a theory which has nothing to do with the oracles of the main text. Thus, in the hexagrams, the unbroken lines were denoted as *Yang*, the broken lines as *Yin*, and the former conceived as *strong* and *hard*, the latter as *weak* and *soft*—qualities which, strictly speaking, only belong to the Yin and Yang substances (*b*). Thus the

---

(*y*) *Yiking*, p. 358, Note.

(*z*) *Yiking*, App. IV., p. 414. 乾 卦。潛 龍 勿 用 陽 氣 潛 藏.

(*a*) *Yiking*, App. II., p. 268, 1. 坤 卦。象 曰。履 霜 堅 冰 陰 始 凝 也.

(*b*) Cf. *Yiking*, Introd., p. 16.

words Yin and Yang, heaven and earth, are applied to
nature as well as to the symbols of the Yiking, which easily
causes confusion. The Yang lines are always regarded as
odd, the Yin lines as *even*, because the former always consist of one stroke or an odd number of strokes, the latter
of two strokes or an even number (*c*).

XII. YIN AND YANG IN MEDICINE (SU-WÊN).

The human body, as we saw, is built up from the Yin
and Yang fluids. Consequently the conditions of the body,
its well-being, and especially its diseases, depend on the two
fluids. The oldest Chinese system of medicine, for which
the *Su-wên* is the fundamental work, is closely connected
with the Yin-yang theory.

According to the Su-wên, a young man reaches his
puberty with $2 \times 8 = 16$ years. Then the Yin and Yang are
in perfect harmony, and the generative power is fully
developed. With 6×8, i.e., 48 years, the Yang fluid begins
to be exhausted, the face dries up, and the hair turns
grey (*d*).

Since the Yang reigns in spring and summer, and the
Yin in autumn and winter, the sage cultivates these forces
during their seasons. Living accordingly, he enjoys
immunity from maladies, otherwise he is liable to attacks
upon his health and other disasters (*e*).

(*c*) *Yiking*, App. III., p. 388, 29. 繫辭下傳。其故何也陽
卦奇陰卦耦.

(*d*) *Su-wên* 上古天眞論。丈夫二八腎氣盛天癸至
精氣溢寫陰陽和故能有子六八陽氣衰竭於上
面焦髮鬢頒白.

(*e*) *Eod.* 四氣調神大論。所以聖人春夏養陽秋
冬養陰以從其根 . . . . 逆之則災害生從之則苛
疾不起.

The Yang prevailing, the Yin suffers; and the Yin predominating, the Yang suffers. Excessive Yang evokes heat, and excessive Yin cold, of the body. Heat is usually combined with obstruction of the pores, dryness of the skin, and heavy breathing. Cold leads to a secretion of sweat, shivers, and convulsions. Sudden anger injures the Yin, sudden joy the Yang (*f*).

As regards epileptic fits, the Su-wên distinguishes such as are connected with heat and those combined with cold. The former are said to be produced when the Yin fluid in the lower part of the body is spoiled, and the latter when the Yang fluid is used up. The heat comes forth at the soles; the cold advances from the feet up to the knees (*g*).

Raving madness also has its cause in the Yang fluid, which breaks forth all of a sudden and cannot be deflected quickly enough (*h*). Insanity comes from the entire Yang being concentrated in the upper part of the body, and the entire Yin in the lower part; for thus the body is full above and empty in its lower part, Yin admittedly corresponding to vacuity (*i*).

XIII. YIN AND YANG IN WARFARE.

The speculations about the activity of the dual forces had become so familiar to the Chinese that even in warfare

---

(*f*) *Eod.* 陰陽應象大論。陰勝則陽病陽勝則陰病陽勝則熱陰勝則寒暴怒傷陰暴喜傷陽.

(*g*) *Su-wên* 厥論。陽氣衰於下則爲寒厥陰氣衰於下則爲熱厥帝曰熱厥之爲熱也必起於足下者何也‥‥陰氣勝則從五指至膝上.

(*h*) *Eod.* 病能論。帝曰陽何以使人狂岐伯曰陽氣者因暴折而難決故善怒也病名曰陽厥.

(*i*) *Eod.* 陽盡在上陰氣從下下虛上實故狂巓疾也.

they occasionally made use of them. In the oldest work on tactics by *Sun-tse*, sixth century B.C., we read that the armies are fond of altitudes and dislike depths; that they appreciate the Yang and disdain the Yin (*k*).

In the *Kuo-yü* (fifth century B.C.), during a war against *Wu*, *Fan Li* says to the King of *Yüeh* : " In days of yore good generals took the regular course of heaven and earth as their model, and in concert therewith executed their movements.   Falling back they utilised the *Yin* (of obscurity), and advancing, the *Yang* (of light).   In the vicinity they employed *softness*, at a distance *hardness*. Unless the retreat be covered by Yin, and unless in the advance Yang show the way, the sacrifice of men is of no avail " (*l*).   The reference to softness and hardness, the two well-known attributes of Yin and Yang, seems to imply that he who is attacked in his own country has to limit himself to the defensive or inactivity, while the enemy arriving from afar exhausts his forces in useless attacks. In pursuance of this principle, the King of Yüeh did not accept battle until, after three years, the army of Wu was completely disorganised.

B. MODERN TIMES.

The Yin-yang theory was further developed and expanded during the Sung epoch ; but by no means was it propounded then for the first time, as is often wrongly assumed.   Its fundamental principles were long known. The Sung scholars attempted to give it a better philosophical basis, and took great pains to scrutinise the origin of the two fluids.

(*k*) *Sun-tse* 孫子。凡軍好高而惡下貴陽而賤陰.

(*l*) *Kuo-yü*　越王謂范蠡曰 . . . . 古之善用兵者因天地之常與之俱行後則用陰先則用陽近則用柔遠則用剛後無陰蔽先無陽察用人無蓺.

I. Evolution of Yin and Yang from the Primordial
Principle.

The most important source for the question about the
origin of the Yin and Yang is the *T'ai-chi t'u.* According
to this text, the Yang springs from the motion, and the
Yin from the repose, of the primary principle or the
Absolute, *T'ai-chi.* " The Absolute moves and engenders
Yang. The movement having reached its climax, rest
ensues. From rest springs Yin, and, when rest has reached
its utmost limit, again movement follows. So we have
alternately now movement, now rest. They together form
the basis from which by separation grow Yin and Yang,
so that these are the two modes " (*m*).

In a similar way already by *Lü Pu-wei,* in the *Liki*
and in a *Yiking* commentary, creation was described (*n*).
Yang was always thought of as activity and motion, Yin
as passivity and rest. Just these two attributes of the dual
forces henceforth appear in the foreground; the notion of
substantiality, i.e., fire and water, is not forgotten, but less
insisted upon in the disquisitions of the Sung time.

From the above statement it might appear as though
the Absolute were something material. This idea, however,
is opposed by *Chu Hsi* holding that the Absolute is
an immaterial principle. Motion and rest adhere to the
primary fluid *Ch'i,* in which the immaterial principle has
its seat (*o*). Properly speaking, Chu Hsi assumes but *one
single fluid,* of which Yin and Yang merely constitute two

(*m*) *Hsing-li ching-i* I., 5 v. 宋 周 子 太 極 圖。太 極 動 而
生 陽 動 極 而 靜 靜 而 生 陰 靜 極 復 動 一 動 一 靜 互
爲 其 根 分 陰 分 陽 兩 儀 立 焉.

(*n*) *Vid.* pp. 36 and 39.

(*o*) *Chu Hsi,* '49, 32 v. 陰 陽。太 極 只 是 理 . . . . 理 寓 於
氣.

phases, and quotes the *T'ai-chi t'u* as nis authority.   Both
fluids change one into the other.   Th Yin fluid flowing
and extending becomes Yang, and the Yang fluid congealing
and contracting turns into Yin (*p*).

Of the Yang fluid between heaven and earth there are
six strata or layers tending to rise upwards, so that there
grows a void below and in this void the Yin.   The Yang
fluid proceeds only as far as the surface of the earth;
consequently it freezes in the earth, for there prevails
Yin (*q*).   *Chu Hsi* compares the two fluids to expiration
and inspiration.   The expiration, which, of course, causes
an expansion of the air, is Yang; the inspiration and the
contraction of air is Yin (*r*).

II. QUALITIES OF THE TWO PRIMARY FLUIDS.

In their attempts to conceive and define the nature of
Yin and Yang the scholars of modern times emphasise
either the one or the other of the well-known qualities of
these fluids as their main attributes.   Accordingly we can
distinguish the following lines of thought.

(1) The Old Notion of Substantiality.

We find this formulated, perhaps most pregnantly, by
Ch'êng-tse : "Of the Yin and Yang fluids, that which is
permanent and never scatters, is the sun and the moon;
that which continually grows and decreases is heat and

(*p*) *Chu Hsi, eod.* 49, 34 r. 陰陽只是一氣陰氣流行卽
爲陽陽氣凝聚卽爲陰非直有二物相對也.

(*q*) *Hsing-li ta-ch'üan*, 27, 18 r. 朱子曰。陽氣只是六層
只管上去上盡後下面空闕處便是陰 .... 天地
間只有六層陽氣到地面上時地下便冷.

(*r*) *Loc. cit.* 這只是個噓吸噓是陽吸是陰.

cold " (s). Heat and cold appear in the sky as the sun and the moon, and on éarth as fire and water, of which professedly the sun and the moon are formed.

(2) *Expansion and Contraction.*

Chu Hsi works mainly with these notions : " Although Yin and Yang are two different words," he says, " it is actually but the shrinking and growing of one fluid, an advancing and retreating, a shrinking and expanding. The advancing is Yang, the retreating Yin; the growing Yang and the shrinking Yin. It is only a process taking place between heaven and earth incessantly from times immemorial through the shrinking and expanding of this one fluid. Therefore one may say, Yin and Yang are one, but one may also say that they are two things " (t). Further, Chu Hsi calls the activity of the Yang an expansion and dispersion, that of the Yin a contraction and accumulation; and he compares the Yang to the breath issuing from the nostrils, and the Yin to the breath reverting into them. Both forces are like a snail issuing from its shell and again retiring into it. It cannot issue farther and farther, for then it would die; but the part emitted must be taken back again. Similarly the primordial fluid would perish if it only extended itself, whereas life is its real nature (u):

(s) *Eod.* 27, 15 v. 程子曰。陰陽之氣有常存而不散者日月是也有消長而無窮者寒暑是也.

(t) *Chu Hsi,* 49, 30 r. 陰陽. 曰陰陽雖是兩箇字然却只是一氣之消息一進一退一消一長進處便是陽退處便是陰長處便是陽消處便是陰只是這一氣之消長做出古今天地間無限事來所以陰陽做一箇說亦得做兩箇說亦得.

(u) *Chu Hsi,* eod. 49, 30 r. v. 又問氣之發散者爲陽收斂者爲陰否曰也是如此如鼻氣之出入出者爲

T'sai Ch'ên, a disciple of Chu Hsi, gives utterance to the same sentiment : " Yang is air exhaled, and Yin inhaled. The exhaled air emits (the seed), the inhaled air transforms. Yang emits, and Yin transforms. On this is based the course of human life, and all things are produced thereby in multitudes " (*x*).

(3) *Motion and Rest.*

Motion and rest are, to *Shao-tse,* the chief characteristics of Yin and Yang, but he effaces their distinctions completely. His statements are somewhat mystical. The spirit, he says, cannot exist without the body, and the body cannot live without the spirit. Yang has Yin as its body, and Yin has Yang as its body—one expects that he would say as spirit. That which is moving is the spirit; that which is at rest is the body. In heaven Yang is moving and Yin at rest; on earth, however, Yang is at rest and Yin moving (*y*). One does not see why Yin and Yang in heaven and earth act quite differently. If they are both bodies, now moved, now motionless, as a matter of fact, there is no real difference between them.

Hsü San-chung, in the *Hsin-ku yü-lun,* gives a clearer statement to the effect that Yang is the movement of Yin,

---

陽 收 回 者 爲 陰 入 息 如 螺 螄 出 殼 了 縮 入 相 似 是 收 入 那 出 不 盡 底 若 只 管 出 去 不 收 便 死 矣 . . . . 那 氣 又 只 管 生.

(*x*) *Hsing-li ta-ch'üan*, 24, 10 r. 洪 範 皇 極. 內 篇。陽 者 吐 氣 陰 者 含 氣 吐 氣 者 施 含 氣 者 化 陽 施 陰 化 而 人 道 立 矣 萬 物 繁 矣.

(*y*) *Hsing-li ta-ch'üan*, 11, 21 r. 皇 極 經 世. 觀 物 外 篇。性 非 體 不 成 體 非 性 不 生 陽 以 陰 爲 體 陰 以 陽 爲 體 動 者 性 也 靜 者 體 也 在 天 則 陽 動 而 陰 靜 在 地 則 陽 靜 而 陰 動.

and Yin the rest of Yang. Movement is Yang and rest is Yin. Rest and Yin spring from the highest degree of movement, and have Yang as their root. Contrariwise, movement and Yang spring from the highest degree of rest, and have their root in Yin (z), i.e., each fluid, after attaining its climax, turns into its opposite.

(4) *Manifestation and Body.*

Motionlessness or rest now became conceived of as a body. Torpor or inertia has always been considered a chief attribute of the body in Europe as well, and many have taken it for the inner nature of bodies. "Rest," remarks Hsü San-chung, "in view of its retiring and concealing itself, is designated as *body*, and motion because of its coming forth and extending as *manifestation*" (a).

Wu of *Lin-ch'uan* (1247—1331 A.D.) calls Yang a fluid and Yin a fine substance. At the production of organisms Yang gives the shape and Yin the body; activity depends on Yang and the body on Yin (b). Accordingly, the Yang is something easily movable, flowing, air-like, while the Yin is something corporeal, endowed with natural inertia.

(5) *Spirit and Body.*

If one thinks of the Yin as a body, the next step is to regard its correlate, the Yang, as a spirit. Provided that the unmoved is the body, then that which gives motion to

---

(z) 徐三重信古餘論 論陰陽。陽卽陰之動者陰卽陽之靜者動則爲陽靜則爲陰陰由動極而靜是陰根陽也陽由靜極而動是陽根陰也.

(a) *Hsü San-chung, loc. cit.* 靜以斂藏而言體動以發散而言用.

(b) *Hsing-li ta-ch'üan*, 27, 19 v. 臨川吳氏曰。陽爲氣陰爲精陽成象陰成形陽主用陰主體.

it must be the spirit, for the vital force in former times was generally identified with the spirit or the soul. This step is taken by *Ho T'ang*. His words are : " The Yang is moving, the Yin at rest, the Yang is enlightened, the Yin in obscurity, the Yang has consciousness, the Yin has not, the Yin has a form, the Yang has not, the Yang has no body and uses the Yin as its body, the Yin is without activity and requires the Yang to become active. Both being united, creatures are alive; when they separate, creatures die " (*c*).

This idea that the Yang is a spirit and the Yin a body is something quite novel. In ancient times we find nothing of the kind. It comes near to the modern conception of heaven as a spirit, being the same idea only differently expressed (*d*). Therefore it is most vigorously impugned by *Wang T'ing-hsiang* as Non-Confucian, and of Taoist or Buddhist origin. In accordance with the old sources, spirit, he says, is but the unexplicable working of the Yin and Yang, and therefore belongs to both. The spirit can only exist in conjunction with a material fluid, without which it perishes. In the original *aurae* all future things were contained already. There were hot vapours and moist ones ; the hot vapours were very agile, they formed the Yang and fire, the moist ones dropped down and formed the Yin and water (*e*). This is again the old, well-known theory.

Furthermore, the Sung scholars assign to Yin and Yang the same qualities always ascribed to them. According to *Chu Hsi* the Yang has its position on the *left*; its activity

---

(c) *Hsü Hsing-li hui-t'ung* 何塘陰陽管見。陽動陰靜陽明陰晦陽有知陰無知陰有形陽無形陽無體以陰爲體陰無用待陽而用二者相合則物生相離則物死.

(d) See p. 118 *seq.*

(e) *Hsü Hsing-li hui-t'ung*　廷相陰陽管見辯.

is *giving life, nourishing, growing,* its nature *hard, bright, public-spirited, just*; it is the principle of the *superior* man. The Yin has always its seat on the *right* side. *Injuring, hurting, killing* is its way; it is *soft, dark, selfish, egoistic*— the principle of the mean man (*f*). *Li* of *Yen-p'ing* professes that the nature of Yang is *burning,* its number *odd.* It is *hard, hot, round, swimming above, bright, moving* and *pouring out.* The Yin, in turn, is by nature *moist,* and its number is *even.* Moreover, it is *soft, cool, square, sinking down, dark, still, contracting* (*g*). Other contrasts for which, in the Sung time, Yin and Yang were used are : *day* and *night, full* and *empty, straight* and *crooked, right* and *divergent.*

III. Relations between and Combinations of Yin and Yang.

Yin and Yang not only change into one another as phases of one and the same substance, but in the opinion of many scholars they also appear in manifold compounds, so that a pure Yang or an unalloyed Yin are rather rare.

Shao-tse affirms that in every Yang there is Yin, and in every Yin Yang, but he likewise assumes other combinations, and draws therefrom the most peculiar consequences. The sun is Yang in Yang, and the moon is Yin in Yang, and, owing to its being Yang, also can be seen in daytime. If heaven is considered as Yang, the sun as fire and the moon as water, we can understand that the sun is defined as Yang in Yang and the moon as Yin in Yang. But the inference drawn respecting the moon, where Yang suddenly is taken in the acceptation of daylight, is wrong. Further on it is said that the stars are Yang in Yin, wherefore they

---

(*f*) *Chu Hsi,* 49, 35 v.

(*g*) *Hsing-li ta-ch'üan,* 27, 17 r. 延平李氏 A.D. 1033-1163, a teacher of *Chu Hsi.*

shine at night.   Here, again, Yang means brightness and Yin darkness—the stars shine in darkness.   The celestial spaces finally, representing the soil of heaven, are Yin in Yin (*h*).   This entire division is nothing but a play of fancy.   Elsewhere *Shao-tse* calls the sun and the moon the Yin and Yang of heaven, water and fire the Yin and Yang of earth, the stars and celestial spaces the hard and soft of heaven, and stones and earth the hard and soft of earth (*i*), regarding the hard and soft as fundamental principles like Yin and Yang, as we remember.

Other *savants* put forth quite different combinations of the two elements.   Thus *Tse-hua-tse* holds that Yang in Yang is fire, and Yin in Yin water.   Yin in Yang gives wood and Yang in Yin metal, as we shall see later.

In contrast to this *Ho T'ang* asserts : "Heaven is Yang in Yang, therefore it is a spirit and bodiless.   Earth is Yin in Yin, therefore it has a body, but no spirit.   Fire is Yin in Yang, therefore it is visible, but has no body.   Water is Yang in Yin, therefore it is changeable, but it has no consciousness " (*k*).

The conception of water as Yang in Yin, and of fire as Yin in Yang, may be based on the view that all the Five

---

(*h*) *Hsing-li ta-ch'üan*, 11, 33 r. ; *Huang-chi ching-shih* 觀 物 外 篇。陽 中 有 陰 陰 中 有 陽 天 之 道 也 陽 中 之 陽 日 也 暑 之 道 也 陽 中 之 陰 月 也 以 其 陽 之 類 故 能 見 於 晝 陰 中 之 陽 星 也 所 以 見 於 夜 陰 中 之 陰 辰 也 天 壤 也.

(*i*) *Loc. cit.* 日 月 天 之 陰 陽 水 火 地 之 陰 陽 星 辰 天 之 剛 柔 土 石 地 之 剛 柔.

(*k*) *Hsü Hsing-li hui-t'ung* 何 塘 陰 陽 管 見。天 陽 之 陽 也 故 神 而 無 形 地 陰 之 陰 也 故 形 而 不 神 火 陽 之 陰 也 故 可 見 然 終 無 形 也 水 陰 之 陽 也 故 能 化 然 終 無 知 也.

Elements consist of two parts, a *fluid* and a *substance*, of which we shall hear more when dealing with the Five Elements. Accordingly, the fluid of water would be Yang, its substance Yin, and of fire the opposite would hold good.

Chou-tse inverts all this, declaring water to be the moist fluid (Yin) in Yang and fire to be the dry fluid (Yang) in Yin. All these divisions are perfectly arbitrary, for every possible combination has its advocates. We find fire defined as Yang in Yang, Yin in Yang, and Yang in Yin, and with water it is the same.

Chu Hsi makes the relations between Yin and Yang still more complicated, if possible, saying : " In Yin, of course, one distinguishes Yin and Yang, and in Yang there are also Yin and Yang. The celestial principle produces the male and the terrestrial principle the female. But although men belong to the Yang, one cannot affirm that they have no Yin, and although women depend on Yin, one cannot contend that they are without Yang. The bodily fluid of man belongs to Yang, but yet his breath contains Yin and Yang (inspiration and expiration). Blood belongs to Yin, but yet it has Yin as well as Yang " (*l*).

IV. LOCALISATION OF YIN AND YANG ACCORDING TO QUARTERS AND SEASONS.

The seasons are, as we saw, the result of the growing and decreasing of the two fluids struggling for supremacy, so that now the one, now the other, get the better. But this never goes so far that one destroys the other completely. Even if it seems to be gone, there still remains a

---

(*l*) *Chu Hsi*, 49, 33 r. 陰陽。統言陰陽只是兩端而陰中自分陰陽陽中亦有陰陽乾道成男坤道成女男雖屬陽而不可謂其無陰女雖屬陰亦不可謂其無陽人身氣屬陽而氣有陰陽血屬陰而血有陰陽.

residue which grows again, and in the progress of time outclasses the other fluid, when the same process sets in anew (*m*).

Pursuant to the common view, the Yang is permanently connected with the *South* and the Yin with the *North*, for the South is hot and the North is cold. This view, however, is again modified by *Shao-tse*, who always walks in his own ways. " The Yang of heaven," he opines, " is in the South and its Yin in the North, but the Yang of earth is in the North and its Yin in the South, and the Yang of man is above and his Yin below. When uniting the Yang is below and the Yin above " (*n*). There is hardly any conclusive reason for inverting the directions with earth. Perhaps Shao-tse imagined that earth, being the counterpart of heaven, everything concerning her must be inverted also. With man the upper part of the body is always looked upon as Yang or the nobler. Why at the union of Yin and Yang their usual position, Yang above and Yin below, must be abandoned, is not apparent.

This notion that the fluids have their seat in a certain quarter was already in antiquity superseded by a conception propounded by *Tung Chung-shu*, according to which Yin and Yang travel round the horizon following the seasons. The temporary position of the Yang was admittedly pointed out by the constellation of the " Bushel " (Great Bear). On the question where the fluids have their smallest and where their biggest quantitative expansion, opinions are at variance.

Chu Hsi claims that the Yang originates in the N., develops in the E., and attains its climax in the S. The

---

(*m*) *Loc. cit.* 49, 36 r.

(*n*) *Hsing-li ta-ch'üan,* 11, 29-30; *Huang-chi ching-shih* 觀 物 外 篇。天 之 陽 在 南 而 陰 在 北 地 之 陰 在 南 而 陽 在 北 人 之 陽 在 上 而 陰 在 下 旣 交 則 陽 下 而 陰 上.

Yin comes out in the S., is of medium strength in the W., and finishes in the N. (*o*). The Yang, as we saw, in winter, to which the N. corresponds, when the Yin has reached its climax, is already in its embryonic state, but it becomes perceptible only in spring and in the E., and appears in all its fullness in summer and in the S. Just so the Yin originates already in summer and in the S., but it obtains full sway only in winter in the N.

Chu Hsi observes that, about the localisation of the fluids, opinions disagree. The *Liki exponents* assume that the warm fluid develops in the S.E. and the icy one in the N.W. In opposition to this the *astronomers* make the Yang appear in the N. and the Yin in the S., which tallies with Chu Hsi's own view. The *calendar experts* seem to have supposed that the Yang begins in the N. and ceases in the S.S.E., whereas the Yin commences in the S. and ends in the N.N.W. The *meteorologists* in turn assert that Yang starts in E.N.E. and finishes in S.S.W., while Yin starts in W.S.W. and reaches the goal in N.N.E. (*p*). Chu Hsi endeavours to reconcile these conflicting views. The commencements in N. and S. are said to refer to the embryonic state of the still hidden fluids, E.N.E. and W.S.W. to the time when both actually become visible in nature. S.S.E. and N.N.W. mark the climax of Yin and Yang, S.S.W. and N.N.E. the real end of their manifestations.

V. Yin and Yang the Constituent Parts of Weather.

Yin and Yang are responsible for weather conditions, but as to the reason opinions differ as much as they did in ancient times.

(*o*) *Chu Hsi*, 49, 35 v. 陰 陽。陽 生 於 北 長 於 東 而 盛 於 南 陰 始 於 南 中 於 西 而 終 於 北.

(*p*) *Chu Hsi*, 49, 37 v.

1. *Wind.*

Wind is believed to be produced when the Yin is within and the Yang without. The latter cannot enter into the Yin, and therefore turns round it without ceasing (*Chang-tse*). According to the *Hung-fan huang-chi* the Yin is outside and the Yang, which is very weak, fills the centre. *Shao-tse* makes the laconic remark that when Yin seizes the Yang, wind is the result.

2. *Thunder and Lightning.*

Yang enclosed in the congealed Yin, through which it is unable to break, causes thunder and lightning (*Chang-tse*). The *Hung-fan huang-chi* likewise makes the Yin keep the Yang imprisoned in its interior, whereupon the latter forcibly breaks through as thunder. According to the peculiar theory of *Shao-tse*, thunder is the seizing of the Hard by the Soft. The Hard is thunder or Yang, the Soft the rain or Yin. All the three statements mean the same after all.

3. *Clouds.*

When the Yin is seized by the Yang it whirls up in the shape of clouds (*Chang-tse*). In *Shao-tse's* terminology clouds are produced by the seizure of the Soft by the Hard, which amounts to the same, the Soft corresponding to Yin and the Hard to Yang.

4. *Rain and Dew, Frost and Snow.*

Yang pressed together by Yin falls down as rain (*Chang-tse*). Conversely, *Shao-tse* lets the Yin be seized by the Yang. On the other hand, rain and dew are considered the harmonious union of Yang with Yin, and frost and snow the harmonious union of Yin with Yang. The preceding fluid seems to be paramount in the compound (*Hung-fan huang-chi*). Yet rain, dew, hoar-frost and snow are also regarded as the harmonious diffusion of the fluids (*Chang-tse*).

5. *Vitiated Air.*

Vitiated air, by which most likely miasms are understood, and dust storms, are said to be the outcome of the unharmonious union (*Chang-tse*), or the unharmonious separation, of Yin and Yang (*Hung-fan huang-chi*) (*q*).

VI. FURTHER DIFFERENTIATION OF YIN AND YANG.

From the two primary substances the Five Elements were evolved, of which Book IV. treats more in detail. Properly speaking, these elements are nothing else than the *Four Forms* (*sse-hsiang*) (*r*)—the abundant Yang (Fire), the abundant Yin (Water), the scanty Yang (Wood), and the scanty Yin (Metal), to which is still to be added Earth, which is said to be sometimes Yin and sometimes Yang, at least in the outline given by *Tse-hua-tse*. Furthermore, according to *Ho T'ang*, the *Eight Diagrams* (*pa-kua*) (*s*) are supposed to proceed from Yin and Yang, viz., *Heaven, Earth, Water, Fire, Wind, Thunder, Mountains, Lakes.* This derivation is not very logical, notably as regards mountains and lakes, which are merely parts of earth.

Ho T'ang supports the peculiar view that out of the condensation of terrestrial water comes fire (*t*). *Tai T'ing-huai* fancies that from Yin and Yang, by duplication, grow the 4 seasons, which trebled give the 12 months,

---

(*q*) *Hsing-li ta-ch'üan*, 11, 27; *Huang-chi ching-shih* 觀 物 外 篇; *eod*. 5, 9 *seq*; *Chang-tse chêng-mêng* 參 兩 篇; *eod*. 24, 9 v.; *Hung-fan huang-chi* 內 篇.

(*r*) 四 象.

(*s*) 八 卦.

(*t*) *Hsü Hsing-li hui-t'ung* 何 塘 陰 陽 管 見。地 水 相 結 爲 火.

which doubled become the 24 periods, and the latter trebled result in the 72 sections of the year (*u*). Needless to say that, in a strict sense, more or less substantial fluids cannot be transformed into periods of time. The author probably harboured the thought that, during all the enumerated sections of the year, there are Yin and Yang in quite determinate mixtures, and in so far one may say that all these different mixtures determinating the sections of the year are developed from Yin and Yang.

VII. Yin and Yang as Correlates.

Through the wide extension of the notions Yin and Yang on all kinds of relations exhibiting only some distant analogy with the two primary substances, these notions almost entirely melt away, and we arrive at the most poignant contradictions. The same object may be Yin and Yang at the same time, according to the point from which it is viewed. Ultimately, Yin and Yang do not mean anything in themselves at all, being only employed to express a relation; one notion is the opposite of the other, the one is positive, the other negative.

The consequences to which the unlimited extension of the notions Yin and Yang must lead are brought home to us in the *Chang Huang T'u-shu pien* (*x*) : Heaven and the sun, spring and summer, east and south are Yang, the earth and the moon, autumn and winter, west and north are Yin. But during the day heaven and earth are both

---

(u) 經濟文輯. 戴庭槐氣候總論。一歲之間本一氣之周流耳一氣分而爲二則有陰陽二倍而爲四則有四時三四一十二則又有十二月十二倍而爲二十四則有二十四氣復三其二十四而爲七十二候.

(x) 章潢圖書編。陰陽五行八卦.

Yang, and at night they are both Yin. In spring and summer heaven and earth, the sun and the moon are all Yang, in autumn and winter they are all Yin. In the east and the south the four seasons are always Yang, in the west and the north they are always Yin. The left hand is Yang, the right one Yin, in this no change is possible, but raise both hands, then they are both Yang, and put them down, and they are both Yin, and no matter whether you raise them or put them down, when they are hot they are both Yang, and when they are cold they are both Yin.

VIII. PLANTS, ANIMALS AND MEN PRODUCED BY YIN AND YANG.

The moderns also make the vegetable and animal kingdoms grow from the two primary principles, but in details they differ a great deal from their older predecessors.

According to *Shao-tse* the union of Yin and Yang engenders animals with hoofs and horns and Hard and Soft together produce roots and nuts. In this process the Yang and Hardness are decisive. Yin joined with Yang produces birds, Soft along with Hard produces branches and trunks. In this the influence of the Yin and Softness preponderate. Consequently Yin and Yang produce only birds and animals, whereas the vegetable kingdom owes its origin to the Hard and Soft. Leaves are Yin in spite of that, and blossoms and fruits are Yang. At the same time leaves and branches are considered soft, and roots and trunks hard (*y*).

(*y*) *Hsing-li ta-ch'üan*, 11, 23 r.; *Shao-tse*; *huang-chi ching-shih* 觀物外篇。陽交於陰而生蹄角之類也剛交於柔而生根荄之類也陰交於陽而生羽翼之類也柔交於剛而生枝幹之類也。葉陰也華實陽也枝葉軟而根幹堅也.

The single parts of the body *Shao-tse* presumes to be generated in a similar manner by the co-operation of two of his four principles, besides some parts are said to produce others in turn : Yang and Hardness combined produce the heart and the lungs, Yang with Softness the liver and the gall, Softness and Yin together form the kidneys and the bladder, Hardness and Yin the spleen and the stomach. These inner parts having been created, they produce the outer ones, namely, the heart produces the eyes, the gall the ears, the spleen produces the nose, the kidneys the mouth, the lungs the bones, the liver the flesh, the stomach the marrow, and the bladder the blood (z).   All this is a mere play of fancy, and reasons are not given.

Ho T'ang informs us that when Yang, the spiritual substance, and Yin, the corporeal one, are blended, man is produced. When they separate again, he dies. Yang is spirit, but simultaneously the heavenly fire; Yin is body and also the terrestrial water. Out of the heavenly fiery spirit grows the human spirit, and from the terrestrial water blood and flesh are formed (a).

IX. Yin and Yang in Zoology and Botany.

In the descriptive, natural sciences the Chinese have made many good observations and theirs are no mean attainments, notably in the field of botany.   It goes with-

---

(z) *Loc. cit.* 11, 24 r. 體必交而後生故陽與剛交而生心肺陽與柔交而生肝膽柔與陰交而生腎與膀胱剛與陰交而生脾胃心生目膽生耳脾生鼻腎生口肺生骨肝生肉胃生髓膀胱生血.

(a) *Hsü Hsing-li hui-t'ung, Ho T'ang yin-yang kuan-chien*. 陽神合則人生所謂精氣爲物也離則人死所謂遊魂爲變也 .... 化生人物其心性之神則皆天火之神所爲也其血肉之形則皆地水之形所爲也.

out saying that here also they have made attempts to avail themselves of the Yin-yang theory with a view to accounting for the observed natural facts. How they proceeded may be gathered from the following extract from the *Ching-chi wên-chi.*

" Birds, beasts, plants and trees obtain the Yin and the Yang fluid and are determined by them. The eagle plans murder and in autumn pounces upon its prey. The mouse is full of greed and goes out at night (*b*). In the fourth and the fifth months they can transform themselves into a turtle-dove and a quail, for in the fourth and fifth months Yang is powerful and Yin can be transmuted by Yang (*c*). The sparrows brood on their eggs and congregate in spring; the pheasant searches for its mate and cries in the morning (*d*). In the 11th and and 12th months they can transform themselves into frogs and shells (*e*), for in these months the Yin reaches its climax, and the Yang then can be changed by the Yin " (*f*).

" The hibernating insects open their holes, when thunder is heard, and come out along with the Yang. They close their holes when thunder ceases to sound, and retire together with the Yin. At the commencement of spring the otter sacrifices fish. At this time the fish follow the

---

(*b*) Both are Yin animals, for murder, autumn, greed, and night are Yin.

(*c*) According to the *Yüeh-ling* (Liki), the eagle in the middle of spring changes into a pigeon, and the mole = 田鼠 into a quail, *Liki* I., 258, 263.

(*d*) Both are Yang animals : spring and morning are Yang.

(*e*) Cf. *Yüeh-ling, Liki* I., 292, 297.

(*f*) *Ching-chi wên-chi* 戴庭槐氣候總論。陰陽之氣鳥獸草木得之爲先鷹主殺而秋擊鼠主貪而夜出卯辰之月能化鳩鴽者以卯辰者陽之壯陰爲陽所化也爵乳子而春集雉求雌而朝呴而戌亥之月能爲蛤蜃者以戌亥者陰之極陽爲陰所化也．

Yang fluid and swim up the river. When autumn closes the wolf immolates animals, for then the animals are affected by the Yin fluid and are doomed to die " (*g*).

" In spring the wild geese fly to and the swallows come from the north, the former travelling from the south to the north and the latter from the north to the south. Both fly with the Yang fluid, which is to their advantage. In autumn, on the contrary, the wild geese arrive and the swallows depart, the geese going from north to south, the swallows in the opposite direction, but both make use of the convenient Yin fluid to fly upon " (*h*).

" In the 2nd month the mango birds sing and in the 4th the green frogs croak, viz., with the Yang. In the 5th month the first Yin appears, then the shrike sings once and becomes silent again. In the 7th month the cicadas sing, viz., with the Yin. In the 11th month the first Yang appears and the nightingale sings, but as soon as it is affected by the Yang it does not sing any more " (*i*).

(*g*) 蟄蟲啓戸者雷發聲之時與陽俱出也蟄蟲坯戸者雷收聲之時與陰俱入也孟春而獺祭魚者此時魚逐陽氣而上遊也季秋而豺祭獸者此時獸感陰氣而見殺也. Sacrificing means that the first seized fishes and animals are not devoured, but, so to speak, left to the gods. The Yin fluid in autumn denotes death, but our author forgets that the Yang fluid in spring likewise brings about the death of the fish.

(*h*) 春而鴻鴈北元鳥至者鴈自南而來北燕自北而來南各乘其陽氣之所宜也秋而鴻鴈來元鳥歸者鴈自北而來南燕自南而來北各乘其陰氣之所宜也. It may be convenient for wild geese to fly with the Yang fluid, i.e., the south wind northward, but it can hardly be advantageous for swallows to fly against the wind.

(*i*) 二月而倉庚鳴四月而螻蟈鳴者鳴以陽也及五月一陰始生鵙一鳴而反舌則無聲矣七月而寒蟬鳴者鳴以陰也及十一月一陽始生鶡鴠能鳴而

"In the 4th month earth-worms come forth : the Yin is coiled up, but when it obtains Yang it expands. In the 11th month earth-worms coil themselves up. Although the Yang is already created, the Yin is still rolled up. At the summer solstice Yin first comes out, and stags shed their horns, for they are Yang-like animals. At the winter solstice Yang first comes forth, and elks shed their horns, for they are Yin-like animals " (*k*).

"That plants and trees can sprout in the 1st month is due to the union of Yin and Yang, which causes their development. In the 9th month they fade and lose their leaves, because then the Yin increases and the Yang vanishes, so that they are destroyed. Peaches and *Elaeococca* blossom in spring conformably to the abundance of Yang, the asters bloom in autumn in accord with the plenitude of Yin. In the 4th month delicate plants die, because the Yin is not defeated by the Yang. In the 11th month the *lichi* come out. The Yang makes its first appearance again in the Yin " (*l*).

"Wheat has Yin seed, therefore it grows under the sway of metal and dies under the rule of fire. Its crop is

---

感陽則不鳴矣. It is not quite certain whether the nightingale is intended. Anyhow, it is a bird singing only during the night.

(*k*) 四月而蚯蚓出者陰之屈者得陽而伸也十一月而蚯蚓結者陽雖生矣而陰尚屈也夏至得一陰而鹿角解者鹿陽獸也冬至得一陽而麋角解者麋陰獸也. The new-growing Yin is supposed to cause the loss of the horns of the stags; with the elks it is the Yang.

(*l*) 草木正月而萌動者陰陽氣交而爲泰也九月而黃落者陰長陽消而爲剝也桃桐華於春者應陽之盛也黃菊華於秋者應陰之盛也四月而靡草死者陰不勝於陽也十一月而荔挺出者陽初復於陰也.

in the 4th month. Rice has Yang seed, therefore it grows under the rule of wood and ripens under the dominion of metal. The rice crop is in the 7th month " (*m*).

" When rotten, plants become glowworms, plants are changed into animals and inanimate things into animate ones. Is that not because the brightness of Yang has reached its acme, so that also things of the dark Yin adhere to and change into it? Generally, the two fluids Yin and Yang are immaterial and move quietly in the interior, whereas wind, rain, dew, thunder, insects and plants have form and change outwardly " (*n*).

We see from these extracts how far the Chinese still were from the knowledge of the real laws of nature.

X. Analogies to Yin and Yang in other Countries.

The well-known *Persian Dualism*, the combat between *Ahuramazda*, the god of light and principle of good, and *Ahriman*, the god of darkness and evil, bears some slight resemblance to the Yin-yang theory. This great war is at length decided by the destruction of Ahriman with all his attendants, when a time of bliss begins (*o*). Like Yin and Yang, the Persian deities represent light and darkness, good and evil, but in the fundamental ideas both nations differ to such an extent that a mutual influence can hardly

---

(*m*) 麥得陰之穉也故金王而生火王而死而麥秋在於四月也禾得陽之穉也故木王而生金王而熟而禾登在於七月也·

Of the Five Elements wood reigns in spring, fire in summer, metal in autumn, and water in winter.

(*n*) 至於腐草之爲螢則植物之變爲動物無情之變爲有情豈非陽明之極而陰幽之物亦隨之以化哉大抵陰陽二氣無形而默運於內風雨露雷昆蟲草木有形而改換於外·

(*o*) *Troels Lund*, pp. 36-39.

be thought of. Moreover, the conception of gods of light and darkness, of which the former, of course, are regarded as the good and beneficent, is so generally human that a fortuitous coincidence would not prove anything. In point of fact the Yin-yang theory is purely physical, the Persian conception religious-mystical, and where the former overlaps the sphere of religion, it distinguishes itself quite clearly from the Persian dualism. Heaven and Earth, the manifestations of Yin and Yang, are to the Chinese not two enemy powers, but a married couple which generate all living beings. The dual forces are in conflict, it is true, insomuch as now the one, now the other, is paramount, but it is never a war to the knife leading to the complete annihilation of one party. The Yin is looked upon as something less noble and less good than the Yang, or even as bad, but no Chinese would admit that Earth is something bad that ought to be destroyed. Yin and Yang have contradictory qualities. As mother of everything living Earth is revered, and yet from another point of view the Yin is accounted bad, being always the opposite of Yang, which is good. This wickedness is only a technicality, required by theory, and not a moral one like that of Ahriman, the spirit of evil.

The great similarity of the physical views of *Anaxagoras* with the Yin-yang doctrine has already been pointed out. From chaos the Greek thinker causes two masses to separate : the *Thick* and the *Thin*, the *Cold* and the *Warm*, the *Dark* and the *Bright*, the *Moist* and the *Dry*. These are all fundamental attributes of the Yin and the Yang. Anaxagoras does not define his two substances as fire and water, but as ether and air (*p*).

The primogenial elements of *Parmenides* are very much alike. He is said to have taken the *Fiery* for the *active*

_____

(*p*) *Zeller* I., 897.

and the *Dark* for the *passive* or material principle. This latter he identified with the earth, denoting the fire as *light*, and the earth as *darkness* (*q*). "The mixture of light and darkness he represented symbolically as sexual intercourse."

Pythagorism is much less closely related to the Yin-yang doctrine than are the systems of Anaxagoras and Parmenides, though it shows some remarkable agreement. *Gladisch* attempted to prove that Pythagorism is derived from China (*r*), a view controverted by *Zeller* with good reasons (*s*). To the Pythagoreans the *number* constitutes the entity of all things, and, since all numbers consist of *odd* and *even*, the Pythagoreans concluded that odd and even are the constituent parts of all things. The odd was identified with the limited, the even with the unlimited, and in conformity with the popular belief the limited and odd was considered better and more perfect than the even and unlimited. With the aid of the holy decad the Pythagoreans then formed ten contrasts, regarding one quality as good and the opposed one as bad. These two series are as follows :—

(a) *Limit, Odd, One, Right, Male, Quiet, Straight, Light, Good, Square.*

(b) *Unlimited, Even, Multitude, Left, Female, Moved, Crooked, Darkness, Bad, Rectangle* (*t*).

Series (a) are Yang qualities, series (b) Yin qualities. The Chinese did not consider the contrasts : limit—un-

---

(*q*) *Zeller* I., 522. *Alex. in Simpl. Phys.* 9, 9, 1 : κατὰ δὲ τὴν τῶν πολλῶν δόξαν καὶ τὰ φαινόμενα φυσιολογῶν . . . ἀρχὰς τῶν γενομένων ὑπέθετο πῦρ καὶ γῆν, τὴν μὲν γῆν ὡς ὕλην ὑποτιθείς, τὸ δὲ πῦρ ὡς ποιητικὸν αἴτιον, καὶ ὀνομάζει, φησί, τὸ μὲν πῦρ φῶς τὴν δὲ γῆν σκότος.

(*r*) *Gladisch*, Die Pythagoraeer und die alten Chinesen, Posen, 1844.

(*s*) *Zeller* I., 28 *seq.*

(*t*) *Zeller* I., 325. *Arist. Metaph.* I., 5, 986a, 22 : ἕτεροι δὲ τῶν αὐτῶν τούτων τὰς ἀρχὰς δέκα λέγουσιν εἶναι τὰς κατὰ συστοιχίαν λεγομένας, πέρας καὶ ἄπειρον, περιττὸν καὶ ἄρτιον, ἓν καὶ πλῆθος, δεξιὸν καὶ ἀριστερὸν, ἄρρεν

limited, one—multitude. Instead of multitude they would say " two." Quite different is the Chinese conception of the Left as Yang and good, and the Right as Yin and bad (*u*), of the Male as moving, and the Female as quiet, and in lieu of Square and Rectangle they would say Circle and Square. Still a great similarity between the ten Pythagorean contrasts and the Chinese contrasts of the Yin and Yang qualities cannot be denied. Some Pythagoreans have expanded the table of ten by adding : *Above —Below, Anterior—Posterior* (*x*), which again falls in with the Chinese theory. According to the Pythagorean doctrine the *Day* is considered as odd, the *Night* as even. *Dry Warmth* corresponds to the Male and *Wet Cold* to the Female (*y*).

But all these agreements cannot alter the fact that Pythagorism in its essence is entirely different from the Chinese doctrine. To the Pythagorean the number is the real substance of all things, which for that reason are reduced to numbers and classified under the two heads, odd and even. The Chinese presume things to spring from two primary elements, the fiery Yang and the moist Yin. Both are denominated odd and even in the Yiking commentary, but only in respect of the broken and unbroken lines used in divination. In the further development of the theory this division into odd and even is of no consequence and does not touch the core of the doctrine at all.

καὶ θῆλυ, ἠρεμοῦν καὶ κινούμενον, εὐθὺ καὶ καμπύλον, φῶς καὶ σκότος, ἀγαθὸν καὶ κακὸν, τετράγωνον καὶ ἑτερόμηκες.

(*u*) The Right is always given the preference over the Left by Occidentals. On this is based the defence of the Romans to put the left leg on the right one. *Zeller* I., 327.

(*x*) *Zeller, loc. cit. Arist. in Simpl. De caelo*, 173a, 11 *Schol. in Arist.* 492 a, 24 : τὸ οὖν δεξιὸν καὶ ἄνω καὶ ἔμπροσθεν ἀγαθὸν ἐκάλουν, τὸ δὲ ἀριστερὸν καὶ κάτω καὶ ὄπισθεν κακὸν ἔλεγον, ὡς αὐτὸς 'Αριστοτέλης ἱστόρησεν ἐν τῇ τῶν Πυθαγορείοις ἀρεσκόντων συναγωγῇ.

(*y*) *Bouché-Leclercq*, p. 155, 2.

Book IV.

THE FIVE ELEMENTS.

BOOK IV.*

THE FIVE ELEMENTS.

The theory of the Five Elements is no doubt of Chinese origin and its existence in ancient times proved by many old documents. We read in one of the first books of the *Shuking*, the " Counsels of the Great *Yü* " 大 禹 謨:

" *Yü* said (*a*), ' Well! may Your Majesty think of it. Virtue implies good government, and government consists in nourishing the people. *Water, fire, metal, wood, earth,* and grain must be attended to. The rectification of virtue, the supply of all useful things, and ample provision for the necessaries of life must be well balanced. These nine achievements succeed each other, and the nine successive steps are praised in songs. Caution the people with kindness, govern them with majesty, and incite them with the nine songs, in order that there may be nothing amiss.'

" The emperor (*b*) said, ' Yes (*c*), the earth is undis-

---

* Already published as Appendix I. in my translation of the *Lun Hêng*, Part II., 1911.

(*a*) 禹曰, 於帝念哉, 德惟善政, 政在養民, 水火金木土穀, 惟修, 正德利用厚生, 惟和, 九功惟敍, 九敍惟歌, 戒之用休, 董之用威, 勸之以九歌, 俾勿壞.

(*b*) *Shun*, thus apostrophised by *Yü*.

(*c*) 帝曰, 俞, 地平天成, 六府三事允治, 萬世永賴, 時乃功.

turbed now, heaven is in perfect order, and the six treasuries and three affairs properly managed. Ten thousand generations may perpetually rely on them. All this is your doing ' '' (*Legge, Classics*, Vol. III., Part I., p. 85 *seq.*).

What does it mean that the Five Elements : *water, fire, metal, wood,* and *earth* must be controlled by the emperor? How can he exercise any power on nature? By regulating his administration on the natural sequence of the elements, doing only those things which are in harmony with the element ruling for the time being. Natural phenomena are thus affected by the actions of the Son of Heaven, being either disturbed or kept in their regular course. The *Liki* will give us the necessary details.

The elements are here enumerated in the series in which they overcome or destroy one another, for which the terms 勝 or 克 are used. This part of the theory of the Five Elements seems to have been known to the compilers of the *Shuking.*

The above passage is quoted and explained by the *Tso-chuan*, Duke *Wên*, 7th year, and its genuineness thus firmly established. The corresponding passage of the *Tso-chuan* reads thus :

" The book of *Hsia* (*d*) says, ' Caution the people with kindness, govern them with majesty, and incite them with the nine songs, that there may be nothing amiss.' The virtues of the nine achievements may be sung, and are called the nine songs. The six treasuries and the three affairs are called the nine achievements. *Water, fire, metal, wood, earth* and grain are called the six treasuries. The rectification of virtue, the supply of all useful things,

---

(*d*) The '' Counsels of the Great *Yü*,'' *Yü* being the founder of the *Hsia* dynasty.

and ample provision for the necessaries of life are called the three affairs" (*e*). (Cf. *Legge, Classics,* Vol. V., Part I., p. 247.)

In another book of the *Hsia* dynasty, entitled 甘 誓 "the Speech at *Kan,*" the following words are attributed to the Emperor *Ch'i* 啟 who is supposed to have spoken them in 2194 B.C. :

"The Lord of *Hu* offers violence and insult to the *Five Elements,* and neglects and discards the three commencements (of the seasons). Therefore Heaven employs me to destroy and cancel his appointment. Now I merely reverently mete out the punishment of Heaven" (*f*). (*Legge, Classics,* Vol. III., Part I., p. 153.)

Legge rightly observes that the crime of the Lord of *Hu* is stated in a somewhat obscure and mystical language. The Five Elements are not to be taken in the simple physical sense, for then they could not be outraged by a sovereign, but are metaphysical terms, equivalent almost to the four seasons 四 時, as one commentator points out. The seasons are nothing else than the result of the revolutions of the Five Elements, and a ruler commits a crime if, for his administrative acts, he does not choose the proper time, neglecting the seasons. At all events there is some theory at the bottom of the very concise expression.

Another criminal of this sort is introduced to us in the chapter *Hung-fan* (The Great Plan) of the *Shuking,* where

---

(e) 夏書曰, 戒之用休, 董之用威, 勸之以九歌, 勿使壞, 九功之德, 皆可歌也, 謂之九歌, 六府三事, 謂之九功, 水火金木土穀, 謂之六府, 正德, 利用, 厚生, 謂之三事.

(f) 有扈氏, 威侮五行, 怠棄三正, 天用勦絕其命, 今予惟恭行天之罰.

the Viscount of *Chi* says : "I have heard that of old *K'un* by damming up the Great Flood *threw the Five Elements into confusion.* God was highly incensed at him, and did not grant him the Great Plan with the nine divisions" (g). (*Legge, Classics*, Vol. III., Part II., p. 323.)

I suppose that the imaginary guilt of *K'un* did not so much consist in his illtreating the element water as in not observing the propitious time for his draining work, thereby disturbing the Five Elements, i.e., the Five Seasons, and thus bringing down calamities upon his people.

Further on the *Hung-fan* informs us of the nature of the Five Elements, the fullest description to be found in the *Shuking* :

"First the Five Elements : the first is termed *water;* the second, *fire;* the third, *wood;* the fourth, *metal;* the fifth, *earth.* Water is described as soaking and descending; fire as blazing and rising; wood as crooked and straight; metal as yielding and changing; whereas the nature of earth appears from sowing and reaping. That which is soaking and descending becomes *salt;* that which is blazing and rising becomes *bitter;* that which is crooked and straight becomes *sour;* that which is yielding and changing becomes *acrid;* and the produce of sowing and reaping becomes *sweet*" (h). (*Legge, Classics*, Vol. III., Part II., p. 325.)

The sequence of the Five Elements is different from that in the *Hsia-shu*, insomuch as here wood precedes metal.

(g) 箕子乃言曰, 我聞在昔, 鯀陻洪水, 汩陳其五行, 帝乃震怒, 不畀洪範九疇.

(h) 一五行, 一曰水, 二曰火, 三曰木, 四曰金, 五曰土, 水曰潤下, 火曰炎上, 木曰曲直, 金曰從革, 土爰稼穡, 潤下作鹹, 炎上作苦, 曲直作酸, 從革作辛, 稼穡作甘.

It is the sequence in which originally the elements were created. This at least is the opinion of *Chu Hsi,* which we shall examine later on. The nature of the *Five Elements* is described, and another category, that of the *Five Tastes:* *salt, bitter, sour, acrid,* and *sweet* connected therewith, i.e., we have here the first classification based on the five elements. From this one to the others the transition is easy. It is just this book of the *Shuking* which shows us the great partiality of the ancient Chinese for numerical categories and classifications. We find already the 五 事 *Five Businesses :* 貌 言 視 聽 思 *demeanour, speech, seeing, hearing,* and *thinking,* immediately following upon the five elements, and further on the 五 徵 *Five Manifestations,* or 五 氣 *Five Atmospheric Influences* as they are now called, viz., 雨 暘 燠 寒 風, *rain, sunshine, heat, cold,* and *wind* (*Legge, loc. cit.,* p. 339), which subsequently were combined with the Five Elements. The love of symbolism and the tendency of discovering analogies between natural and moral phenomena appears already in what the *Hung-fan* has to say on the *Five Manifestations :*

" There are the auspicious manifestations :—selfpossession is related to seasonable rain ; orderliness, to seasonable sunshine ; judiciousness, to seasonable heat ; discretion, to seasonable cold ; and sageness, to seasonable wind. There are likewise the evil manifestations :—excitement is related to incessant rain ; confusion, to incessant sunshine ; fickleness, to incessant heat ; impetuosity, to incessant cold ; and dullness, to incessant wind.

" It is said that the emperor pays attention to the year ; his ministers and high officers, to the months ; and the petty officials, to the single days. When, during a year, a month, or a day, the seasonableness does not change, then all the crops ripen, the administration is enlightened, excellent persons become illustrious, and the people enjoy peace and happiness. But when, during a day, a month, or a year, the seasonableness changes, then the crops do not ripen, the administration is beclouded and unenlightened, excellent persons remain in obscurity, and the people do not enjoy quietude " (*i*). (*Legge, loc. cit.*, p. 340 seq.)

Already at the beginning of the *Chou* dynasty, in the eleventh century B.C., the Chinese had discovered some resemblance between heaven and earth, and the four seasons with the six ministries, which appears from the names of these departments recorded in the *Chou-li*. There is the prime minister, the chief of the Civil Office, 冢 宰 or 天 官 Officer of Heaven; the minister of the interior and of revenue, 司 徒 or 土 官 Officer of Earth; the minister of ceremonies, 宗 伯 or 春 官 Officer of Spring; the minister of war, 司 馬 or 夏 官 Officer of Summer; the minister of punishments, 司 寇 or 秋 官 Officer of Autumn; and the minister of works, 司 空 or 冬 官 Officer of Winter.

We learn from the same source that the vice-president of the Board of Ceremonies " erected altars to the *Five Emperors* in the four suburbs " (Cf. Le *Tcheou-li*, par E. *Biot*, Vol. I., p. 421, 441, and Vol. II., p. 324). These Five Emperors were five old rulers subsequently deified and venerated as the deities of the *Five Points*.

(i) 曰 休 徵, 曰 肅, 時 雨 若, 曰 乂, 時 暘 若, 曰 晢, 時 煥 若, 曰 謀, 時 寒 若, 曰 聖, 時 風 若, 曰 咎 徵, 曰 狂, 恆 雨 若, 曰 僭, 恆 暘 若, 曰 豫, 恆 煥 若, 曰 急, 恆 寒 若, 曰 蒙, 恆 風 若.

曰, 王 省 惟 歲, 卿 士 惟 月, 師 尹 惟 日, 歲 月 日, 時 無 易, 百 穀 用 成, 乂 用 明, 俊 民 用 章, 家 用 平 康. 日 月 歲, 時 既 易 百 穀 用 不 成, 乂 用 昏 不 明, 俊 民 用 微, 家 用 不 寧.

These are two more corner stones added to the system of the Five Elements. We have no literary evidence to show that this was done already at the commencement of the *Chou* epoch, although there is nothing against such a supposition. At all events this step had been taken some centuries later, for in the *Tso-chuan* we see the theory pretty well evolved from the nucleus observed in the older sources.

We read under *Chao-Kung*, 29th year : " Therefore there were the *officers of the Five Elements*, who accordingly were called the Five Officers. They, in fact, received their family and clan names, and were appointed high dignitaries. As divine spirits they were sacrificed to, and honoured, and venerated at the altars of the Spirits of the Land and Grain and the Five Sacrifices. The ruler of wood was called *Kou Mang*, that of fire *Chu Yung*, of metal *Ju Shou*, of water *Hsüan Ming*, and of earth *Hou T'u*. . . . Viscount *Hsien* inquired of which families were these Five Officers partaking of the oblations of the Spirits of the Land and Grain and the Five Sacrifices. *Tsai Mê* replied : ' At the time of *Shao Hao* there were four men : *Ch'ung, Kai, Hsiu*, and *Hsi*, who were able to regulate metal, wood, and water. *Ch'ung* was made *Kou Mang*, *Kai* was made *Ju Shou*, and *Hsiu* and *Hsi*, *Hsüan Ming*. They never were remiss in discharging their duties and in assisting *Ch'iung Sang* (*Shao Hao*). For these are the Three Sacrifices. *Chuan Hsü* had a son named *Li*, who became *Chu Yung; Kung Kung* had a son named *Kou Lung*, who became *Hou T'u*. For these are the two sacrifices. *Hou T'u* became Spirit of the Land and Grain and director of the fields.' "

Here we have five sons of old legendary rulers raised to the dignity of spirits of the Five Elements after their deaths. They partake of the Five Sacrifices offered to the Five Emperors in the four suburbs and the centre, i.e., they are assistant deities of the Five Points. That they were, moreover, regarded as genii of the seasons appears from their names, for *Kou Mang,* "Curling fronds and spikelets" evidently points to spring, and *Ju Shou,* "Sprouts gathered," designates autumn. *Chu Yung,* referring to heat, may well denote summer, and *Hsüan Ming,* "Darkness obscure," winter. Thus we have the *Five Elements* and their deities connected with the *Five Points* and the *Five Seasons.*

But the most important testimony of the *Tso-chuan* is to be found in the following passage, Duke *Chao,* 25th year :

" *Chien Tse* said, ' I venture to ask what is meant by propriety?' *Tse T'ai Shu* replied, ' I heard the former great officer *Tse Ch'an* say : Propriety is the principle of Heaven, the rule of Earth, and the basis of human conduct. This principle of Heaven and Earth is imitated by the people conforming to the luminaries of Heaven and agreeing with the nature of Earth. The *Six Fluids* are produced and the *Five Elements* made use of. The fluids become the *Five Tastes,* manifest themselves as the *Five Colours,* and appear as the *Five Sounds* ' " (*k*).

And farther on we read : " People feel love and hatred, pleasure and anger, sorrow and joy, which feelings are produced from the *Six Fluids*. Therefore one carefully imitates relations and analogies, in order to regulate these *Six Impulses* " (*l*).

(*k*) 簡子曰, 敢問何謂禮. 對曰, 吉也聞諸先大夫子產, 曰, 夫禮天之經也, 地之義也, 民之行也, 天地之經, 而民實則之, 則天之明, 因地之性, 生其六氣, 用其五行, 氣爲五味, 發爲五色, 章爲五聲.

(*l*) 民有好惡, 喜怒, 哀樂, 生於六氣, 是故, 審則宜類, 以制六志.

By the Six Fluids or atmospherical influences are understood : 陰 陽 風 雨 晦 明 the *Yin* principle, the *Yang* principle, *wind, rain, darkness,* and *light,* a classification somewhat different from that of the Five Fluids of the *Shuking.*

In the above-quoted passage the Five Elements are combined with the Five Tastes, the Five Colours, and the Five Sounds on the one side, and with the Six Fluids and the Six Impulses on the other. After all there are but five entities which appear to us under different forms, either as substances or as atmospherical fluids, or as tastes, colours or sounds. And even human feelings are nothing else but manifestations of these fluids.

Elsewhere the *Tso-chuan* informs us that " the former kings constituted the *five tastes* and harmonised the *five sounds*. It is by these that they made their minds equable and regulated their administration. Sounds are nearly related to tastes " (*m*). (*Tso-chuan,* Duke *Chao,* 20th year.)

That the antagonism of the elements was well known at the time of the *Tso-chuan* we infer from the following passages : " Water overcomes fire " (*n*) (Duke *Ai,* 9th year), and " Fire overcomes metal " (*o*) (Duke *Chao,* 31st year). The meeting of two opposed elements is compared to a marriage, and the stronger element subduing the weaker, called the husband, the weaker being looked upon as the wife. " Water is the husband of fire " (*p*) (Duke *Chao,*

(*m*) 先 王 之 濟 五 味, 和 五 聲 也, 以 平 其 心, 成 其 政 也, 聲 亦 如 味.

(*n*) 水 勝 火.

(*o*) 火 勝 金.

(*p*) 水, 火 之 牡 也.

17th year), and "Fire is the wife of water" (*q*) (Duke *Chao*, 9th year).

Finally the Five Elements are connected with the cyclical signs of the Ten Stems and the Twelve Branches. A disaster is predicted on a *Ping-tse* or a *Jên-wu* day, because on these there is a meeting of water and fire (*r*), *ping* corresponding to fire, and *tse* to water, *jên* to water, and *wu* to fire. Since these cyclical signs serve to denote the points of the compass, the Five Elements must be referred to them also. So we read that "*tse* is the position of water" (*s*) (Duke *Ai*, 9th year), i.e., that water is placed in the North.

The *Tso-chuan* states that the Five Elements manifest themselves as the Five Colours, but does not assign the different colours to the various elements. This is done in the *Chi-chung chou-shu* (*t*), a collection of ancient texts excluded by *Confucius* from the *Shuking*, and consequently prior in time to the sixth century B.C. (Cf. *Chavannes*, *Mém. Hist.*, Vol. V., p. 457.) There we read : " Among the Five Elements the first, the *black* one, is water; the second, the *red* one, is fire; the third, the *green* one, is wood; the fourth, the *white* one, is metal; and the fifth, the *yellow* one, is earth " (*u*).

Resuming the adduced old testimonies, we may assert that, at the time of *Confucius* and before, the theory of the

---

(*q*) 火, 水 妃 也.

(*r*) 丙 子 若 壬 午 作 乎, 水 火 所 以 合 也.

(*s*) 子 水 位 也.

(*t*) 汲 冢 周 書.

(*u*) 五 行 一 黑 位 水, 二 赤 位 火, 三 蒼 位 木, 四 白 位 金, 五 黃 位 土.

Five Elements was known and developed in all its chief features. The elements are roughly described and conceived as partly physical, partly metaphysical entities. They vanquish one another in a certain order already given in the *Shuking*. The weaker element in such a contest is termed the wife, the stronger the husband. The atmospherical fluids, closely connected with the elements, affect mankind, in so far as they are believed to produce impulses and sensations, and, conversely, human actions may influence these fluids. The sovereign especially regulates the elements by the virtue displayed in his administration. There are five officers or deities presiding over the elements and, at the same time, venerated as genii of the seasons, in the five directions, together with the Five Emperors, ruling over the five points of the compass. Thus we have a link between the elements, the seasons, and the five directions. Moreover, the fluids and the elements manifest themselves under the form of the five tastes, the five colours, and the five sounds. Tastes and colours are enumerated and assigned to the respective elements, and we may assume that the same was done with the five sounds, although we have no literary evidence to prove it. By their combination with the signs of the denary and duodenary cycles, the five elements were again located in those points of the compass to which these signs correspond.

In the Appendix to *Couvreur's Dictionary* there is a table of the Five Elements and their corresponding categories, altogether twelve columns. Of these we have so far traced nine ; only the five heavenly Emperors, the five planets, and the five viscera have not yet been mentioned. But these also were referred to the elements in the *Chou* dynasty, as we shall see from the *Liki* and other works.

A short sketch of a natural philosophy is given in the chapter *Li-yün* of the *Liki* (*Legge, Sacred Books,*

Vol. XXVII. p. 380 *seq.*), in which the Five Elements play a part. Man is said to be the product of the forces of heaven and earth by the interaction of the *Yin* and the *Yang*, the union of the animal and intelligent spirits, and the finest matter of the Five Elements (*x*). This, of course, would account for the many relations existing between the elements and the human body, as well as human actions. Moreover, the Five Elements are distributed over the four seasons (*y*). They are in constant movement, and alternately exhaust one another. Each of them becomes in its turn the fundamental one, just like the four seasons and the twelve months (*z*). It is not expressly stated that the five sounds, the five tastes, and the five colours are identical with the five elements; but they are mentioned in close connection with the elements and declared to undergo similar regular revolutions, by which each sound, taste, and colour for a certain time becomes the principal one. Throughout the whole treatise we notice the intimate relation of human life to all the forces of nature, the elements included.

The chapter *Li-yün* is by some attributed to *Tse Yu*, a disciple of *Confucius*, or to his disciples, and regarded as one of the most valuable parts of the *Liki*. I do not share *Legge's* view that the ideas about elements, numbers, colours, &c., are Taoistic admixtures to the commonsense of Confucianism, for we have met them all in the Confucian Classics. (Cf. *Legge's Liki*, Introduction, p. 24.)

(*x*) 故 人 者, 其 天 地 之 德, 陰 陽 之 交, 鬼 神 之 會 五 行 之 秀 氣 也.

(*y*) 播 五 行 於 四 時.

(*z*) 五 行 之 動, 迭 相 竭 也, 五 行 四 時 十 二 月, 還 相 爲 本.

How the elements and their correlates were distributed over the twelve months we learn from another book of the *Liki*, the *Yüeh-ling* (*Legge, eod.*, p. 249 seq.) embodying the fullest scheme of this theory in classical literature. It is a sort of a calendar clearly showing us how much the doctrine of the Five Elements was interwoven with the life of the ancient Chinese. For each of the four seasons it is stated that the Grand Annalist informed the Son of Heaven of the day on which the season began, and of the element ruling over the three months composing the season. The element earth alone had no proper season.

About the first month of *spring* we learn that its days are *chia* and *yi* (*a*), its *divine ruler* is *T'ai Hao*, and the attending *spirit Kou Mang*. Its *creatures* are the *scaly*, its *musical note* is *chio*, its *number* 8 (*b*), its *taste* is *sour*, its *smell* is *rank*. Its *sacrifice* is that at the *inner door* (*c*), and for this the *spleen* of the victim is essential. The *east winds* resolve the cold. The Son of Heaven occupies the apartment on the left of the *Ch'ing-yang Fane* (*d*), and

---

(*a*) The two first of the ten cyclical signs.

(*b*) This number is said to refer to the vernal element wood. The Five Elements are counted in the sequence of their creation (see above. p. 231) :—Water, fire, wood, metal, earth. Now the last only is given its natural number 5. All the other elements have their number in the series plus 5.

(*c*) One of the five sacrifices of the house. The correspondence of these offerings with the seasons and elements is obvious. The door symbolises the opening of the year and the display of the energies of nature. The outer door, or the gate, is the counterpart of the inner door, and therefore connected with the autumn sacrifice. The sacrifice to the hearth goes well with fire, that to the inner court with earth or the centre, and that of the well with water. Our text of the *Liki* reads " path " 行 for 井 " well " (cf. *Legge, loc. cit.* p. 297, note 1). I follow *Wang Ch'ung* I., p. 510.

(*d*) The eastern part of the Hall of Distinction, where the Emperor went on the first day of the month. *Ch'ing-yang* 青 陽 means " green and bright."

rides in a carriage drawn by *green dragon* horses, carrying a *green* flag and wearing *green* robes and pieces of *green* jade. His food consists in *wheat* and *mutton*. At the head of his ministers and the feudal princes, the emperor meets the spring in the *eastern* suburb. The inspectors of the fields are ordered to reside in the lands having an *eastward* exposure. They instruct the people, and see that all the necessary measures for cultivating the fields be taken. Prohibitions are issued against cutting down trees and the killing of young animals, birds, or insects. No fortifications are to be erected, no warlike operations to be undertaken, for they would be sure to be followed by the calamities from Heaven. I refrain from quoting all the other prescriptions and defences, and would only draw attention to the characteristical last paragraph of this

TABLE OF THE FIVE ELEMENTS, THE FOUR SEASONS.

Five Elements 五行	Four Seasons 四時	Five Emperors 五帝	Five Spirits 五神	Five Sacrifices 五祀	Five Animals 五牲	Five Grains(e) 五穀	Five Intestine 五臟
wood	spring	*T'ai Hao*	*Kou Mang*	inner door	sheep	wheat	spleen
fire	summer	*Yen Ti*	*Chu Yung*	hearth	fowl	beans	lungs
earth	...	*Huang Ti*	*Hou Tu*	inner court	ox	panicled millet	heart
metal	autumn	*Shao Hao*	*Ju Shou*	outer door	dog	hemp	liver
water	winter	*Chuan Hsü*	*Hsüan Ming*	well	pig	millet	kidneys

(e) The correspondences of the Five Grains do not quite agree with the and *millet* with fire. His translation of 稷 by rice instead of "panicl "stomach" as *Mayers* does.

section, which has its counterpart in all the other months.

" If in the first month of spring the governmental proceedings proper to summer were carried out, the rain would fall unseasonably, plants and trees would decay prematurely, and the States would be kept in continual fear. If the proceedings proper to autumn were carried out, there would be great pestilence among the people; boisterous winds would work their violence; rain would descend in torrents; orach, fescue, darnel, and southernwood would grow up together. If proceedings proper to winter were carried out, pools of water would produce their destructive effects, snow and frost would prove very injurious, and the first sown seeds would not enter the ground."

In a similar way the other months are described. We abstract therefrom the following Table :

ᴺᴰ OTHER CORRESPONDENCES ACCORDING TO THE LIKI.

Five Numbers (五 數)	Ten Stems 天干	Five Colours 五色	Five Sounds 五音	Five Tastes 五味	Five Smells 五臭	Five Points 五方	Five Creatures 五蟲
8	*chia yi*	green	*chio*	sour	goatish	east	scaly
7	*ping ting*	red	*chih*	bitter	burning	south	feathered
5	*wu chi*	yellow	*kung*	sweet	fragrant	centre	naked
9	*kêng hsin*	white	*shang*	acrid	rank	west	hairy
6	*jên kuei*	black	*yü*	salt	rotten	north	shell-covered

ᴇn in *Mayers' Manual*, p. 316, in as far as he combines *beans* with water, let" is not quite correct. It is also better to render 脾 by " spleen " for

The *Yüeh-ling* is now universally ascribed to *Lü Pu-wei* of the third century B.C. (*Legge, Liki*, Introduction, p. 20); but there is no reason to suppose that it was invented by him, and that it is not a calendar of the *Chou* period, for its contents accords very well with other sources, and was, at all events, regarded as a genuine record of old customs by the compilers of the *Liki*.

The literary evidence of ancient texts collected above is more than sufficient, I trust, to establish the fact that the theory of the Five Elements is of Chinese origin. This has been contested by no less an authority than *Ed. Chavannes*, who is of opinion that the Chinese have borrowed it from the Turks (cf. *Ed. Chavannes*, "*Le cycle turc des douze animaux*," *T'oung-pao*, Série II. Vol. VII. No. 1, pp. 96— 98). His view can hardly be upheld against the old texts. *L. de Saussure* ("*Les Origines de l'astronomie chinoise*," *T'oung-pao*, 1910, Vol. XI. pp. 265—288) has already disposed of it. To his counter-arguments, with which I concur in general, some more may be added. It is rather surprising that of all the Chinese authors who have written on the Five Elements almost nobody refers to *Tsou Yen*, whom *Chavannes* believes to have been the first exponent of the Turkish theory in China. They all go back to the old Chinese sources quoted above. In the fourth or the fifth centuries B.C., when the Turkish theory must have found its way into China, the Turkish tribes, *Hsiung-nu* or *Scythians*, bordering on the Chinese empire, were practically barbarians, from whom the Chinese could not learn much. In the *Shi-chi*, chap. 110, they are described as nomads without cities, who could not write and did not care for the moral laws. The accounts found in *Herodotus*, Book IV., seem to confirm that, at that early age, the Turkish tribes lived in a very primitive state of culture, and it is highly improbable that the theory of the interaction of the elements, supposing a mystical sympathy of all the forces of nature, an attempt at a natural philosophy, should have been devised by an uncivilised people like the early Turks. To the Chinese mind such sorts of speculations have been familiar from time immemorial. In ancient times the Turks most likely received the little culture they had from their neighbours, the Chinese, and when, subsequently, the *Sakas* made their incursions into Bactria and India, from the Greeks and Indians. When, many centuries later, they went over from Buddhism to the Islam, their language as well as their civilisation fell under the influence of the Arabs and Persians. They possessed very little originality, wherefore the invention of the theory of the Five Elements cannot well be set down to their credit.

I strongly doubt that, at the time of *Tsou Yen*, the *Hsiung-nu* already possessed any notion of the elements, which require a more advanced state of civilisation than theirs was. Their descendants, the *Uigurs*, know four elements. But which? *Fire, wind, water and earth* (*Kudatku Bilik*, by *H. Vámbéry*, pp. 75, 78). They are the same as those of the Greeks and Indians, and they evidently learned them from these directly or through the Arabs, as they must have borrowed the seven planets and the twelve signs of the zodiac from the same source. After deducting these foreign loans, there remains nothing originally Turkish.

Even if the four elements, *fire, wind, water,* and *earth,* were of Turkish invention, it would not help us much, for the four elements of the *soi-disant* semi-Turkish *Ch'in* dynasty, according to Chavannes, must have been *fire, wood, metal,* and *earth,* i.e., besides two elements occurring in Europe as well, they embrace two characteristically Chinese elements, *wood* and *metal,* unknown in Europe and India.

I should say that the principal passage on which *Chavannes* bases his belief in the Turkish origin of the theory of the Five Elements admits of a totally different interpretation than that of the eminent sinologist. The Emperor *Han Kao Tsu* expressed his astonishment that in *Ch'in* only four heavenly emperors were sacrificed to, since he had heard that there were five in heaven (*Mém. Hist.* Vol. III. p. 449). In my opinion, this means to say that the emperor knew that before the *Ch'in* epoch there were five emperors worshipped under the *Chou*, and that he simply reverted to the old custom, changed by the *Ch'in*, by instituting a sacrifice to the black emperor, the representative of *water*.

At first sight the theory of the Five Elements, and the classification ingrafted thereon, may seem strange to us, and one of the many Chinese peculiarities; but sociology teaches us that similar classifications, though based on other principles of division, are common all over the world, and among people not connected with one another. Such classifications must therefore be a product of human nature, which is more or less the same everywhere. Consequently, we need not look for a foreign origin of the Chinese theory.

Most *Australian* natives divide up the things of the world conformably to their clans and fraternities, which, each of them, have their special totems. All things belonging to the same group are allied and, so to say, the same reality under different forms. Animals of the same class must not be eaten by their kindred (*E. Durkheim* and *M. Mauss, De quelques formes primitives de classifications,* in *L'Année Sociologique* (Paris, 1901—02), Vol. 6, p. 17). The totems are not only animals but also plants, fruits, and other objects. They may be natural phenomena as well, such as *wind, water*, the *sun, clouds* amongst the *Aruntas* (p. 28, note 2). With the totem *fire* are connected the branches of eucalyptus, the red leaves of the érémophile, the sounds of trumpets, warmth, love (p. 31).

A tribe of the *Sioux* in North America has grouped all objects according to the position occupied by their clans in their camp, viz., *right*, *left*, in the *front*, and in the *rear* (p. 47).

Another tribe of the North American Indians, the *Zuñis*, have taken the seven directions—*north, south, west, east, the zenith, the nadir,* and *the centre*—as the basis for their classifications, and filled them up with all the things in which they are specially interested. Thus they have the following equations :

North : Wind, winter, the pelican, the crane, the green oak, strength, destruction, yellow.

West : Water, spring, moist wind, the bear, the wild dog, vernal herbs, peace, hunting, blue.

South : Fire, summer, agriculture, medicine, red.

East : Earth, seeds, frost, the buck, the antelope, the turkey, magic, religion, white, &c. (p. 35 *seq.*).

The *Dacotahs* have a similar division, but they have lost their clans. The Australian *Wotjoballuk* have distributed their clans and their correlates over thirteen points of the compass (p. 51).

The classifications according to clans and totems appear to be the more primitive ; and those starting from the points of the compass are probably derived from the grouping of the clans in the camp.

It is owing to the preponderance of astrology amongst the *Chaldeans* that with them and their successors, *Greeks* and *Romans*, the planets have become the corner stones of very similar classifications. The *Chaldeans* have attributed the following colours to the planets :

Saturn = *black*, Jupiter = *light red*, Mars = *purple*, the Sun = *golden*, Venus = *white*, and Mercury = *blue*.

Ptolemy gives them somewhat different colours :

Saturn = *a livid grey*, Jupiter = *white*, Mars = *red*, the Sun = *golden*, Venus = *yellow*, and Mercury = *changing colours*.

The scholiasts also differ, and only agree in the colours of *Mars* (red) and the *Sun* (golden) (*A. Bouché-Leclercq, L'Astrologie Grecque* (Paris, 1899), pp. 313, 314).

In addition to colours, *metals*, *plants*, and *animals* are also classified under these planets. Thus mercury is the metal of the homonymous planet ; dragons, snakes, foxes, cats, night birds, donkeys, and hares are linked to Saturn ; wild beasts, monkeys, pigs, to Mars (pp. 317, 318). Moreover, *Ptolemy* has distributed the *parts of the body* and the *senses* among the seven planets according to the following scheme :

Saturn : The right ear, the bladder, the spleen, the phlegm, the bones.

Jupiter : The sense of touch, the lungs, the arteries, the semen.

Mars : The left ear, the kidneys, the veins, the testicles.

Sun : The eyes, the brain, the heart, the nerves—all the chief organs.

Venus : The smells exciting love, the liver, the seat of prophecy, the flesh.

Mercury : The tongue, the gall.

Moon : The taste, the stomach, the womb (p. 321).

This system has undergone a great many modifications at the hands of later authors ; for instance, *Demophilus* and *Hermippus*.

Proclus teaches that the different spheres of the human spirit correspond to the spheres of the stars : *Fixed stars* = intellectual life, *Saturn* = contemplation, *Jupiter* = political and social instincts, *Mars* = passionateness, *Sun* = perceptive faculties, *Venus* = desires, *Mercury* = faculty of speech, *Moon* = vegetative life (p. 325).

In the Middle Ages the *Kabbala* sets forth various systems of classification simultaneously. According to the *Sepher Jezirah* (ninth to tenth century A.D.), the world has been built up by the *Three Elements* named the Three Mothers—*fire* is the substance of heaven, *water* that from which the earth was produced, and both antagonistic elements are separated by the third element, *air*. These Three Elements govern the *Three Seasons—summer*, the *rainy season*, and the *cool season*, and the *Three Parts* of the *Body*, the *head*, the *breast*, and the *belly*. This gives the following table :

Three Elements	Three Seasons	Three Parts of the World	Three Parts of the Body
fire	summer	heaven	head
water	rainy season	earth	breast
air	cool season	void	belly

Besides there are the "*Seven Double Ones*," being partly good and partly wicked. These are the *Seven Planets*, and corresponding to them the *Seven Days* and the *Seven Nights* of a week, and the *Seven Orifices of the Head*.

The "*Twelve Single Ones*" are the *Twelve Months* combined with the *Twelve Signs of the Zodiac* and the

Twelve Human Activities—sight, hearing, smell, touch, speech, nutrition, generation, motion, anger, laughing, thought, and sleep (*A. Lehmann, Aberglauben und Zauberei* (2nd ed.), translated by Petersen, Stuttgart, 1908, p. 145 *seq.*).

At the end of the Middle Ages, these classifications received their highest development in Europe by the mystic *Agrippa von Nettesheim* (1456—1535 A.D.), who, in his great work " *De occulta philosophia,*" combined the Physics of *Aristotle,* the astronomy of *Ptolemy,* the *New Platonism,* and the *Kabbala,* with his own observations and fanciful ideas. His works, and those of his contemporaries, show us that in the beginning of the sixteenth century people in Europe were not a whit farther advanced in natural science than the Chinese philosophers of the Sung epoch or those of to-day. Many of the arguments of *Agrippa* remind us of similar ones of the Chinese theorists of the Five Elements.

Agrippa maintains that everything is subject to a planet or a constellation. Thus, fire and blood are *solar,* and the same is said of gold and of the precious stones—pyrope, heliotrope, jasper, emerald, ruby, the sun-flower, the lotus flower; and the big and audacious animals—the lion, the crocodile, the ram, the bull, the phoenix, the eagle, the cock, the raven. Similar lists are given for all the planets.

Everything on earth is classified according to fixed numbers. *Agrippa* has established groups and classes of one to twelve links each, and combined them to systems, following perhaps the precedent of the *Kabbala.* As a specimen I give his table of the Seven Planets.

In the world of	Zaphkiel	Zadkiel	Chamael	Raphael	Haniel	Michael	Gabriel	God's name in seven letters
archetypes	A Sh R A H J H = Asher Eheie							seven angels before God's face
ideas	Saturn	Jupiter	Mars	Sun	Venus	Mercury	Moon	seven planets
the heavenly world	whoop	eagle	vulture	swan	pigeon	stork	night-owl	seven planetary birds
the elementary world	cuttle-fish	dolphin	pike	seal	shad-fish	blenny	sea-cat	seven planetary fish
	mole	stag	wolf	lion	ram	monkey	cat	seven planetary animals
	lead	tin	iron	gold	copper	mercury	silver	seven planetary metals
	onyx	sapphire	diamond	pyrope	emerald	agate	crystal	seven planetary stones
the world of men	right foot	head	right hand	heart	pudenda	left hand	left foot	seven members
	right ear	left ear	right nostril	right eye	left nostril	mouth	left eye	seven orifices of the head
the infernal world	Gehenna	gate of death	shadow of death	well of death	slough	perdition	abyss	seven dwellings of the damned

After this historical and sociological excursion we return to the *Chou* period where we left the subject. We possess still more sources dating from that time, though not classical ones, proving that already then the table derived from the *Liki* was still further developed.

The Taoist writer *Ho Kuan-tse* (*f*) (fourth century B.C.) arranges the Five Elements according to the position taken by soldiers in a camp, referring them to the human body, and not to the four quarters. "In choosing a position," he says, "one must take advantage of the ground and select it according to the Five Elements. Wood is on the *left* side, metal on the *right*, fire in *front*, water in the *rear*, and earth in the *centre*. In army camps, and in marshalling troops, this order must be observed. These five divisions being well defined, everything may be undertaken with safety" (*g*). This arrangement of the elements agrees with their positions in the four quarters if the observer turns his face to the chief quarter, which for the Chinese is the south. Then fire is in the front or in the south, water in the rear or in the north, wood on the left side or in the east, metal on the right side or in the west, and earth, in both cases, remains in the centre.

The *Su-wên* devotes several chapters to the theory of the Five Elements. This theory has remained the basis of all Chinese medicine up to the present day. As appears from the title of the work, it consists of questions addressed by *Huang Ti* to his assistant, *Ch'i Po*. This, of course, is fiction.

"*Huang Ti* asked in what manner cold and heat, dryness and moisture, wind and fire operated on man, and how

---

(*f*) 鶡 冠 子.

(*g*) 定 下 因 地 利, 制 以 五 行, 左 木, 右 金, 前 火, 後 水, 中 土, 營 軍 陳 士, 不 失 其 宜, 五 度 旣 正, 無 事 不 舉.

they produced the transformations of all things " (h).
Ch'i Po replied about the operation of these six atmospherical influences in the five quarters. For our purpose it
suffices to consider what he says about heat and cold, and
their derivates. A strict parallelism goes through all his
deductions : " The south produces heat, heat produces fire,
fire produces bitterness, bitterness the heart, the heart
blood, and blood the spleen. In heaven it is heat, on earth
it is fire, and in the body, the veins. As a breath it
respires, and among the viscera, it is the heart. Its nature
is hot, its quality effulgence, its manifestation drying up.
Its colour is red, its transformation luxuriance, its creatures
the feathered ones, its government enlightenment, its
weather sultry, its sudden change burning, its calamity a
conflagration. Its taste is bitter, its sentiment joy. Joy
injures the heart, but fear overcomes joy. Heat injures
the breath, but cold overcomes heat, and bitterness injures
the breath, but salt overcomes bitterness " (i).

" The north produces cold, cold produces water, water
produces salt, salt the kidneys, the kidneys produce bones
and marrow, the marrow produces the liver. In heaven it
is cold, on earth it is water, and in the body the bones.
As a breath it is hard, and among the viscera it is the
kidneys. Its nature is glacial, its quality cold, and its

(h) 帝曰, 寒, 暑, 燥, 濕, 風, 火, 在人合之奈何, 其於
萬物何以生化.

(i) 南方生熱, 熱生火, 火生苦, 苦生心, 心生血,
血生脾, 其在天爲熱, 在地爲火, 在體爲脈, 在氣
爲息, 在藏爲心, 其性爲暑, 其德爲顯, 其用爲躁,
其色爲赤. 其化爲茂, 其蟲羽, 其政爲明, 其令鬱蒸,
其變炎爍, 其眚燔炳, 其味爲苦, 其志爲喜, 喜傷
心, 恐勝喜, 熱傷氣, 寒勝熱, 苦傷氣, 鹹勝苦.

manifestation . . . (*l*). Its colour is black, its transformation frost, its creatures are the shell-covered, its government is quiet, its weather . . . , its sudden change is freezing, its calamity ice and hailstones. Its taste is salt, its sentiment fear. Fear injures the kidneys, but desire overcomes fear. Cold injures the blood, but dryness overcomes cold. Salt injures the blood, but sweetness overcomes salt " (*m*).

Ch'i Po winds up by saying : " The Five Fluids come forward in turn, and each of them takes precedence once. When they do not keep in their proper spheres, there is disaster; when they do, everything is well ordered " (*n*).

The *Su-wên* adds some more categories to those given by the *Liki* : The five styles of government 五 政—*relaxation, enlightenment, carefulness, energy* and *quietude* (*o*); the five impulses 五 志—*anger, joy, desire, sorrow* and *fear* (*p*); and the five constituent parts of the body 五 體—*muscles, veins, flesh, skin and hair,* and *bones* (*q*). The five intestines or viscera are the same as those of the *Liki,* but their sequence is different, and in each class, in addition

---

(*l*) *Lacuna* in the text.

(*m*) 北方生寒, 寒生水, 水生鹹, 鹹生腎, 腎生骨髓, 髓生肝, 其在天爲寒, 在地爲水, 在體爲骨, 在氣爲堅, 在藏爲腎, 其性爲凜, 其德爲寒, 其用爲 ○ 其色爲黑, 其化爲肅, 其蟲鱗, 其政爲靜, 其令 ○ ○ 其變凝冽, 其青冰雹, 其味爲鹹, 其志爲恐, 恐傷腎, 思勝恐, 寒傷血, 燥勝寒, 鹹傷血, 甘勝鹹.

(*n*) 五氣更立, 各有所先, 非其位則邪. 當其位則正.

(*o*) 散, 明, 謐, 勁, 靜.

(*p*) 怒, 喜, 思, 憂, 恐. The five impulses partly correspond to the six impulses of the *Tso-chuan.* See above, p. 234.

(*q*) 筋, 脈, 肉, 皮, 毛, 骨.

to the principal intestine, a secondary one is introduced, viz., every secondary one is the principal intestine of the next class.

As to the theory of the Five Elements, the medical work agrees with the *Shuking* and the *Tso-chuan*, whose general hints it specifies. It distinguishes three spheres of the elements, which in each of them appear in different forms, the spheres of heaven, of earth, and of man, just as *Agrippa* has seven spheres. The original form of the elements is that of the Six Fluids or atmospheric influences—*cold* and *heat, dryness* and *moisture, wind* and *fire* (r). They produce the five elements on earth, but in combining each element with a fluid the author drops *fire*. All the other diverse forms of the elements are the result of constant transformations, which to us appear very strange. How can fire produce bitterness, bitterness the heart, the heart blood, and blood the spleen? The qualities and manifestations of the elements described in the work are more in accordance with nature.

But what does it mean that "fear injures the kidneys, but desire overcomes fear. Cold injures the blood, but dryness overcomes cold. Salt injures the blood, but sweetness overcomes salt," and the like passages under the other heads? These are merely equations deduced from the theory of the antagonism of the elements, and seem to be the basis for the medical treatment of the parts of the body. We know that fear may affect the kidneys, and that a strong desire may vanquish fear. The last conclusion, however, the Chinese theorist probably did not draw from practice, but from the premises that desire corresponds to earth, and fear to water. Consequently, earth overcoming

---

(r) The Six Fluids of the *Tso-chuan*, not expressly mentioned, would be different if the commentators are right. Cf. p. 235. But they practically agree with the Five Fluids of the *Shuking* :—*rain, sunshine, heat, cold,* and *wind* (see above, p. 231), leaving aside *fire.*

water, desire must vanquish fear likewise. In the same manner cold (water) injures the blood (fire), and dryness (metal) again overcomes cold (water), not directly, it is true, but indirectly, for metal overcomes wood, wood earth, and earth water. Moreover, salt (water) injures the blood (fire), but sweetness (earth) vanquishes salt (water).

The new classes of the *Su-wên* are thus grouped :

Five Fluids	Five Elements	Five Parts of Body	Five Intestines	Five Impulses	Five Styles of Government
五 氣	五 行	五 體	五 臟	五 志	五 政
wind	wood	muscles	liver (heart)	anger	relaxation
heat	fire	veins (blood)	heart (spleen)	joy	enlighten-ment
moisture	earth	flesh	spleen (lungs)	desire	carefulness
dryness	metal	skin and hair	lungs (kidneys)	sorrow	energy
cold	water	bones (marrow)	kidneys (liver)	fear	quietude

Each element preponderates during one season, and, while so doing, it may be well balanced and have its proper quantity, it may be excessive or deficient. Excess and deficiency both entail calamities affecting the vegetation and the human body. In the latter case we have all kinds of diseases and maladies. All these states are minutely described, and still more categories added. Each element in its proper state of equilibrium is said to be governed by a part of a body different from those already mentioned —the eye, the tongue, the mouth, &c. Moreover, it is connected with two sorts of fruits, a fleshy and a not-fleshy— wood, for instance, with a plum and a nut—and with a domestic animal like the dog, the horse, &c. Even in its felicitous state each element has a special sickness assigned to it : palpitations and convulsions belong to fire, coughing to metal, constipation to earth. The classes of the *Liki* are again ascribed to the elements well balanced, but not in the proper order. Thus, e.g., wood is combined with hemp, the hairy creatures, and the liver; fire has as correlates wheat, feathered creatures, and the heart.

In case a ruling element be excessive or insufficient, two or more things of the same sort are made to correspond to it, whereas as a rule there is only one. There may be two fruits, two animals, two colours, two tastes corresponding to one element; even three are combined, probably to show the irregularity of the ruling element. At the same time, the Five Planets are introduced as correlates of the elements, mostly two or three connected with one element. Thus we find Jupiter and Venus in connection with excessive wood, Mars and Mercury combined with excessive fire, Venus and Mars together with insufficient wood, and Mars, Mercury and Saturn together with insufficient fire.

All irregularities of the elements entail a great variety of diseases. Whenever wood is superabundant, earth and the spleen have to suffer. This leads to pains in the limbs, flatulency, diarrhoea, and vomiting. A scarcity of wood is accompanied by pains of the ribs and the stomach, by coughs and catarrhs, eruptions, scarlatina, sores and ulcers. A scarcity of fire causes pains in the breast, the back, the shoulders, the arms, the heart, rheumatism, cramps, paralysis of the legs, dumbness, swooning, &c.

Whereas the *Su-wên* insists upon the effects of the irregularities of the elements upon man, the philosopher *Kuan-tse*, of the seventh century B.C., attempts to show how natural events, connected with the elements, are influenced by the government of the emperor.

" *Yin* and *Yang*," says *Kuan-tse*, " are the great principles of heaven and earth, and the Four Seasons are the warp in the web of *Yin* and *Yang*. Punishments and rewards are the correlates of the Four Seasons (*s*). Their conformity to the seasons brings about happiness, their discrepancy leads to misfortune " (*t*) (*Kuan-tse* XIV. 7 r.). Then *Kuan-tse* proceeds to describe the seasons in a similar way as the *Liki* does, but, whereas the *Liki* distinguishes but *Four Seasons*, earth having no special one and belonging to all, *Kuan-tse* gives Five Seasons (*u*), each lasting seventy-two days. Besides, he joins a special heavenly body to every quarter—the centre corresponds to the *earth*, the south to the *sun*, the north to the *moon*, the east to the *stars*, and the west to the *zodiacal signs* (*x*). For each of the Four Seasons five administrative measures 五 政 are prescribed, the carrying out of which ensures felicity, whereas their omission or change is fraught with disaster. In the opinion of one commentator each season would have counted ninety days, and to each of the five administrative measures eighteen days would have been allotted. Thus the author says in regard to winter :

" In the three winter months, on the *jên-kuei* (*y*) days five administrative measures are carried out. The first is

---

(*s*) 陰 陽 者, 天 地 之 大 理 也, 四 時 者, 陰 陽 之 大 經 也, 刑 德 者, 四 時 之 合 也, 刑 德 合 於 時, 則 生 福, 詭 則 生 禍.

(*t*) As will be seen in the following, rewards are in accordance with spring and summer, punishments with autumn and winter. From time immemorial capital punishment in China has been meted out in autumn and winter, so that the Chinese have come to consider this the natural course of nature.

(*u*) In the chapter on the Five Elements, XIV., 16 v. *seq.* In the preceding one on the Four Seasons, XIV., p. 8 v., he still adheres to the theory of the Four Seasons, stating that *earth*, the element of the centre, helps the Four Seasons 輔 四 時.

(*x*) 土, 日, 月, 星, 辰.

(*y*) See below, p. 259, note (*h*).

providing for orphans and destitute persons and succouring the old and the aged; the second is conforming to the *Yin*, preparing the sacrifices for the spirits, bestowing titles and emoluments, and conferring ranks; the third is verifying accounts, and not to exploit the treasures of mountains and rivers; the fourth is rewarding those who seize runaway criminals and arrest robbers and thieves; the fifth is prohibiting the moving about of the people, stopping their wanderings, and preventing their settling in other parts of the empire (z). If these five measures are taken at the proper time, so that the affairs of winter are not disregarded, one obtains one's wishes, and that which one dislikes does not take place " (a).

Kuan-tse then proceeds to show how an emperor should act conformably to the Four Seasons :

" If plants wither in spring and blossom in autumn, if it thunders in winter, and there is frost and snow in summer, all this is harm caused by the fluids. If regarding rewards and punishments the periods are changed, and the natural order is confounded, then injurious fluids quickly arrive,

---

(z) 冬三月, 以壬癸之日發五政, 一政曰, 論孤獨, 恤長者, 二政曰, 善順陰, 修神祀, 賦爵祿, 授備位, 三政曰, 效會計, 毋發山川之藏, 四政曰, 捕姦遁, 得盜賊者有賞, 五政曰, 禁遷徙, 止流民, 圍分異, 五政苟時, 冬事不過, 所求必得, 所惡必伏.
Kuan-tse, XIV., 11 r.

(a) The Chinese probably discovered some analogies between these measures and winter, and for that reason prescribed them :—There is some similarity between the desolateness of winter and destitute persons. Winter, being the end of the year, may be compared with old and aged persons. We ourselves personify it by an old man, and spring by a young boy. In winter the *Yin* principle is at its height, and incorporeal spirits belong to it. Accounts are usually settled at the end of the year. The hidden treasures of mountains and rivers 藏 must not be moved, because hiding and torpidity is the nature of winter. The forces of nature do not move ; hence the moving about of the people is prohibited. Criminals, as we have seen, are called to account in autumn and winter.

and, upon their arrival, the State is visited with many disasters. Therefore a wise emperor observes the seasons and accordingly regulates his administration. He provides education and makes his warlike preparations, offers sacrifices and thereby establishes virtue. It is by these three things that a wise emperor puts himself into harmony with the movement of heaven and earth " (*b*).

" The sun governs the *Yang*, the moon the *Yin*, the stars govern harmony. *Yang* produces rewards, *Yin* punishments (*c*), and harmony makes business possible. Consequently when there is an eclipse of the sun (*d*), a State that has failed in its rewards is to be blamed for it. When there is an eclipse of the moon (*e*), a State that has failed in its punishments is responsible. When a comet puts in an appearance, a State that has lost harmony is guilty, and when wind fights with the sun for brightness, a State that has failed in productiveness is answerable (*f*). Wherefore, at an eclipse of the sun, a wise emperor improves rewards; at an eclipse of the moon, he improves punishments; when a comet becomes visible, he improves harmony, and when wind and sun fight together, he

---

(*b*) 故春凋秋榮冬雷夏有霜雪, 此皆氣之賊也, 刑德易節失次, 則賊氣遫至, 賊氣遫至, 則國多菑殃, 是故聖王務時而寄政焉, 作敎而寄武, 作祀而寄德焉, 此三者聖王所以合於天地之行也.

(*c*) The *Yang* is warm, and thus may be symbolised by warmth of heart, benevolence, and rewards. *Yin* is cold, and has an analogy in cold-hearted severity and punishments.

(*d*) An eclipse of the sun, the chief representative of *Yang*, means that rewards have been incomplete.

(*e*) The moon again represents the *Yin* fluid and punishments. Its partial annihilation shows that punishments have been insufficient.

(*f*) Wind is the fluid of spring, the characteristic feature of which is productiveness. Fighting for brightness must signify that wind chasing the clouds attempts to obscure the brightness of the sun, which now and then breaks through the clouds.

improves production. By these four measures the wise emperor avoids the punishments of heaven and earth " (*g*).

The disasters which may befall a sovereign not conforming to the seasons in his administration are thus described :

" When we see the cyclical sign *chia-tse* (*h*) arrive, the element wood begins its reign. If the Son of Heaven does not bestow favours or grant rewards and, contrariwise, extensively allows cutting, destroying, and wounding (*i*), then the sovereign is in danger, and should he not be killed, then the heir-apparent would be in danger, and some one of his family or his consort would die, or else his eldest son would lose his life. After 72 days this period is over. When we see the cyclical sign *ping-tse* arrive, the element fire begins its reign. In case the Son of Heaven be anxious to take hurried and hasty measures (*k*), an epidemic would

---

(*g*) 日掌陽, 月掌陰, 星掌和, 陽爲德, 陰爲刑, 和爲事, 是故日食, 則失德之國惡之, 月食, 則失刑之國惡之, 彗星見, 則失和之國惡之, 風與日爭明, 則失生之國惡之, 是故聖王, 日食, 則修德, 月食, 則修刑, 彗星見, 則修和, 風與日爭明, 則修生, 此四者, 聖王所以免於天地之誅也. *Kuan-tse*, XIV., 11 v.

(*h*) This is the cyclical sign of the day beginning the period of seventy-two days assigned to the element wood. Here we have a key to the understanding of the pairs of cyclical signs joined to each element in the *Liki*, the meaning of which was not clear to *Legge*. The days of spring are *chia*, and *yi* (cf. p. 241) means nothing else than that the first and the second days of this season bear these signs, being in the sexagenary cycle *chia-tse* and *yi-chou*. Summer begins when we arrive at the sign *ping-tse*, after having passed through the entire cycle of sixty, adding twelve, i.e., after seventy-two days. The second day of summer or of the element fire is a *ting-chou* day, so that the *Liki* may say that the days of summer are *ping* and *ting*, &c. Of course, the assigning of three full months to each season by the *Liki* is not in keeping with these cyclical signs, which can only be applied to seasons of seventy-two days.

(*i*) Spring is the time of growth, but not of destruction.

(*k*) According to a commentator, this is the season of ease and indulgence.

be caused by a drought (*l*), plants would die, and the people perish by it. After 72 days this period is over. When we see the sign *wu-tse* arrive, the element earth begins its reign. If the Son of Heaven builds palaces or constructs kiosks, the sovereign is in danger, and if without city walls are built (*m*), his ministers die. After 72 days this period is over. When we see the sign *kêng-tse* arrive, the element metal begins its reign. Should the Son of Heaven attack the mountains and beat the stones (*n*), his troops would be defeated in war, and his soldiers die, and he would lose his sway. After 72 days this period is over. When we see the sign *jên-tse* arrive, the element water begins its reign. If the Son of Heaven cuts the dykes and sets the great floods in motion, his empress or his consort die, or else the eggs of birds become addled, the hairy young are miscarried, and pregnant women have an abortion. Plants and trees are spoiled in the roots. After 72 days this period is over " (*o*).

Among the authors of the *Han* time *Huai-nan-tse* and

(*l*) A drought is a consequence of too much heat symbolised by hurried and hasty actions.

(*m*) By building the element earth is disturbed.

(*n*) This, again, would mean a disturbance of the metal hidden in the mountains.

(*o*) 睹甲子, 木行御, 天子不賦不賜賞, 而大斬伐傷, 君危不殺, 太子危, 家人夫人死, 不然則長子死, 七十二日而畢. 睹丙子, 火行御, 天子敬行急政, 旱札, 苗死民厲, 七十二日而畢. 睹戊子, 土行御. 天子修宮室, 築臺榭, 君危, 外築城郭, 臣死, 七十二日而畢. 睹庚子, 金行御, 天子攻山擊石, 有兵作戰而敗士死, 喪執政, 七十二日而畢. 睹壬子, 水行御, 天子決塞, 動大水, 王后夫人薨, 不然則羽卵者毈, 毛胎者瀆, 腫婦銷弃, 草木根本不美, 七十二日而畢也. *Kuan-tse* XIV., 18 v. (*Shih-tse ch'üan-shu*).

Tung Chung-shu, both of the second century B.C., have written more or less systematically on the theory of the Five Elements, to which several chapters of their chief works are devoted. *Liu Hsiang*, in the first century B.C., composed the *Wu-hsing-chih* (*p*), a treatise on the Five Elements, which has not come down to us. *Pan Ku*, of the first century A.D., discourses at some length on the subject in his *Po-hu-t'ung*. Afterwards it was taken up by a great many writers, and forms an important part of the disquisitions of the philosophers of the *Sung* dynasty.

We are now going to consider the results at which these writers and their predecessors have arrived.

I. Various Terms for the Elements.

The modern work, *Chang-huang t'u-shu pien* (*q*), states that in the *Yiking* the Five Elements are named 五 位 *Wu-wei*, *Five Positions* (*r*), in historical works 五 材 *Wu-ts'ai*, *Five Materials*, in chronicles or essays 五 物 *Wu-wu*, *Five Things*, and in medical works 五 運 *Wu-yün*, *Five Revolutions*. *Mayers* (Manual, p. 313) gives some more terms : 五 節 *Wu-chieh*, *Five Sections*, 五 美 *Wu-mei*, *Five Excellencies*, and 五 氣 *Wu-ch'i*, *Five Fluids*. They are descriptive of the elements under various aspects, as substances formed of matter, as fluids or vapours, as moving and revolving, or as keeping certain positions. But by far the commonest expression is 五 行 *Wu-hsing*, on the meaning of which the Chinese and foreign authorities are agreed. 行 *hsing* is "to act" and "to move," the *Wu-hsing* are, therefore, the five essences which are always active and in motion. *Mayers* (*loc. cit.*) calls them the

---

(*p*) 五 行 志.

(*q*) 章 潢 圖 書 編.

(*r*) The utterances of the *Yiking* are very obscure, and I doubt whether they really refer to the elements.

primordial essences or perpetually active principles of nature. The term is all but equivalent to 五 運 *Wu-yün*, the *Five Revolutions*.

II. WHAT ARE THE FIVE ELEMENTS?

The designation *Wu-hsing* goes back to the *Shuking* and implies that at these remote times the elements were conceived already as ever active essences, which again supposes the existence of some sort of a theory devised to explain the phenomena of nature. In the most ancient description of the elements contained in the *Shuking* (cf. above, p. 230) they are considered from the physical point of view as natural substances :—water has the tendency of descending and soaking other stuffs, fire that of rising and blazing; wood is characterised as crooked and straight, which seems to refer to the appearance of the branches of trees; metal is said to be yielding and changing, which is only true of metal in a liquid state; earth is not described any further, and its nature found in its generative and productive power. At all events, the authors of the Classic had not some metaphysical entities in view, but the substances usually understood by the names :—water, fire, wood, metal, and earth.

As to the impressions produced by these elements upon our senses and resulting in the categories of *colours, sounds, tastes,* and *smells,* the *Shuking* concerns itself with tastes only :—Water becomes salt, fire bitter, wood sour, metal acrid, and cereals, the produce of earth, sweet. Of course pure water is not salt, but tasteless, yet, as the commentators remark, it becomes salt in the ocean, a wrong notion. Fire we would rather describe as burning than bitter, and wood as bitter instead of sour. The acrid taste of metals and the sweet one of cereals, such as rice and millet, may pass. It is difficult now to say which considerations led the ancient Chinese to attribute just these tastes to the five elements. Since the five tastes are always given in the series :—*salt, bitter, sour, acrid, sweet,* it is not impossible that the ancients merely coupled them with the five elements of the *Shuking* in the same order, without any regard to their natural relations.

In the same superficial manner the five colours :—*black, red, green, white* and *yellow* may have been connected with the five elements, although the correspondencies have been explained :—Fire may well be described as red, though yellow would seem more appropriate. Wood appears green at least outwardly in plants and trees, whereas inwardly it is mostly white or yellow. The colours of metals are manifold, only their glittering may be said to be white. Earth is not yellow in most countries, but it was so in the *loess* regions in *Honan* and *Shansi* where the Chinese were first settled. How can water be called black, however, a colour it almost never shows? It seems to refer to the *Yin* fluid preponderating in winter, the time of the element water. *Yang* is light and sunshine, *Yin* darkness, *Yang* day-time, and *Yin* night. These correspondences are universally accepted, but I met with one exception in the " Sayings of the School of Confucius," *K'ung-tse chia-yü* (s), chap. 6, p. 1, from which we learn that the *Hsia* dynasty reigned by the virtue of *metal* and of the colour most appreciated *black,* the *Yin* dynasty reigned by *water* and appreciated *white,* the *Chou* by *wood* with the *red* colour. *Yao's* element was *fire,* and his colour *yellow.* *Shun's* element *earth,* and his colour *green.* These different combinations of elements and colours show the arbitrariness of the whole scheme. It is impossible to find one colour for each element, because each embraces many species with different colours :—Water

---

(s) I doubt whether this chapter 五 帝, treating of the Five Elements, really goes back to *Confucius*, since he is made to say that he was informed about the elements by *Lao-tse.*

may appear pellucid, white, green, blue, red, yellow, grey, black; earth may be black, brown, yellow, red, blue, white, etc. (*t*); and so different substances burn with different lights. Therefore to ascribe one colour to each element cannot but be arbitrary.

The *Zuñis* of North America have no elements (*u*), but they have attributed certain colours to their seven points of the compass. Their reasons for doing so are not very convincing either :—The *North* is yellow, because at sunrise and sunset the sunlight appears yellow. The *West* is blue, the colour of the evening light. The *East* is white, the colour of day, the *South* red, because it is the seat of summer and of the red fire. The *Zenith* is multicoloured like the clouds, the *Nadir* black, and the *Centre* has all colours. (*Année Sociologique*, Vol. VI., p. 35 *seq.*)

Of the *Five Smells* only *burning* and *fragrant* seem to refer to the corresponding elements fire and earth (cereals). *Goatish, rank,* and *rotten* have nothing to do with wood, metal, and water. They probably apply to the Five Animals joined to these elements :—the *sheep* (goat), *dog*, and *pig*.

On the principle by which the *Five Sounds* have been combined with the elements I am unable to express any opinion.

Kuan-yin-tse has amplified the statement of the *Shuking* about the rising and descending of fire and water :—" That which rises, he says, is fire; that which descends, water. That which would like to rise, but cannot, is wood; and that which would like to descend, but cannot, is

---

(*t*) If we speak of the green earth, we regard its coat, the green vegetation, as part of it.

(*u*) That is to say, they have not conceived the idea of the elements, but ascribe the single ones to the four quarters like the Chinese—wind belongs to the north, water to the west, fire to the south, and earth to the east.

metal " (x). This depicts fairly well the tendency of plants of growing up and that of metals of sinking down. These tendencies, however, are restricted and less free than those of fire and water which, endowed with a greater agility as air and fluid, can follow their propensities and rise and fall.

The *Chang Huang t'u-shu pien* makes an attempt to distinguish between the different *forms* of the elements :— water is level, fire is pointed, earth is round, wood crooked and straight, and metal square (y). These are indeed the forms under which these substances often appear to us. Whereas water shows a level surface, a flame rises and seems pointed. Clods of earth are more or less round, and ore has often angular and square shapes. The description of wood as crooked and straight is taken from the *Shuking*.

It is but natural that the Chinese should have connected their Five Elements with the two principles of nature established by their old philosophers, the *Yin* and *Yang*, and derived them therefrom. *Tung Chung-shu* says in his *Ch'un-ch'iu fan-lu* XIII., 5 v., that the fluid of Heaven and Earth united is one. But it splits into *Yin* and *Yang*, becomes divided into the Four Seasons, and separated into the Five Elements (z). *Yin* and *Yang*, which we may here translate by *cold* and *heat*, are the primogenial essences

---

(x) 升者爲火, 降者爲水, 欲升而不能升者爲木, 欲降而不能降者爲金.

(y) 水之平也, 火之銳也, 土之圜也, 木之曲直也, 金之方也. 此其以形言也. In another chapter the same author gives 尖, 圓, 方, 直, 曲 as the shapes of the elements. 直 " straight " seems to stand for " level," and 曲 " crooked " alone for " straight and crooked," the shape of wood.

(z) 董仲舒, 春秋繁露, 五行相生。天地之氣, 合而爲一, 分爲陰陽, 判爲四時, 列爲五行. (Han-Wei ts'ung-shu).

from which the Five Elements are produced in the following way :—Water has its seat in the north which is governed by the *Yin* fluid. Wood is placed in the east, which is likewise under the sway of the *Yin*, but the *Yang* begins to move already. Fire occupies the south where the *Yang* reaches its climax. Metal rests in the west, and is governed by the *Yang*, but the *Yin* begins to stir. Consequently " Fire is *Yang*, it is noble, and therefore rises ; water is *Yin*, it is mean, and therefore goes down ; wood is a scanty *Yang*, and metal a scanty *Yin* " (*a*). (*Pan Ku's Po-hu-t'ung* II., 1.) The idea is quite clear, if we take into consideration the Four Seasons with which the elements are combined. In summer ruled by fire, *Yang*=heat prevails, in winter ruled by water, *Yin*=cold. In spring and autumn, when wood and metal are paramount, *Yin* and *Yang*, heat and cold fight together, so that one may speak of a scanty *Yang* or an incomplete *Yin*. The element earth which does not well agree with the Four Seasons is left out by *Pan Ku*.

Later authors have gone more into details. *Tse-hua-tse* (*Sung* dynasty) characterises fire as an abundant *Yang*, and water as an abundant *Yin*, wood as a scanty *Yang*, metal as a scanty *Yin*, and earth as sometimes *Yin* and sometimes *Yang*.

" The *Yang* in the *Yang* is fire, he says, the *Yin* in the *Yin* is water, the *Yin* in the *Yang* is wood, the *Yang* in the *Yin* is metal. Earth keeps in the middle between the two essences and thus governs the four quarters :—in the *Yin* it is *Yin*, and in the *Yang* it is *Yang* " (*b*). (*Tse-hua-tse* II., 11 v.)

(*a*) 班固, 白虎通, 五行。火者陽也, 尊故上, 水者陰也, 卑故下, 木者少陽, 金者少陰.

(*b*) 子華子, 北宮意問。陽中之陽者火是也, 陰中之陰者水是也, 陽中之陰者木是也 陰中之陽

" In the north the extreme *Yin* resides. It produces cold, and cold engenders water. In the south the extreme *Yang* resides, which produces heat, and heat produces fire. In the east the *Yang* is set in motion. It disperses and calls forth wind, which again produces wood. In the west the *Yin* stops and gathers. It thus causes dryness, which produces metal. In the centre the *Yin* and the *Yang* mix and produce moisture, which engenders earth " (*c*).

In other words fire is considered to be *Yang* throughout, *Yang* in *Yang*, i.e., an unalloyed *Yang*; water, a pure and genuine *Yin*. Wood is also *Yang*, but with an admixture of *Yin*; metal is *Yin*, but with an alloy of *Yang*. Earth may be both.

Chu Hsi and his school take a somewhat different view. They look upon the Five Elements as created by Heaven and Earth alternately, Heaven and Earth thus taking the the place of the *Yin* and the *Yang*. " Heaven first creates water, Earth secondly creates fire, Heaven thirdly creates wood, Earth fourthly creates metal " (*d*). This idea seems to have originated from an obscure passage of the *Yiking* believed to refer to the Five Elements (*e*). *Chu Hsi* quotes the famous *Su Tung-p'o* (1036—1101 A.D.) as his authority, who says that water is the extreme *Yin*, but it requires

---

者 金 是 也, 土 居 二 氣 之 中 間, 以 治 四 維, 在 陰 而 陰, 在 陽 而 陽.

(c) 北 方 陰 極, 而 生 寒, 寒 生 水, 南 方 陽 極 而 生 熱, 熱 生 火, 東 方 陽 動 以 散 而 生 風, 風 生 木, 西 方 陰 止 以 收 而 生 燥, 燥 生 金, 中 央 陰 陽 交 而 生 濕, 濕 生 土. (*Tse-shu po-chia*).

(d) 朱 子 全 書。天 一 生 水, 地 二 生 火, 天 三 生 木, 地 四 生 金 (T'u shu chi-ch'êng).

(e) 易 經, 繫 辭 上 傳。天 一, 地 二, 天 三, 地 四, 天 五, 地 六, 天 七, 地 八, 天 九, 地 十.

Heaven to co-operate before it can be produced. *Yin* alone without *Yang* cannot produce it. Fire is the extreme *Yang*, but it likewise requires the co-operation of Earth to come into existence. And so it is with all the Five Elements, they all cannot be created unless the *Yin* and *Yang* are both at work. When the *Yang* is added to the *Yin*, water, wood, and earth come forth, and when the *Yin* is added to the *Yang*, fire and metal are produced (*f*).

About the creation of the elements and their nature *Chu Hsi* further asserts that by the joint action of *Yin* and *Yang* water and fire are first produced. Both are fluids flowing, moving, flashing, and burning. Their bodies are still vague and empty, and they have no fixed shape. Wood and metal come afterwards. They have a solid body. Water and fire are produced independently, wood and metal need earth as a substratum from which they issue (*g*). Heaven and Earth first generate the light and pure essences, water and fire, afterwards the heavy and turbid ones, wood, metal, and earth. The last is the heaviest of all. As to their density, water and fire are shapeless and unsubstantial fluids, fire, hot air in the atmosphere, wood is a soft substance, metal a hard one.

Chou-tse, a predecessor of *Chu Hsi*, gives still another formula for the elements :—water is the moist fluid in the *Yang*, fire the dry fluid in the *Yin*, wood the moist fluid

---

(*f*) 水至陰也, 必待天一加之, 而後生者, 陰不得陽, 則終不得而成也, 火至陽也, 必待地二加之, 而後生者, 陽不得陰, 則無所得而見也。五行皆然, 莫不生於陰陽之相加, 天加陰, 則爲水爲木爲土, 陰加陽, 則爲火爲金.

(*g*) 陽變陰合, 初生水火, 水火氣也, 流動閃鑠, 其體尙虛, 其成形猶未定。次生木金, 則確然有定形矣, 水火初是自生, 木金, 則資於土。

in the *Yang* but expanded, metal the dry fluid in the *Yin* contracted, earth the *Yin* and the *Yang* blended and condensed, so as to become a substance. *Yang* and *Yin*, heat and cold, are allotted to the Five Elements in the same manner as by *Chu Hsi*, but as a secondary constituent we have moisture and dryness. These are the same principles from which *Aristotle* has evolved his Four Elements :— earth, water, fire, and air. The Chinese have become acquainted with his theory by the geographical work *K'un-yü t'u-shuo* (*h*), written by the Jesuit father *Verbiest* about the end of the 17th century and cited by the *T'u-shu chi-ch'êng*. According to the Aristotelian theory dryness and cold produce earth, moisture and cold produce water, moisture and heat give air, dryness and heat give fire (*i*). The result arrived at by *Chou-tse* is different, he only composes earth similarly, namely, by heat and cold (*Yin* and *Yang*). His water consists of moisture and heat (*Yang*) instead of cold, and his fire of dryness and cold (*Yin*) instead of heat. The Aristotelian view appears more natural than that of *Chou-tse*, who is under the spell of the *Yiking*. Perhaps *Tse-hua-tse* agrees with the Greek philosopher, for his above-mentioned dictum that fire is the *Yang* in the *Yang*, and water the *Yin* in the *Yin*, may be understood to mean that fire is dryness in heat, and water moisture in the cold, *Yang* denoting heat as well as dryness and *Yin* cold and moisture.

III. Fluids, Substances, and Seasons.

Originally the elements were not combined with the Seasons. The fact that there always have been Five Elements, but Four Seasons, and that our oldest sources

---

(*h*) 坤輿圖說.

(*i*) 乾冷成土, 濕冷成水 .... 濕熱成氣 .... 乾熱成火。

do not allude to such a connection, tells against it. On the other side the term "*Wu-hsing*" makes it plain that the Five Elements were conceived already in times immemorial as something more than simple substances. From the passage of the *Tso-chuan* where the elements are mentioned together with the heavenly fluids, which become the Five Tastes, the Five Colours and the Five Sounds, and even manifest themselves in human affections (cf. p. 234), we may gather that, at a very early date the elements were identified with the heavenly fluids or atmospherical influences. These are in the *Shuking* :—*rain, sunshine, heat, cold,* and *wind*. They again, I presume, formed the link with the Four Seasons, which in the opinion of the Chinese, who did not know the real cause of the seasons, are the result of the regular changes of the heavenly fluids. In the *Liki* elements and seasons are linked together already. *Kuan-tse,* **XIV.,** 7 *seq.,* asserts that *wind* produces *wood,* the *Yang* fluid *fire,* the *Yin* fluid *metal,* and *cold, water*. Earth has no special fluid.

The *Sung* philosophers were the first clearly to point out the difference of *substances* 質 and *fluids* 氣. Substances are produced, says *Chou-tse,* by the interaction and coagulation of the *Yin* and the *Yang,* whereas the Fluids are the regular revolutions of these two primary essences (k). *T'sai Ch'ên,* a disciple of *Chu Hsi,* holds that in heaven the Five Elements are the Five Fluids :— rain, sunshine, heat, cold, and wind, and on earth the Five Substances :—water, wood, fire, metal, earth. Of the Five Heavenly Fluids rain and sunshine are the substances, which seems to imply that they are more substantial than heat, cold, and wind—and of the Five Substances of Earth water and fire are the fluids—possessing more the

---

(k) 性理會通. 五行. 周子曰。質則陰陽交錯凝合而成. 氣則陰陽兩端循環不己。

nature of fluids than of substances, a view held by *Chu Hsi* also, as we have seen above (*l*). Another writer maintains that the substances adhere to and have their roots in the earth, and that the fluids revolve in heaven. The latter generate, the former complete all organisms (*m*), i.e., the fluids give the first impulse to every new creation and the substances complete it. It may not be out of place to point out that the afore-mentioned *Agrippa* puts forward quite similar ideas. The elements in the lower worlds he declares to be coarser and more material, whereas in the higher spheres they appear only as forces or qualities. (*Lehmann, Aberglaube*, p. 198.)

This view has again been modified, all elements being held to be compounded of substance and fluid. There is a difference between the various elements insomuch as they are more substantial or more ethereal. " Fire and water have much fluid and little substance, wherefore they were produced first. Metal and wood have much substance and little fluid, and for this reason were created later. In earth substance and fluid are equally balanced, consequently it came after water and fire, but preceded metal and wood " (*n*).

" The fluid of water is *Yang*, its substance *Yin*. The nature of *Yin* is procreative, therefore water produces wood. The fluid of fire is *Yin*, its substance *Yang*. Since

---

(*l*) 蔡氏曰. 五行在天. 則爲五氣. 雨暘煥寒風也。在地. 則爲五質. 水木火金土也。天之五氣. 雨暘質也. 地之五質. 水火氣也。

(*m*) 章潢圖書編. 五行氣質。質根於地. 氣運於天 …. 生之者氣. 成之者質。

(*n*) 性理會通. 膚語。水火氣多而質少. 故生成居先。金木質多而氣少. 故生成居後。土氣質均當. 後水火. 而先金木。

the nature of *Yang* is burning and destructive, fire cannot produce metal. As regards earth, its fluid is *Yang* and its substance *Yin*. Consequently it makes use of the *Yang* of fire to produce the *Yin* of metal " (*o*). Here we have again the mysticism of the *Yiking*.

Fire and earth together produce metal, and water and earth combined produce wood. In both cases earth is indispensable. When wood produces fire, and metal water, earth is not required.

Regarded as the ultimate causes of the seasons the elements were also invested with the qualities which, properly speaking, belong to the seasons alone. These characteristic features of the seasons are, according to *Pan Ku's Po-hu-t'ung* :—*generating, growing, reaping,* and *hiding* (*p*). *Tung Chung-shu* already gives similar attributes to the elements. " Wood," said he, " is the generative nature of spring and the basis of agriculture. Fire is the growing of summer, earth the maturing of the seeds in mid-summer, metal the deadly breath of autumn, and water the hiding in winter and the extreme *Yin* " (*q*).

IV. TRANSFORMATIONS OF THE ELEMENTS.

(a) *In Heaven:—The Celestial Bodies and the Five Planets.*

The whole universe, the material as well as the intellectual world, are nothing else than transformations of the

---

(o) 水 氣 陽 而 質 陰. 陰 之 性 滋. 故 水 生 木。火 氣 陰 而 質 陽. 陽 之 性 烈. 故 火 不 生 金。地 也 者. 氣 陽 而 質 陰 者 也. 故 接 火 之 陽 而 生 金 之 陰。

(p) 春 生. 夏 長. 秋 收. 冬 藏 —*Kuan-tse* XIV., 8 v., has nearly the same attributes : 春 贏 育. 夏 養 長. 秋 聚 收. 冬 閉 藏。

(q) 木 者 春 生 之 性. 農 之 本 也。火 者 夏 成 長。土 者 夏 中 成 熟 百 種。金 者 秋 殺 氣 之 始 也。水 者 冬 藏 至 陰 也。

Five Elements. The world has been evolved from the primary essences the *Yin* and the *Yang*, of which the elements are derivates or compounds.

We have seen that *Kuan-tse* (p. 256) joined the heavenly bodies to the different quarters :—the earth to the centre, the sun to the south, the moon to the north, the stars to the east, and the zodiacal signs to the west. It is natural that the earth should be regarded as the centre of the universe and the sun be connected with the south, the seat of heat and light. The moon then had to go to the opposite direction, the north, where cold and darkness reign. Then the stars had to take the two remaining quarters, the east and west. Fire being the element of the south and water that of the north, the celestial bodies were believed to be formed of the element belonging to their quarter. The earth consists of earth, the element of the centre. Then the stars must be of wood and the zodiacal constellations of metal.

But the combination of the Five Planets with the Five Quarters of the Five Elements is much more common than that of the celestial bodies in general. *Huai-nan-tse* III., 3 r. *seq.*, declares the *Five Planets* :—*Jupiter, Mars, Saturn, Venus,* and *Mercury* (r) to be the spirits of the Five Quarters. The *Shi-chi,* chap. 27, says that the Five Planets are the elements of the Five Quarters ruling over the Seasons, e.g., " Mars is said to be the fire of the south and governs summer " (s) (*eod.* p. 18 v.). Of course one may translate that Mars *corresponds* to the fire, but the literal translation seems to me preferable and more in accordance with the materialistic views of the Chinese to whom Mars, the Fire Star, 火 星, is made of fire, and Jupiter, the Wood Star, 木 星, is made of wood. These characteristic

---

(r) 歲 星, 熒 惑, 鎮 星, 太 白, 辰 星.

(s) 熒 惑, 曰 南 方 火, 主 夏

terms of the Planets are frequently used in the *Shi-chi.* The *Chin-shi* (fourteenth century A.D.) distinctly states that in heaven the fluid of the essence of the Five Elements becomes the Five Planets, on earth the Five Substances, and in man the Five Virtues and the Five Businesses (*t*). From another modern treatise we learn that looking up to the Five Planets at dusk we see their five colours quite clearly, without the least confusion, because they are the essences of the Five Elements (*u*). Here again we notice quite analogous conceptions in *Agrippa* (*loc. cit.*, p. 198), who likewise takes the planets for products of the elements. Mars and the Sun he pronounces to be fiery, Jupiter and Venus to be airy, Saturn and Mercury to be watery, and the Moon to be earthy.

We do not know which consideration led to the connection of each element with each planet. Probably it was in the different colours of the planets that the Chinese imagined they recognised the five colours :—green, red, yellow, white, and black of the elements. That at dusk we see the five colours quite distinctly, without the least confusion, as the above-quoted Chinese author would have us believe, is out of the question. The ancients as well as the moderns are at variance in regard to the colours of the planets (see above, p. 246). There only seems to be some unanimity about the red colour of Mars and the white one of Venus.

Valens goes so far as to give the reasons why the planets logically must have the colours which he assigns to them :—Saturn, he says, is black, because it is Time or *Kronos* which obscures everything. Jupiter is radiant, because he

---

(*t*) 金史, 五行志序。五行之精氣, 在天為五緯, 在地為五材, 在人為五常及五事.

(*u*) 王文祿, 補衍五德主運篇. 每仰觀五星, 初昏即見五色, 朗然不亂, 是五行之精也.

cares for glory and honour. Venus shows various colours owing to the various passions which she excites, and Mercury is yellow, for he governs the gall which is yellow (*x*). These arguments are very queer, but quite in the Chinese way of reasoning, and it would not be surprising to find them, slightly modified, in an ancient Chinese writer.

As we have learned from *Huai-nan-tse* in the *Chou* epoch already, the Five Planets were regarded as the spirits of the Five Quarters. As such they were venerated and named the "*Five Emperors.*" They were distinguished by their colours as the Green Emperor = Jupiter, the Red Emperor = Mars, the Yellow Emperor = Saturn, the White Emperor = Venus, and the Black Emperor = Mercury. (Cf. *Shi-chi*, chap. xxviii.; *Chavannes, Mém. Hist.*, Vol. III., p. 449.)

(b) *On Earth:—The Inorganic and the Organic Kingdom; Man.*

The element earth embraces all kinds of earth and stones; metal, the various metals; so the entire inorganic kingdom is the outcome of these two elements. Of water different kinds are distinguished according to their origin, such as spring water, rain water, water from ditches, lakes, the sea, &c. Fire may take its origin from wood, from oil, from stones or other substances, from lightning, or it may be the glowing of insects, or a will-o'-the-wisp. The whole flora belongs to the element wood, which includes trees, plants, and flowers. But here we meet with a difficulty. If all plants are produced by the element wood, how is it that in the *Liki* the five kinds of grain :—wheat, beans, millet, &c., are connected with the Five Elements and not with wood alone, so that beans correspond to fire, and millet to water? A Chinese philosopher would prob-

---

(*x*) *Bouché-Leclercq, Astrologie Grecque*, p. 314.

ably reply that all these cereals issue from the element wood, but have an admixture of one of the other elements. So wheat would be wood in wood, beans fire in wood, and millet water in wood.

It would be logical if the whole animal kingdom were classed under one chief element also, but they are distributed among the Five Elements, and it is difficult to understand the plan of this division. The scaly creatures, fishes, and reptiles, e.g., snakes and dragons, belong to the element wood, the shell-covered or crustaceous animals, turtles, crabs, oysters, &c., to the element water. The element earth embraces all naked creatures, among which are found toads, earthworms, silkworms, spiders, eels, and *man*. Fire is the element of all feathered animals or birds, and metal that of all hairy ones or beasts (*y*). Consequently, the Five Sacrificial Animals, sheep, cock, ox, dog, and pig, should be looked upon as transformations of the element metal, save the cock corresponding to fire, but the *Liki* makes them correspond to all the Five Elements, and we would again have combinations of two elements : metal and wood=sheep, metal and earth=ox, &c.

Here the views of *Agrippa von Nettesheim* (*loc. cit.* p. 198) are very instructive. He teaches us that from the Four Elements of Aristotle issue the four principal divisions of nature : stones, metals, plants, and animals. Each of these groups consist of all the elements combined, but one predominates. Stones are earthy, metals watery, because they can be liquefied, and by the Alchemists are declared to be the products of living metallic water (mercury); plants depend upon air, and animals upon fire, their vital force.

Among stones which as such are earthy, the opaque

(*y*) See the list of living beings 五行動物屬圖 in the 性理會通.

ones are earthy, the pellucid ones and crystal which have been secreted from water, are watery, those swimming on water like sponges are airy, and those produced by fire, like flints and asbestos, are fiery. Lead and silver are earthy, mercury is watery, copper and tin are airy, and iron and gold are fiery.

As regards animals, vermin and reptiles belong to earth, fish to water, and birds to the air. All animals with great warmth or with a fiery colour, such as pigeons, ostriches, lions, and those breathing fire, belong to this element. But in each animal the different parts of its body belong to different elements—the legs belong to earth, the flesh to air, the vital breath to fire, and the humours to water.

Man is treated in the same manner by the Chinese. As the foremost among the three hundred and sixty naked creatures he belongs to the element earth, but the parts of his body and his moral qualities are connected with the different elements, and produced by them. From the *Liki* and the *Su-wên* (p. 254) we have learned the correspondences of the Five Constituent Parts of the body—muscles, veins, flesh, skin and hair, and bones—and of the Five Intestines with the elements. An inner reason for this classification is difficult to discover, but there has certainly been one, although it may not tally with our ideas of a scientific classification.

The transition of the Five Elements from the material into the spiritual world is by some writers believed to be a direct one, whereas others see in the parts of the human body the connecting links. *Ch'u Yung*, of the *Sung* period, informs us that the Five Elements are the Five Organs of the human body, and that the fluids correspond to the Five Intestines (z). The Five Organs are the ear,

---

(z) 宋 儲 泳. 論 劉 向 災 異 五 行 志。五 行 者, 人 身 之 五 官 也. 氣 應 五 臟.

the eye, the nose, the mouth, and the body serving to produce the five sensations. *Wang Ch'ung* (Vol. I., pp. 194, 381) is of opinion that the Five Virtues are closely connected with the Five Intestines, which are their necessary substrata. By a destruction of these inner parts of the body the moral qualities of man are destroyed as well. According to this view the elements appear as moral qualities only after having been transmuted into parts of the human body. Other writers assume a direct process of transformation. We have seen the *Chin-shi* maintaining that in heaven the fluid of the Five Elements becomes the Five Planets, on earth the Five Substances, and in man the Five Virtues and the Five Businesses (above p. 274). The Taoist *T'an Ch'iao* (tenth century) also merely states that the Five Virtues are the Five Elements, setting forth the following classification : " Benevolence is equivalent to fostering and growing, therefore it rules through wood. Justice means assistance of those in need, therefore it rules through metal. Propriety is enlightenment, whence it rules through fire. Wisdom denotes pliability, whence it rules through water, and faith is the same as uprightness, wherefore it rules through earth " (*a*). The reasoning is rather weak, but we find the same distribution of the Five Virtues in the following list of the *Sung* school of thought (*b*). That its classification does not quite agree with that of the *Liki* and the *Su-wên* given above is not to be wondered at, since in reality the elements have nothing

---

(a) 南唐. 譚子化書. 五行相濟相伐。五常者. 五行也. 仁發生之謂也. 故君于木. 義救難之謂也. 故君于金. 禮明白之謂也. 故君于火. 智變通之謂也. 故君于水. 信愨然之謂也. 故君于土.

(b) 五行人體性情圖.

to do with moral qualities, and the supposed relations are pure imagination :

Five Elements	Five Parts of Body	Five Intestines	Five Souls (c)	Five Senses (d)	Five Impulses	Five Virtues
wood	muscles	liver	mind	smell	joy	benevolence
fire	hair	heart	spirit	vision	gaiety	propriety
earth	flesh	spleen	reason	touch	desire	faith
metal	bones	lungs	animal soul	taste	anger	justice
water	skin	kidneys	vitality	hearing	sorrow	wisdom

We have seen above (p. 246) how *Ptolemy* joined the parts of the body and the senses to the Seven Planets, and how *Proclus* made the different spheres of the human mind correspond to the spheres of the stars. In this respect they were only the successors of the *Chaldeans* and *Egyptians*, who first connected the parts of the human body with the Twelve Signs of the Zodiac. A human body was thought extended over the vault of heaven, its head resting on Aries. Then its neck lay on Taurus, its shoulders and arms on Gemini, the breast on Cancer, the flanks on Leo, the stomach and the bladder on Virgo, the buttocks on Libra, the genitals on Scorpio, the thighs on Sagittarius, the knees on Capricorn, the legs on Aquarius, and the feet on Pisces. In the *Kabbala* the three elements, fire, water, and air, were combined with the three parts of the body, the head, the breast and the belly. The Seven Planets correspond to the Seven Orifices of the Head, and the

---

(c) 魂, 神, 意, 魄, 精.

(d) 臭, 色, 形, 味, 聲.

Twelve Signs of the Zodiac to the Twelve Human Activities (p. 248). These ideas were taken up by *Agrippa*, as appears from his table (p. 249). A similar scheme was in vogue among the *Central American Mayas* (cf. *P. Carus, Chinese Thought* (1907), p. 87). The Chinese do not lay much stress upon the relation between the parts of the human body and the planets, but it exists, since the planets are nothing else than manifestations of the Five Elements in the celestial sphere; the parts of the body, its sensations, feelings, and moral qualities being manifestations of the same elements in the human sphere.

V. Local and Numerical Relations of the Elements.

It has been shown that at a very early date the Five Elements were referred to the Four Seasons, a fact evidenced by the *Tso-chuan* and the *Liki*. It is not difficult to guess—strict proofs we have not—how the elements were assigned to the seasons. Fire could only be joined to the hottest time of the year, when the sun sends its fiery rays, summer. Conversely, water, considered as the extreme *Yin* and the product of cold, had to be combined with the coldest and darkest season, winter. Wood could serve to symbolise the new growing of the vegetation in spring, and metal the cutting of the cereals and other plants, used by man, in autumn. For earth there was no special season first.

The obvious analogy between the Four Seasons and the Four Quarters then led to the connection of the elements with the Four Points of the Compass. Within the space of a year the four seasons, spring, summer, autumn and winter, follow one another, and during one day the sun successively passes from the east, through the south and the west, to the north, to begin the same course on the following morning. What more natural than the equation :

$$\left.\begin{array}{l} Wood, \ fire, \ metal, \ water \\ \text{Spring, summer, autumn,} \\ \qquad \text{winter} \end{array}\right\} = \begin{array}{l} East, \ south, \ west, \\ \qquad north. \end{array}$$

With spring the new year begins, as in the east the sun begins its course; in summer, and in the south the sun is hottest, summer being the season, and the south the region of the greatest heat; in autumn, and when the sun is in the west, its heat decreases; in winter, and in the north, the heat is gone, and we then arrive at the cold season and the region of cold. Here we have a seat for earth also, viz., the centre, so that the Five Elements correspond to the Five Points. Our point of observation is the centre, and we have earth under our feet. The south is filled with the element fire, the north with water, whereas wood permeates the east, and metal the west. Facing the south, the chief direction according to the Chinese view, we have fire in the *front* and water in the *rear*, wood on our *left*, metal on our *right side*, and earth in the *centre* where we stand. These positions, first assigned to the elements by *Ho Kuan-tse* (p. 250), are merely derived from their combinations with the Five Points.

The Four Quarters, or, more correctly speaking, the Four Quadrants of Heaven, 四 宮 *Sse-Kung*, have been symbolised by four fancy animals—the *Green Dragon* in the east, the *Scarlet Bird* in the south, the *White Tiger* in the west, and the *Black Warrior* or the *Black Tortoise* in the north—to which *Huai-nan-tse* still adds the *Yellow Dragon*, corresponding to the centre (*e*). Each of these four animals embraces seven of the twenty-eight Constellations or Solar Mansions. We find the same names in the *Shi-chi*, chap. xxvii. (*Chavannes, Mém. Hist.*, Vol.III.,

---

(*e*) *Huai-nan-tse*, III., 3 v. : 蒼 龍, 朱 鳥, 白 虎, 元 武, 黃 龍

p. 343 *seq.*), and in the *Lun Hêng*, Vol. I., pp. 106, 534 (*f*). *Wang Ch'ung* seems to regard them as heavenly spirits formed of the fluids of the Five Elements and as constellations at the same time. *Pan Ku* likewise speaks of the essence of these animals, but instead of the Scarlet Bird he gives the Yellow Thrush and the Phoenix (*g*). It is not improbable that the ancient Chinese really saw the shapes of animals in these constellations, and took them for celestial animals imbued with the fluids of the four elements, wood, fire, metal, and water; for the Yellow Dragon of *Huai-nan-tse* belongs to the earth, and is no constellation. The classes, as well as the colours of these four animals, harmonise with those of the *Liki*. The dragon is a scaly animal, the scarlet bird feathered, the tiger hairy, and the tortoise shell-covered; and their colours are green, red, white, and black, like wood, fire, metal, and water. The yellow colour of the thrush and that of the phoenix or argus pheasant, though not red, would still accord more or less with the colour of fire.

From the *Tso-chuan* and the *Liki* onward, the *Ten Stems*, or cyclical signs of the cycle of ten, have been combined with the elements. The principle has been explained above (p. 259, note (*h*)). To distinguish each of the Five Seasons of seventy-two days governed by one element, a couple of these signs, as they follow one another in the regular series, are used. The days are numbered by means of the sexagenary cycle, and each Season or element is designated by the two Stems beginning the compound number of the first and second day of the season. The two first days of spring are *chia-tse* and *yi-ch'ou* (*h*),

---

(*f*) The translation " Blue Dragon " must be changed into " Green Dragon."

(*g*) *Po-hu-t'ung* II., 2 v. : 青 龍. 鳥 離. 鸞. 白 虎. 玄 武.

(*h*) 甲 子. 乙 丑.

therefore the whole season and its element would have the cyclical signs *chia* and *yi*. The first and the second days of summer are after the sexagenary cycle a *ping-tse* and a *ting-ch'ou* (i) day, therefore the whole season of summer and its element fire are connected with the Stems *ping* and *ting*. The second characters of the component numbers belonging to the Twelve Branches, *tse* and *ch'ou*, are left out of account. So the Ten Stems, *chia yi* (wood —spring), *ping ting* (fire—summer), *wu chi* (earth—latter part of summer), *kêng hsin* (metal—autumn), *jên kuei* (water—winter), serve to denote the commencements of the seasons or the periods when each element begins its reign; they are time marks so to say.

In the *Liki* only the *Ten Stems* are thus used. *Huai-nan-tse*, moreover, conformably to the method alluded to in the *Tso-chuan*, joins a couple of the *Twelve Branches* to the Five Elements. Their meaning is quite different, they are local marks showing the point of the compass where the respective element is located, for the Chinese denote the Four Quarters and their subdivisions by means of these Branches. According to the position of the elements, the Branches designating the east, south, west, and north points, and the intermediary points nearest to these, are added to them. So we have : wood = *yin mao*, E.N.E. and East ; fire = *sse wu*, S.S.E. and South ; metal = *shên yu*, W.S.W. and West ; water = *hai tse*, N.N.W. and North.

With good reason *Huai-nan-tse* III., 17 v., leaves out earth, on the ground that it belongs to all the four seasons. Earth being in the centre cannot well be combined with a sign connoting a point of the compass on the periphery. Later authors have done it all the same. *Tai T'ing-*

(i) 丙 子. 丁 丑.

huai (*k*) attributes to earth the four remaining cyclical signs—*shên, hsü, ch'ou,* and *wei* (*l*), viz., E.S.E., W.N.W., N.N.E., S.S.W. If this has any sense at all, it can only mean that earth is to be found in every direction, approximately denoted by the four characters. In *Couvreur's* Table only the signs *ch'ou* and *wei* are assigned to earth.

It is well known that the Twelve Branches also serve to mark the twelve double hours of the day, but I doubt whether all sinologists are aware of the reason of this peculiar use. Even when denoting the hours of day and night, the Branches have not temporal, but only a local value, marking the direction where the sun stands during a certain hour. In spring and autumn, when day and night are nearly of equal length, between 5—7 A.M., the sun stands in, or passes through, *mao* 卯 =East, whence the hour from 5—7 A.M. is called the *mao* hour 卯 時. At noon, 11—1 P.M., it passes through *wu* 午 =South, between 5—7 P.M. through *yu* 酉 =West, and at midnight, from 11—1 A.M., the sun, though not seen by us, traverses *tse* 子 =North. Originally, the Twelve Branches merely mark the points of the compass their designation of the twelve hours is only a secondary use based on the course of the sun through these points.

The *ordinary numerals* attached to the elements in the *Liki*, earth=5, water=6, fire=7, wood=8, and metal =9, are said to refer to the ten stages or turns in which originally the Five Elements were evolved from *Yin* and *Yang*, or Heaven and Earth. This is again in accordance with the above-mentioned obscure passage of the *Yiking*. *Tai T'ing-huai* (*m*) states that :

(*k*) 戴 廷 槐. 五 行 統 論 contained in the 性 理 會 通.

(*l*) 辰, 戌, 丑, 未.

(*m*) 天 一 生 水. 地 六 成 之. 地 二 生 火. 天 七 成 之.

1st. Heaven engendered water.
2ndly. Earth engendered fire.
3rdly. Heaven engendered wood.
4thly. Earth engendered metal.
5thly. Heaven engendered earth.
6thly. Earth completed water.
7thly. Heaven completed fire.
8thly. Earth completed wood.
9thly. Heaven completed metal.
10thly. Earth completed earth.

Now all elements are given the number of their completion—water = 6, fire = 7, wood = 8, metal = 9—except earth, which bears the number of its generation, because, says a commentator, generation is the principal thing for earth (n). This reason is as singular as the whole theory of this creation in ten stages.

VI. THE DIFFERENT MODES OF ENUMERATING THE FIVE ELEMENTS.

There are at least four different ways of enumerating the elements, each series having its special meaning.

(a) The order in which the elements are believed to have originally been created : *Water, fire, wood, metal, earth.*

We found this series in the *Shuking,* p. 230, and the *Chi-chung-chou-shu,* p. 236. Whether it really has the meaning disclosed by the *Sung* philosophers, is open to doubt. According to the *T'ai-chi-t'u,* this series refers to the substances, showing the order in which they were pro-

---

天 三 生 木. 地 八 成 之. 地 四 生 金. 天 九 成 之. 天 五 生 土. 地 十 成 之 *Loc. cit.*

(n) 土 生 數 五, 成 數 十, 但 言 五 者, 土 以 生 爲 本.

duced, in contradistinction to the fluids whose successive revolutions are expressed by series (b) : *wood, fire, earth, metal, water* (o). *Chu Hsi* speaks of the order in which the Five Elements were first created by Heaven and Earth (p). He holds that the vague and shapeless elements water and fire came first, and were followed by the solid substances wood and metal, which required earth as a substratum from which they issued. But in this case earth ought to take the third place in the series and not the last.

(b) The order in which the elements or their fluids follow and produce each other in the course of the seasons : *Wood, fire, earth, metal, water.*

This is the order of the *Liki*. During each season one element predominates. The others are not completely destroyed; but they have dwindled away, and have no power until their turn comes, when they are resuscitated and become preponderant. The elements thus succeeding each other are said to produce one another. Both *Huai-nan-tse* III, 17 v., and *Tung Chung-shu*, XI., 2 v., expressly state that wood produces fire, fire produces earth, earth produces metal, metal water, and water wood. The former regards each element producing another as its *mother*, the latter regards it as its *father*, and the element thus generated as the *son* or child. According to this terminology, wood, for example, would be the mother or the father of fire, and metal the son of earth. This analogy has induced both authors to judge the relations of the elements by the moral and the family laws, which leads to strange consequences. As men under given circum-

----

(o) 周 子, 太 極 圖。以 質 而 語 其 生 之 序, 則 曰 水 火 木 金 土. 以 氣 而 語 其 行 之 序. 則 曰 木 火 土 金 水.

(p) 朱 子 語 類。取 其 天 地 始 生 之 序.

stances act in a certain way, the elements are believed to affect each other in a similar manner. This view has been adopted by other writers, as will appear from some instances given *ad* (c).

The theory that the Five Elements produce each other in the order of this series is to a certain extent based on natural laws. One may say that wood produces fire, and fire leaves ashes or earth. In the interior of the earth metal grows. But how can metal produce water? Here is a hitch. The Chinese try to avoid it by asserting that metal may become liquefied or watery; and in this respect they are at one with *Agrippa*, who likewise, as we saw, looks upon all metals as watery. But liquid metal is not real water, and it can never be transformed into water in the same way as wood becomes ashes or earth metal. Moreover, water alone cannot become wood. There must be earth besides, not to speak of the necessity of a germ; and to produce metal earth and fire must co-operate. This has been pointed out in the *Hsing-li hui-t'ung*, stating that, for the production of metal fire and earth, and for that of wood water and earth, are wanted, so that in both cases earth cannot be dispensed with.

(c) The order in which the elements subdue or overcome each other : *Water, fire, metal, wood, earth.*

This series occurs in the *Shuking* and the *Tso-chuan* (p. 228); and the author of the latter work knows its principle, for he informs us that water overcomes fire and fire metal, and calls the stronger element the husband, the weaker the wife. The full list of the antagonistic elements is given by *Huai-nan-tse* IV., 8 v. (*q*). *Tung Chung-shu* XIII., 5 v., remarks that of the elements in series (b) those placed together produce one another, whereas those separated by

---

(q) 木 勝 土, 土 勝 水, 水 勝 火, 火 勝 金, 金 勝 木.

one place vanquish each other (r). If we take the series, *wood, fire, earth, metal, water*, then wood subdues earth and earth water; fire subdues metal, and metal wood, &c. This series must be regarded as an infinite ring; from the last link one returns to the first.

How this mutual antagonism of the elements is to be understood we best learn from the *Su-wên* : " Wood brought together with metal is felled; fire brought together with water is extinguished; earth meeting with wood is pierced; metal meeting with fire is dissolved; and water meeting with earth is stopped " (s).

In other words, water extinguishes fire, fire melts metal, metal cuts wood. That growing wood perforates the surrounding soil, and that earth stops the course of water, when there is an inundation, for example, seems a little far-fetched; but we must bear in mind that the Chinese reasoning is not always as strict and logical as we would like to have it. The explanation given in the *Su-wên* most likely completely satisfies the Chinese mind. I would prefer the explanation of *de Saussure, T'oung-pao* (1909), p. 259, that earth vanquishes water by absorbing it; and the same thing may be said of the relation of wood and earth, in so far as growing plants draw from the soil all the substances necessary for their development. This may be looked upon as a destruction of earth by wood.

In connection with this theory some writers make interesting observations on the way in which the elements affect each other. Wood, says *Kuan-yin-tse*, when bored, gives fire; when pressed, gives water. Metal is such a substance that, when struck, it produces fire, and when

---

(r) 春秋繁露, 五行相生。比相生而間相勝也.

(s) 黃帝索問, 寶命全形論。木得金而伐. 火得水而滅. 土得木而達. 金得火而欽. 水得土而絕.

melted it becomes water (*t*). The *Chang Huang t'u-shu pien* points out the following changes undergone by the elements when operated upon by one another : Earth becomes softened by water and hardened by fire. Metal becomes liquid by fire and continues unchanged by water. Wood grows by water and is consumed by fire. Fire grows by wood and dies by water. Water is cooled by metal and warmed by fire (*u*). In *Ch'u Yung's Ch'ü-yi shuo* the action of some elements is spoken of in a way that a tacit reproof may be read between the lines : Fire is produced by wood, but it consumes it ; metal grows in earth, but it hoes it, i.e., both elements show a very unfilial behaviour towards their parents. Wood subdues earth, but earth nourishes wood ; earth subdues water, but water irrigates earth (*x*), i.e., earth and water requite the maltreatment by their inimical elements with kindness. *Tai T'ing-huai* is quite outspoken on this subject, and sets forth the curious law that, when an element is vanquished by another, its son always will revenge the wrong inflicted upon the aggressor and subdue him in his turn (*y*). E.g., when water overcomes fire, earth, the son of fire, will subdue water, and when fire overcomes metal, water, the son of metal, will subdue fire. There really is such a

---

(*t*) 關尹子. 二柱篇。木之爲物. 鑽之得火. 絞之得水. 金之爲物. 擊之得火. 鎔之得水.

(*u*) 章潢圖書編. 五行氣質。土得水則柔. 得火則剛. 金得火則流. 得水則止. 木得水則長. 得火則消. 火得木則生. 得水則死. 水得金則寒. 得火則煖.

(*x*) 儲泳. 祛疑說. 五行體象生克之性。火生於木. 而焚木. 金生於土. 而鋤土 ... 木克土. 而土養木. 土克水. 而水澤土.

(*y*) 戴廷槐. 五行統論。有母必能生子, 子必能爲母報讎之義焉.

relation between the various elements according to the Chinese theory of their mutual production and destruction. This destruction is considered a natural rebuff, after an element has been produced and exceeded a certain limit, or it may have been brought about by men on purpose, in order to shape or transform certain substances, or avert calamities. Thus fire is employed to melt metal and cast vessels and utensils, and earth is formed into dikes and embankments to check inundations.

In the occult arts of the Middle Ages the sympathies and antipathies of the elements play an important part. *Agrippa* (*loc. cit.* p. 229) contends that fire is hostile to water, and air to earth. A sympathetic action is exercised by a magnet attracting iron, an emerald procuring riches and health, a jasper influencing birth, and an agate furthering eloquence. Contrariwise, a sapphire is believed to repel plague, ulcers, fever, and eye diseases, amethyst acts against drunkenness, jasper against evil spirits, emerald against wantonness, agate against poison. The panther dreads the hyena so much that, if the skin of a panther be suspended opposite to the skin of a hyena, its hair falls out. In accordance with this doctrine of *Agrippa*, the famous physician *Theophrastus Bombastus Paracelsus* (1493—1541 A.D.) based his cures on the sympathetic action of the elements. Since every part of the body pertained to a planet, all the substances belonging to the same star were considered to be efficacious antidotes against all ailments of the part in question. Gold, e.g., passed for a specific against heart diseases, because gold and the heart both pertain to the sun (*eod.* p. 232). Even animals have recourse to this sort of cures. *Agrippa* relates that a lion suffering from fever cures itself by eating the flesh of a monkey, and that stags, when hit by an arrow, eat white dittany (Eschenwurz), which extracts the arrow.

(d) The order in which the elements are usually

enumerated at present : *Metal, wood, water, fire, earth.*
This series seems to be used for the first time by *Pan Ku*
in his *Po-hu-t'ung* II., 1 r. I found only one attempt
at explaining this order by *Chu Hsi*, which is very unsatisfactory. Metal, he says, is the mother of all fluids, and
the body of Heaven is dry metal (*z*). Because all things
begin to grow after they have received the fluid, therefore
wood follows metal, &c.

Perhaps the principle underlying this series may be
that, first, the two substantial elements are given ; secondly,
their two transformations ; and, thirdly, one second transformation. Metal and wood are transmuted into water
and fire, and fire again is changed into earth (embers).

Accordingly, the above four orders of the elements may
briefly be thus characterised :

   (a) Series of the creation of the elements.
   (b) Series of their mutual production.
   (c) Series of their mutual destruction.
   (d) Series of their transformation.

VII. The Regular Changes of the Elements during the Seasons.

Apart from the transformations which the elements
undergo when meeting, they are subject to regular modifications during the seasons, which repeat themselves every
year. In the course of a year they grow, reach their
climax, and decline again. While one element is at its
height, another has fallen off, and a third is still growing.
The times are usually denoted by the Twelve Branches,
which, as a rule, are merely local marks. Here they are
almost equivalent to the twelve months, for the sun stays
about a month in each of the twelve constellations or
branches, which, therefore, serve to designate the months.

(z) 朱 子 語 類. 金 爲 氣 之 母. 天 體 乾 金 也.

Huai-nan-tse III., 16 r., gives us the following comparative table (*a*) :

Wood is born in *hai* (N.N.W.—10th moon).

Wood is full-grown in *mao* (E.—2nd moon).

Wood dies in *wei* (S.S.W.—6th moon).

Fire is born in *yin* (E.N.E.—1st moon).

Fire is full-grown in *wu* (S.—5th moon).

Fire dies in *hsü* (W.N.W.—9th moon).

Earth is born in *wu* (S.—5th moon).

Earth is full-grown in *hsü* (W.N.W.—9th moon).

Earth dies in *yin* (E.N.E.—1st moon).

Metal is born in *sse* (S.S.E.—4th moon).

Metal is full-grown in *yu* (W.—8th moon).

Metal dies in *ch'ou* (N.N.E.—12th moon).

Water is born in *shên* (W.S.W.—7th moon).

Water is full-grown in *tse* (N.—11th moon).

Water dies in *ch'ên* (E.S.E.—3rd moon).

After this scheme each element is alive nine months, and dead three months. Its body then still exists, but it is lifeless, i.e., inactive. In the next year it is revived again, and the same process, its growing and decaying, begins afresh. Each element is full-grown and shows its greatest development in the second or the middle month of the season over which it rules, wood in the second month of spring, and fire in the second month of summer, or the fifth month. The position assigned to earth is peculiar. It is just one month behind metal, consequently earth would govern a season almost falling together with autumn, but a little later.

Elsewhere *Huai-nan-tse* makes the elements pass through five different stages, adding to those given above " old

---

(*a*) 木 生 于 亥. 壯 于 卯. 死 于 未. 三 辰 皆 木 也. 火 生 于 寅. 壯 于 午. 死 于 戌. 三 辰 皆 火 也. &c.

age " and " imprisonment." Thus we have the following comparative list (*b*).

	strong	old	born	imprisoned	dead
Spring	wood	water	fire	metal	earth
Summer	fire	wood	earth	water	metal
...	earth	fire	metal	wood	water
Autumn	metal	earth	water	fire	wood
Winter	water	metal	wood	earth	fire

Later authors go still more into details. *Sun Chao*, of the *Ming* dynasty, informs us that the " Classic of *Huang Ti* " (*c*) distinguishes twelve changes undergone by each element during a year. He treats the elements like human beings, and therefore takes the names of these changes from human life. They are birth, bathing, being an official, a minister, a sovereign, decline, sickness, death, burial, cessation, stirring up, and growing as an embryo (*d*). *Sun Chao* characterises the twelve stages which follow the Twelve Branches a little differently : (1) Water exists as a sperm in *sse*, (2) in an embryonic state in *wu*, (3) develops in *wei*, (4) is born in *shên*, (5) is washed and bathed in *yu*, (6) receives the cap and the girdle in *hsü*, (7) begins its official career in *hai*, (8) obtains imperial glory in *tse*, (9) becomes old and decrepid in *ch'ou*, (10) sick in *yin*,

---

(*b*) *Huai-nan-tse* IV., 9 r. : 木 壯 水 老 火 生 金 囚 土 死．火 壯 木 老 土 生 水 囚 金 死 &c.

(*c*) 黃 帝 經 the *Huang Ti su-wên* is meant.

(*d*) 明、孫 昭、系 包 考。五 行 十 二 變 曰 生 曰 浴 曰 官 曰 臣 曰 君 曰 委 曰 病 曰 死 曰 藏 曰 止 曰 渾 曰 育.

(11) dies in *mao*, (12) and is buried in *ch'ên* (*e*). The life of each element, its development, its acme, and its decline, in all their phases are compared to the life of man. It is washed like a baby, capped like a youth, must become an official—the ambition of every Chinaman—becomes even an emperor, and then gradually declines. The same list holds good for the other elements likewise, but the cyclical signs indicating the months change. Thus fire exists in a spermatic state in *hai*, wood in *shên*, and metal in *yin*.

VIII. THE ELEMENT EARTH AND ITS SEASON.

When the Five Elements were joined to the Four Seasons, there was one element too much, which could not be combined with a season. This element was earth. Why was just this one left out? Perhaps simply because in the two oldest series, (a) and (c) of the *Shuking*, earth came last. The Chinese give other reasons. Both *Tung Chung-shu* X., 10 r., and *Pan Ku* II., 1 r., urge that earth is the noblest of the elements. Earth (the element) 土, says the latter, is but another name of the Earth 地. As such it governs the other elements, and cannot be classed with them. This is true in so far as Heaven and Earth are held to have produced the elements. Besides, we saw that wood and metal are believed to be products of earth, so that this element must be ranked as a sort of primary element. Though it did not produce water and fire, it supports them, as it does wood and metal.

But although there was no season left for earth, the Chinese did not like to drop this element altogether in

---

(*e*) *Loc. cit.* 其論五行. 一曰水. 其系包在巳. 其胎在午. 其養在未. 其生在申. 其沐浴在酉. 其冠帶在戌. 其臨官在亥. 其帝旺在子. 具衰老在丑. 其病在寅. 其死在卯. 其墓在辰.

their calendars. Since, locally, it was placed in the centre, they also inserted it into the middle of the Four Seasons, between summer and autumn, without attributing a special season to it. This was done in the *Liki* (*f*). Subsequently earth was conceived as the element of "late summer" 季 夏. The next step was to make Five Seasons instead of Four, each of 72 days, and to assign the third, "late summer," to earth. This step was taken by *Kuan-tse* (see above, p. 256), *by Huai-nan-tse* III., 9 v., and by *Tung Chung-shu, Ch'un-ch'iu fan-lu* XIII., 9 v.

IX. The Five Elements under their Religious and Metaphysical Aspect.

The veneration of the Five Elements, or, properly speaking, of the deities presiding over the elements, reaches back to the commencement of the *Chou* dynasty. In the *Chou-li* we met with the Five Sacrifices offered to the Five Heavenly Emperors, the deities of the five directions whose altars were erected in the four suburbs and the centre. They were old legendary rulers deified as the spirits of the Five Points and the Five Elements. Subsequently, they received five assistant spirits, also sons of old emperors, credited with the power of mastering the elements, and therefore revered as the spirits of the Five Elements and the Four Seasons. The spirit of earth alone had no special season. They partook of the sacrifices made to the Five Emperors (p. 233). In the *Liki* each season has a couple of these deities, a Heavenly Emperor or divine ruler and his attendant spirit.

The Five Sacrifices to these deities of the elements were performed by the emperor and the princes in the proper season. The Five Sacrifices of the house, viz., the

---

(*f*) Cf. *Legge's* translation, pp. 280 and 281, note 1.

outer and the inner door, the hearth, the inner court, and the well, were likewise referred to the five elements (cf. p. 239, note (c)). They were offered by the great officers, scholars and common people performing only one or two of them (g). At the sacrifice the part of the victim which is supposed to correspond to the respective element was essential. Besides, the entire ceremonial to be observed by the emperor at these religious functions was more or less connected with the theory of the Five Elements. The hall occupied by the emperor was situated so as to be turned towards the quarter ruled by the predominating element. The colour of his horses, his flag, his robes, and his jade ornaments had to correspond to the colour of the worshipped element. His food, meat as well as vegetables, was similarly determined.

But not the religious life of the ancient Chinese alone, their political life is also overshadowed by the elements. In the *Shuking* already we found the statement that the good qualities of the sovereign :—self-possession, orderliness, judiciousness, discretion, and sageness are related to the seasonable atmospheric influences, i.e., to the fluids of the elements proper to the season, whereas their vices :— excitement, confusion, fickleness, impetuosity, and dullness are the correlates of such fluids as are out of season. Seasonable fluids produce rich harvests, call forth a good government, and make people happy; unseasonable ones have the opposite result (p. 231).

On the other hand, the actions of the sovereign and his administration have an influence upon the seasons and the weather, and thereby may bring down calamities upon his subjects. The *Liki* enumerates all proceedings which may be done during each season and which may not. The

---

(g) See *Liki, Legge's* translation, p. 225, and *Lun Hêng*, Vol. I., p. 519.

latter are not wicked in themselves, but they do not harmonise with the imaginary nature of the ruling element. In spring everything favourable to the cultivation of the fields must be done, and all destructive measures are forbidden. Trees must not be cut, young animals, birds, or insects not be killed. No warlike operations aiming at the destruction of human life are to be undertaken. The *Liki* points out all the natural calamities :—heavy rainfalls, storms, pestilence, &c., caused by unseasonable administrative acts (p. 240).

Kuan-tse prescribes five administrative measures for each season, the observation of which secures happiness and the accomplishment of one's desires, whereas its disregard entails misfortune. Even an eclipse of the sun and the moon and the appearance of a comet are the upshot of unseasonable government. Since malpractices in the rewarding of meritorious actions are the cause of an eclipse of the sun, and since unjust punishments and a want of harmony have brought about the eclipse of the moon and the appearance of a comet, by removing these causes the effects are removed also (p. 257).

According to the *Su-wên* there is felicity only in the case that the element governing a season has its proper quantity, being neither excessive nor defective. That means to say that in summer, for instance, it must not be too hot, but not too cool either, and that in winter it must not be too cold, but, on the other side, not too warm. A cool summer and a warm winter are fraught with all kinds of evils. The vegetation suffers, and especially man is attacked by diseases (p. 254).

Tung Chung-shu, who more than others looks upon the elements as moral entities, puts forward a great variety of cases, in which the principal element of a season comes into collision with the other elements. The terminology sounds very abstract and profound, but the meaning is very simple. *Tung Chung-shu* wants to show the effect of extraordinary changes of the character of the seasons, one season assuming that of another and losing its own nature :

" When (in autumn) metal meets with water, fish become torpid; when it meets with wood, plants and trees sprout again; when it meets with fire, plants and trees blossom in autumn; and when it meets with earth, the Five Grains do not mature (*h*). When (in winter) water meets with wood, the hibernating insects do not hide; when it meets with earth, the insects that ought to become torpid come out in winter; when it meets with fire, a star falls down; and when metal meets with water, winter becomes very cold " (*i*).

Like *Kuan-tse*, *Tung Chung-shu* maintains that natural calamities, the result of irregularities of the elements and the seasons, must be laid to the charge of the sovereign and his administration, and that they will cease as soon as the latter are reformed. Thus he says of spring and summer :—" When *wood* undergoes an extraordinary change, spring withers, and autumn blossoms; there are great floods in autumn, and there is too much rain in spring. This has its cause in excessive personal services.

(*h*) Metal is supposed to meet with the other four elements, or to collide with them, as the text says. That merely signifies that, in consequence of the preponderance of these unseasonable elements, autumn changes its character and in its temperature resembles spring, summer, or winter. In the next clause winter is supposed to undergo similar changes. The consequences of these irregularities of the seasons are, most of them, taken from experience, and not contradicted by facts.

(*i*) 春秋繁露. 治亂五行。水干金. 則魚不爲. 木干金. 則草木再生. 火干金, 則草木秋槃. 土干金. 五穀不成. 木干火. 冬蟄不藏. 土干水. 則蟄蟲冬出. 火干水. 則星墜. 金干水. 則冬大寒. *Tung Chung-shu,* **XIV., 1 r.**

Taxes and imposts are too heavy; the people become impoverished, revolt, and leave the path of virtue, and many starve. This may be remedied by a decrease of the services and a reduction of imposts and taxes, by taking the grain from the granaries and distributing it among the distressed.''

"When *fire* undergoes an extraordinary change, winter becomes warm and summer cool. This is because the ruler is not enlightened; excellent men are not rewarded, bad characters not removed; unworthy persons occupy the places of honour, and worthies live in obscurity. Therefore heat and cold are out of order, and the people visited with diseases and epidemics. This state of affairs may be helped by raising good and wise men, rewarding merit and appointing the virtuous '' (k).

These ideas may seem odd, but they are not illogical. If the virtues of the ruler are manifestations of the Five Elements, an axiom laid down by the old Classics and contested by nobody, then there must be fixed relations between the two, and a change on one side affects the other. Irregularities of the elements and the seasons must also manifest themselves in the conduct of the sovereign and his government, and any deviations of the latter have an influence on the seasons and the weather, with which the happiness of the people living on agriculture was closely connected.

(k) *Loc. cit.* 五行變救。本有變, 春凋秋榮. 秋大水. 春多雨. 此繇役衆. 賦斂重. 百姓貧窮. 叛去道. 多饑人. 救之者省繇役. 薄賦斂. 出倉穀. 賑困窮矣. 火有變. 冬溫夏寒. 此王者不明. 善者不賞. 惡者不紲. 不肖在位. 賢者伏匿. 則寒暑失序. 而民疾疫. 救之者舉賢良. 賞有功. 封有德. *Tung Chung-shu* XIV., 1 v.

X. Wrong Analogies.

The theory of the Five Elements is to a great extent built up on wrong analogies, but few Chinese scholars seem to have become aware of the impossible consequences to which they were led by it. *Wang Ch'ung* does not reject the theory altogether, but very often points out the wrong analogies, e.g., in the chapter on the Nature of Things, Vol. I., p. 105 seq., where he says that there ought to be an internecine strife between the inner organs of man just as there is between the elements, and that the Twelve Animals corresponding to the twelve points of the compass ought to behave quite differently from the way they do, if they were at all influenced by the elements, and in Vol. II., p. 416 seq.

In addition to this theory of the Five Elements the Chinese possess still another somewhat similar, derived from the *Yiking* and based on the Eight Diagrams. It is much less known and less developed than that of the Five Elements, and the correspondences are quite different. The principal ones are enumerated by *De Groot, Relig. System*, Vol. III., p. 964.

HISTORY, PHILOSOPHY AND
SOCIOLOGY OF SCIENCE

Classics, Staples and Precursors

An Arno Press Collection

Aliotta, [Antonio]. **The Idealistic Reaction Against Science.** 1914

Arago, [Dominique François Jean]. **Historical Eloge of James Watt.** 1839

Bavink, Bernhard. **The Natural Sciences.** 1932

Benjamin, Park. **A History of Electricity.** 1898

Bennett, Jesse Lee. **The Diffusion of Science.** 1942

[Bronfenbrenner], Ornstein, Martha. **The Role of Scientific Societies in the Seventeenth Century.** 1928

Bush, Vannevar. **Endless Horizons.** 1946

Campanella, Thomas. **The Defense of Galileo.** 1937

Carmichael, R. D. **The Logic of Discovery.** 1930

Caullery, Maurice. **French Science and its Principal Discoveries Since the Seventeenth Century.** [1934]

Caullery, Maurice. **Universities and Scientific Life in the United States.** 1922

Debates on the Decline of Science. 1975

de Beer, G. R. **Sir Hans Sloane and the British Museum.** 1953

Dissertations on the Progress of Knowledge. [1824]. 2 vols. in one

Euler, [Leonard]. **Letters of Euler.** 1833. 2 vols. in one

Flint, Robert. **Philosophy as Scientia Scientiarum and a History of Classifications of the Sciences.** 1904

Forke, Alfred. **The World-Conception of the Chinese.** 1925

Frank, Philipp. **Modern Science and its Philosophy.** 1949

The Freedom of Science. 1975

George, William H. **The Scientist in Action.** 1936

Goodfield, G. J. **The Growth of Scientific Physiology.** 1960

Graves, Robert Perceval. **Life of Sir William Rowan Hamilton.** 3 vols. 1882

Haldane, J. B. S. **Science and Everyday Life.** 1940

Hall, Daniel, et al. **The Frustration of Science.** 1935

Halley, Edmond. **Correspondence and Papers of Edmond Halley.** 1932

Jones, Bence. **The Royal Institution.** 1871

Kaplan, Norman. **Science and Society.** 1965

Levy, H. **The Universe of Science.** 1933

Marchant, James. **Alfred Russel Wallace.** 1916

McKie, Douglas and Niels H. de V. Heathcote. **The Discovery of Specific and Latent Heats.** 1935

Montagu, M. F. Ashley. **Studies and Essays in the History of Science and Learning.** [1944]

Morgan, John. **A Discourse Upon the Institution of Medical Schools in America.** 1765

Mottelay, Paul Fleury. **Bibliographical History of Electricity and Magnetism Chronologically Arranged.** 1922

Muir, M. M. Pattison. **A History of Chemical Theories and Laws.** 1907

National Council of American-Soviet Friendship. **Science in Soviet Russia: Papers Presented at Congress of American-Soviet Friendship.** 1944

Needham, Joseph. **A History of Embryology.** 1959

Needham, Joseph and Walter Pagel. **Background to Modern Science.** 1940

Osborn, Henry Fairfield. **From the Greeks to Darwin.** 1929

Partington, J[ames] R[iddick]. **Origins and Development of Applied Chemistry.** 1935

Polanyi, M[ichael]. **The Contempt of Freedom.** 1940

Priestley, Joseph. **Disquisitions Relating to Matter and Spirit.** 1777

Ray, John. **The Correspondence of John Ray.** 1848

Richet, Charles. **The Natural History of a Savant.** 1927

Schuster, Arthur. **The Progress of Physics During 33 Years (1875-1908).** 1911

Science, Internationalism and War. 1975

Selye, Hans. **From Dream to Discovery: On Being a Scientist.** 1964

Singer, Charles. **Studies in the History and Method of Science.** 1917/1921. 2 vols. in one

Smith, Edward. **The Life of Sir Joseph Banks.** 1911

Snow, A. J. **Matter and Gravity in Newton's Physical Philosophy.** 1926

Somerville, Mary. **On the Connexion of the Physical Sciences.** 1846

Thomson, J. J. **Recollections and Reflections.** 1936

Thomson, Thomas. **The History of Chemistry.** 1830/31

Underwood, E. Ashworth. **Science, Medicine and History.** 2 vols. 1953

Visher, Stephen Sargent. **Scientists Starred 1903-1943 in American Men of Science.** 1947

Von Humboldt, Alexander. **Views of Nature: Or Contemplations on the Sublime Phenomena of Creation.** 1850

Von Meyer, Ernst. **A History of Chemistry from Earliest Times to the Present Day.** 1891

Walker, Helen M. **Studies in the History of Statistical Method.** 1929

Watson, David Lindsay. **Scientists Are Human.** 1938

Weld, Charles Richard. **A History of the Royal Society.** 1848. 2 vols. in one

Wilson, George. **The Life of the Honorable Henry Cavendish.** 1851